THE HELL THEY CALLE

Edited by Terry Norman:
Armageddon Road: A VC's Diary 1914-16

THE HELL
THEY CALLED
HIGH WOOD

The Somme 1916

TERRY NORMAN

Pen & Sword
MILITARY

First published in Great Britain in 1984 by Patrick Stevens Limited.
Republished in 2003 by Leo Cooper

Published in this format in 2009 and reprinted in 2012 and 2014
Pen & Sword Military
An imprint of
Pen & Sword Books Ltd
47 Church Street
Barnsley
South Yorkshire
S70 2AS

ISBN 978 1 84415 897 3

A CIP catalogue record for this book is
available from the British Library.

Printed and bound in England by
CPI Group (UK) Ltd, Croydon, CR0 4YY

Pen & Sword Books Ltd incorporates the Imprints of Aviation, Atlas,
Family History, Fiction, Maritime, Military, Discovery, Politics, History,
Archaeology, Select, Wharncliffe Local History, Wharncliffe True Crime,
Military Classics, Wharncliffe Transport, Leo Cooper, The Praetorian Press,
Remember When, Seaforth Publishing and Frontline Publishing.

For a complete list of Pen & Sword titles please contact
PEN & SWORD BOOKS LIMITED
47 Church Street, Barnsley, South Yorkshire, S70 2AS, England
E-mail: enquiries@pen-and-sword.co.uk
Website: www.pen-and-sword.co.uk

Contents

Contents

Part I
Into the High Wind

Part II
Encounter of High Wind

List of Plates

The original 47th Division's memorial at High Wood, 1916.
The 51st (Highland) Division's memorial cross.
Unveiling 47th Division's permanent memorial in 1925.
The 1st Cameron Highlanders' memorial at High Wood.
Memorial cairn to the Glasgow Highlanders.
1st Surrey Rifles Association's church parade:
    Camberwell, 1983.
Wreath-laying ceremony at 1st Surrey Rifles' war memorial.

List of Maps

Author's Note

For general comprehension of the various infantry units and formations that went to make up an army of the BEF in 1916, there were 14 men to a section (commanded by a corporal), four sections (plus one officer, sergeant, runner and batman) to a platoon, four platoons to a company (usually commanded by a captain), four companies to a battalion, four battalions to an infantry brigade, three infantry brigades to a division, three divisions (normally) to a corps and, on the morning of 1st July 1916, there were five corps in General Rawlinson's Fourth Army. By late evening there were three, two corps having gone under Lt-General Gough's command to become the Reserve Army and the basis of the BEF's Fifth Army.

A section of 14 men was the establishment figure, but in many cases this figure was lower on the Somme through casualties. With regard to infantry brigades and divisions, each brigade had a trench mortar battery (TMB) and a machine-gun company. A division in its order of battle also had a pioneer battalion, a signals company, three companies of Royal Engineers and four field artillery brigades, each comprising four batteries. An infantry brigade is distinguished in the text as, for example, 53rd Brigade; a division as 18th Division and a corps as XIII Corps. The German equivalents are italicized.

TGN

Hardly any point on the whole Somme battlefield
witnessed more bitter fighting or cost more to take than
High Wood.

C.T.ATKINSON
The Seventh Division,
(1914–18)

Introduction

With the pale autumn sun on his back, 86-year-old ex-Sergeant Harold Silvester, DCM, MM, leaned heavily on his two sticks and slowly negotiated the shallow steps of St Giles Church in Camberwell. As he entered the church to join the congregation, his mind swept back the years to a certain September day on the Somme in 1916. Because of the significance of that day, it merited his attendance at this special memorial service that is held annually on the Sunday nearest to 15th September.

Harold Silvester somehow lived through that September day in 1916, unlike so many of his chums who were with him in the 1st Surrey Rifles. Now he was in church to honour their memory, because he had seen them die by the score that day in a battle known as High Wood.

Dominating the Bazentin Ridge, a maze of trenches linked High Wood with the enemy-held villages of Martinpuich and Flers. With its strongpoints and artillery support, High Wood could be defended on all sides. And it was grimly defended against periodic British infantry attacks and, at one time, a cavalry charge.

High Wood. Even now, it is more than the flickering flame of Great War comradeship that keeps its name alive – with good cause. Because High Wood became the graveyard for numerous young men, whose brief lives were snuffed out by bombs, bullets and shell bursts. In Harold Silvester's battalion alone, just two officers and sixty other ranks emerged unscathed from an attacking force of 567 men. Appalling enough, yet it was not the sum total. The 1st Surrey Rifles were but one of the battalions of the 47th (London) Division, whose awesome task that day was to take High Wood and the defences that snaked through it and beyond it.

Take it they did – what remnants of that proud division were left to take it. They held it, too. They had succeeded where equally gallant men had tried to wrest the wood from a stubborn enemy in two bloody months of fighting. Yet there were no accolades for the successful divisional commander. In one of the most sensational personal episodes of the Great War, he was suddenly dismissed from his post for 'wanton waste of men'. A damning indictment, but was he wholly responsible for the 4,500 casualties incurred when attaining the objective?

That dramatic September day has another connotation: tanks went into battle for the first time in history – ironically, a fact that increased the British casualties at High Wood. Immortalised in verse, it was the last wood to be captured in the Somme campaign and, although a few acres in area, it has been estimated that the remains of thousands of soldiers enrich its scalloped earth which time has reverently blanketed with leaves and has covered with ferns.

Whoever was there and lived, could never forget it. For those young men who fought and died in High Wood and in its surrounding fields; for those fortunate few, such as Harold Silvester, who fought there and miracuously survived, this book is their story and a further testament to their generation.

Acknowledgements

Writing a book of this nature demands much research, which invariably means a heavy reliance on the co-operation of others. This I received in generous measure, not least from Alex Aiken who produced the detail maps of actions at High Wood. I am also indebted to the many people who gave me access to diaries, documents and a diverse number of publications, among which were the transcripts of Fourth Army conferences that were employed for the dialogue between General Rawlinson and his corps commanders in Chapter Nine. I should like to express my appreciation to the Rt Hon Earl Haig OBE, Major Christopher Congreve and Mr Andrew Rawlinson and other copyright holders for allowing me to quote extracts from such sources, as well as my heartfelt thanks to the people who helped me in my research. They include:

Joan Neale, Bramdean, Hants; Monica Ruff, Cheriton, Hants; Marion Edwards and Des Finnigan, Worplesdon, Surrey; Pat Regan, London SE5; Joan and Terry Grantham, Croydon, Surrey; Bill Butler, Hector Arden and Sid Gibson, London SE15; Bert Smith, Bromley, Kent; Dick Stratford, Penrith, Cumbria; Don Lindup, Norfolk; Harold Silvester DCM MM, London SW8; Mrs Clare Soper, London SW9; Bert Mahoney, New Milton, Hants; Vince Collihole, Morden, Surrey; C.E.Couch, London SE23; L.A.Watkins MM, London SE26; Walter Grover MM, Canterbury, Kent; Ernest Collins, Mr and Mrs Reg Collins, West Drayton, Middx; Peter Bryant, Basildon, Essex; Martin Middlebrook, Boston, Lincs; Vincent Lissenden, Brixham, Devon; Walter Nash and L.Ramsey Eveson, Bromsgrove, Worcs; Ray Seaton and Dr Victor Russell, Wolverhampton; Bill Ginn, London SE8; Percy Hannibol, Sandwell, W.Midlands; the late Harry Cohen, Birmingham 27; Arthur Knight and J.L.Gannaway, Sutton Coldfield; Mrs F.Powell, L.D.Phillips and F.G.Bolton, Birmingham; Robert Graves and A.P.Watt Ltd, London WC1, George Tyson, London SW4, T.Kelly, *Daily Mail* Reference Library; Joyce Ligertwood, Falkirk; Major Tom Craze, Royal Green Jackets' Regimental Museum; Colonel Wood, Argyll & Sutherland Highlanders' Regimental Museum; Lt-

Colonel Mike Chard, City of London Headquarters, The Royal Regiment of Fusiliers; Colonel F.W.Cook MBE MC. KOYLI Regimental Museum; Lt-Colonel George Forty, The Tank Museum, Bovington; Sgt Leslie Watling, Regimental Headquarters, Royal Tank Regiment; Geoffrey Jenkens, London SW3; Captain R.G.Appleby, London SW16; Ernest Dormand, Ashtead, Surrey; L.H.Ferne, Worcester Park, Surrey; J.W.A.Burt, Harting, E.Sussex; A.J.Tilley, London W4; S.H.Hopkins, Westcliff on Sea, Essex; Peter Bull, Keston, Kent; T.S.Chance, Cobham, Surrey; Major J.M.A.Tamplin, London SW1; Jack Richbell MM, Basingstoke, Hants; Gwen Edmonds, Faber & Faber Ltd; Correlli Barnet MA and staff of the Archive Centre, Churchill College, Cambridge; J.F.Russell, Dept of Manuscripts, National Library of Scotland; Staff of the Imperial War Museum, London SE1; Charles Messenger, London SW5; Madame G.Mathon, Ferme du Bois des Fourcaux, Somme; Janet and Tom Fairgrieve, Bois Delville, Somme; Nicole Lequette and Guy Dengreville, Méaulte, Somme; Claude Dercourt, Hédanville, Somme; Wendy Bartlett, Long Parish, Hants; Michel Duthoit, Albert, Somme; H.F.Hooton, Northampton; Tony Miles, Ludlow, Shropshire; Diana Jones, Hambledon, Hants; Paul Miles, Shalden, Hants; Donald Macardle, London W8; Patrick Dillon, London SE5; Christopher Skelton, Wellingborough, Northants; John Crosse, Vancouver BC, Canada; Mrs Ivy Brennan, Thornton Heath, Surrey; David M.Griffiths, Warley, West Midlands.

I should like to add that my research was conducted over a long period; during which time I saw some eyewitness accounts from men who fought at High Wood, but who have since passed away and the whereabouts of their next-of-kin are now unknown to me. I, therefore, wish to apologise for any omissions in the Acknowledgements due to this reason.

I
ROUTE TO HIGH WOOD

'All ways seemed to lead to High Wood.'

Lt-Col Graham S.Hutchison DSO MC

Pilgrimage

CHAPTER ONE

Genesis

Perspiring in the grey light of dawn, buffeted and deafened by the tumultuous din of their weapons, British artillerymen rammed shells into the gun breeches for the ultimate bombardment before zero hour. It was the seventh day of the longest artillery barrage then known in the Great War, and the time was 6.25 a.m. The firing reached a crescendo as every artilleryman went to work with renewed vigour, fully supported by trench mortar batteries with a hurricane bombardment as zero hour approached. The air pulsed as shot and shell rained over No Man's Land to fall on to German positions.

For weeks, tunnelling companies had burrowed beneath the surface of No Man's Land and quietly placed tons of high explosive at strategic points below the enemy's front line positions. The first mine was sprung at 7.20 a.m., its eighteen tons of deadly explosive ensuring an awe-inspiring sight from the British trenches opposite as a gigantic column of earth and chalk erupted skywards. Within five minutes, the enemy in that proximity furiously retaliated with machine-gun fire backed by artillery, their fears now confirmed that the moment of truth was near. Except for one mine, whose firing was inadvertently delayed, all remaining mines were detonated at 7.28 a.m., heaving more columns of earth and chalk towards a cloudless sky that promised a fine sunny day. Zero hour came two minutes later, and the guns suddenly ceased firing as gunners elevated their weapons for the first artillery lift beyond the German front line positions.

The few seconds of silence seemed unreal after such a lengthy bombardment which had sent over 1,600,000 shells of various calibre towards the enemy. As the odd incoming shell made its appearance, some 66,000 British infantrymen began to climb up scaling ladders from their trenches or clambered to their feet from where they had lain in No Man's Land. Spearhead of General Sir Henry Rawlinson's Fourth Army and arranged in five corps, with two divisions from the Third Army on their left flank, they shook out in formation and advanced on a fifteen mile front. It was a warm

Saturday morning and the date was 1st July 1916.

Thronging the communication trenches, and pushing their way into the recently vacated assembly trenches, were thousands more of their countrymen and all awaiting their turn to go over the top. Without question, the much heralded Somme offensive had arrived in deadly earnest.

All told, seventeen infantry divisions were committed for the assault that Saturday morning of 1st July. Each division numbered three brigades with four battalions to a brigade. The majority of the battalions comprised youthful faces of Kitchener's New Armies, all of whom had flocked to Britain's recruiting centres in a tidal wave of patriotic fervour, more than replacing the ghastly losses of the original British Expeditionary Force, whose numbers were reduced to a handful by December 1914.

Present also were many of the pre-war part-time soldiers: men of Britain's Territorial Force who were considered to be the nucleus of the country's second line army. To this end, a fortnight under canvas at annual summer camps, plus weekly evening drills and a musketry course yearly was the usual routine until 4th August 1914. On the declaration of war, while the Regular soldiers of the BEF fought side by side (and occasionally alone) with the French and Belgian armies to contain the German advance, the mobilized Territorial battalions underwent intensive training to raise them to the required standard. By October, they were on their way to the Western Front, each man having signed an individual declaration that he was willing to serve abroad.

The Regulars were there too, but in a minority of 47 battalions compared with the combined total of 194 New Army and Territorial battalions. Although of the Regular Army, only a few of the men in those 47 battalions had served with the colours before the war, yet a goodly number had already been blooded in the battles of 1915, at such sanguine places as Festubert, Givenchy and Loos.

With the Regulars in their respective battalions, men of the Territorials and of Kitchener's New Army in theirs, all walked in company formation and in line abreast towards the enemy, each soldier heavily burdened with the accoutrements of war; every one a volunteer. In fact, never before had the British Army ever contained such a patriotic cross-section from every background of life, nor had it seen such a high level of education and physique. Moreover, however inwardly they felt as most soldiers do before battle, battalion morale was terrific. As they marched to the front, did they not see the vast array of *matériel* for the offensive, and had they not found themselves enveloped in the roar of the guns? And had they not witnessed the cruel pounding of the German front? Above all, they had been told that this was to be the big show and they were ready to play their part.

By evening and not a conscript among them, nearly 60,000 had fallen victim to the German defenders who had survived the week-long bombardment, thanks to deep dugouts, untouched machine-gun emplacements and deadly webs of uncut barbed wire. Nor was the assault materially helped by the all too frequent instances of faulty artillery ammunition and fuses – defects that either caused shells to prematurely explode or not to explode at all. The lack of spares for the guns also gave rise to anxiety, especially when over-worked buffer springs broke or lost their resilience from repeated firing. The end result for the poor bloody infantrymen was, mostly, not the promised amble across No Man's Land to occupy pulverised trenches of a beaten enemy, but a desperate fight for every foot of territory.

Such an outcome, particularly to the architects of the Somme offensive, could not be shrugged off as a complete surprise. They knew that the enemy had the luxury of two years in which to prepare an elaborate and potent defence system. French troops certainly knew what faced them when they held the line there before the British take-over. They knew, and it was substantiated later by British raiding parties, that deep dugouts existed; and only the heavier calibre shell or mortar bomb was capable of coming anywhere near to demolishing them. Unhappily, the right type of armament to deal effectively with this problem was in short supply along the British Third and Fourth Army fronts.

On the German side, it was common knowledge for weeks that an Allied offensive would occur that summer. Besides the obvious military build-up behind the Allied lines on the Somme, German agents were busily gleaning intelligence in an effort to discover the actual day. Some agents had heard of the likelihood of a British assault about Whitsuntide: 11th June. Then on 14th June, an enemy agent at the Hague filed a report that the British attaché there had said that 'the offensive in the West will begin next week'. For a while, it was the information concerning the Whitsun date that mainly puzzled German High Command. Everything became apparent when details were received of a speech, given by a British minister to a meeting of owners and workmen of munition factories.

The meeting, held in Leeds, was addressed by Arthur Henderson, MP. During the course of the meeting he had endeavoured to answer a pertinent question on the subject of why Whit Monday, 12th June, was to be a normal working day and not a bank holiday. Fully acknowledging the need for security, Henderson tried to be circumspect, but made a fist of it. 'How inquisitive we all are!' he said. 'It should suffice that we ask for a postponement of the holidays and to the end of July. This fact should speak volumes.'

It did. The significance of his reply escaped the censor's eye and it appeared in the London morning newspapers on 2nd June.

General Fritz von Below, commander of the German *Second Army* who faced Rawlinson's Fourth Army and two of Allenby's divisions that Saturday morning, was in no doubt where the assault would come. He was concerned about the situation, but his superior – General Erich von Falkenhayn – thought differently. He surmised that any Allied offensive would be against the German *Sixth Army*, which was commanded by Crown Prince Rupprecht and situated north of von Below's *Second Army*. To Falkenhayn, it made little sense for the Allies to attack on the Somme. Rupprecht, however, was of the same opinion as Below. The only question that remained was when?

The answer was trawled from various places. Among them were the reports of the German military attaché in Madrid, fully concurred by an agent who agreed that 'the enemy offensive will begin on the 1st July'. This news arrived on 26th June and, on the 27th, fourteen observation balloons were counted north of the Somme, which corresponded to the British fourteen divisions there – all opposite the *Second Army* line. The most critical report emanated from the German *56th Reserve Brigade*'s headquarters at Contalmaison, which sent to its division a part of a message that originated from Rawlinson's Fourth Army headquarters at 10.17 p.m. on 30th June. It wished all infantry units good luck and that they should hold tight to every yard of ground gained. The message was picked up by a listening post and was final confirmation, if confirmation was really needed, that the infantry assault would begin the next day.

A few days previously, however, it was discovered that the assault was scheduled for 30th June. Bad weather though, postponed the date for twenty-four hours. One German unit, not guessing the cause of the delay, cross-examined a captured infantryman on 1st July. He was surprised to be asked why the British had not attacked on 30th June as planned.

Out there in the bullet-torn, shell-pocked terrain of No Man's Land, surrounded by dead and dying comrades, many a bewildered and wide-eyed infantryman might well have asked why it was planned at all. Battalions of volunteers who had gone to war with a cheery song on their lips were halved in number that day. And most of those men scythed down were of the New Army battalions that had not experienced any kind of an assault before.

As night fell on the desolate scene, it became apparent at Fourth Army headquarters that the much vaunted offensive had not gone according to plan. Even though the full reality had yet to strike home, the assault had already met with the tacit approval of one man. He was the French Army Commander-in-Chief, General Joseph Joffre, who now judged that the pressure on his troops at Verdun would ease.

Joffre had, after all, initiated the Somme offensive. Having directed General Foch[1] to make a study for a powerful offensive from the River Somme down to Lassigny, Joffre communicated to Haig in late December of 1915 that any French offensive along that thirty-mile stretch would be greatly assisted by a simultaneous British offensive, and carried out on the north side of the river i.e. between the Somme and Arras. One main reason why he deemed the Somme/Arras area favourable was because it had experienced very little activity for some considerable time. He also thought the ground was generally ideal for a huge offensive.

What Joffre chose to ignore was the fact that, its being a quiet area, the Germans had taken the opportunity to transform many key positions in that part of their front into underground fortresses. Nature helped in this task by presenting the enemy with a massive chalk layer beneath the gentle landscape – perfect for the excavation of deep chambers.

General Sir Douglas Haig, who officially superseded the luckless Sir John French as Commander-in-Chief of the BEF on 19th December, was highly sympathetic towards a simultaneous offensive, but on the Somme? Although he was independent of Joffre's command, policy dictated that there had to be the closest co-operation to effect a united force. Haig, however, would have preferred an offensive in Flanders and near enough to the Channel coast for the Royal Navy to participate. In military terms, any offensive in Flanders made more sense than one on the Somme which was devoid of territorial prizes.

[1] *Commandant le Groupe des Armées du Nord* (GAN).

In his letter to Haig, Joffre had also written that he wanted the French Tenth Army (sandwiched between the British First and Third Armies and holding a twenty-mile front south of Loos) to be replaced by a British force. Haig already knew how Joffre felt about the Tenth Army's situation, but it was a question of finding divisions without depleting the BEF's strength too much in other places. For the sake of co-operation, Haig did agree to take over a section of the Tenth Army's line in order to signify his willingness for a combined Anglo-French offensive.

The idea for this offensive stemmed from a meeting of Allied commanders earlier in December before Haig's promotion. Held at Joffre's headquarters in Chantilly, the meeting consented to a simultaneous offensive on all the three European fronts, namely Russia, Italy and the Western Front; preferably in late March or early April to take advantage of the spring and summer weather. This date, however, was soon found to be impracticable. It was judged that Russia would not be ready before June, nor would the BEF be adequately reinforced before May of 1916. Italy also had her problems.

Political considerations, particularly in Britain, needed to be taken into account too. A fairly strong contingent in Asquith's Coalition Cabinet[2] were reluctant to give *carte blanche* to an early 1916 offensive, or even one at all on the Western Front. Indeed, the bloodletting of 1914 and 1915 had been noted with grave concern. In the event the War Committee of the British Cabinet met on 13th January and amended a recommendation made at a previous meeting on 28th December from: '. . . every effort is to be made for carrying out the offensive operations next spring', to 'Every effort is to be made to prepare for carrying out offensive operations next spring in the main theatre in close co-operation with the Allied Armies, and in the greatest possible strength, although it must not be assumed that such offensive operations are finally decided on.'

Lt-General Sir William Robertson, who became Chief of the Imperial General Staff[3] four days after Haig assumed command of the BEF, was present at the meeting. He promptly wrote to Haig to warn him of the current attitude. He added that some members of the Cabinet, including Lloyd George, wanted no offensive before the

---

[2] A coalition government under Asquith had been formed from the Conservative and Liberal benches in May of 1915.

[3] Hereinafter called the CIGS.

BEF was at full strength, which the dissident Cabinet members calculated would not occur until well into the summer.

It is easy to understand their reasoning. By 31st December 1915 British casualties had risen above the half million mark and, of that figure, about 205,000 had been classified as killed and missing.

The British C-in-C was not alone in feeling the changeable breath of politics down his neck that January. Joffre was receiving similar treatment from members of the French Government. With his casualty list fast approaching two million, he was given to understand that he should try to avoid further heavy losses. Mindful of the political situation, he approached Haig on 20th January and intimated that he would have five offensives prepared by the end of April. The one chosen would depend on the relative military position. Before any main assault, however, he wanted the Germans worn down by preliminary attacks. Joffre thereupon played his joker by prevailing on Haig to mount a large scale attack north of the Somme around 20th April. Not content with that, he wrote to Haig three days later and baldly declared that he regarded it as indispensable that, before the combined assault, the British Army with at least fifteen divisions, 'should seek to wear down the German forces by wide and powerful offensives, as the French Army did in the course of the year 1915.' Hardening on 20th April, he suggested that one of these battles should take place on that date, north of the Somme, followed by another one of the same magnitude in May, but elsewhere along the British line.

Haig was not completely surprised by Joffre's letter. He had heard something in a comparative vein from a staff officer with the British Mission at Chantilly. The same officer also reported that the French felt that the Russians would not be capable of attacking until the end of July. Until then, it was hoped that Britain and Italy would carry out wearing attacks right up to a month before the general offensive. In this way, Joffre could preserve his divisions for the main chance.

For his part, Haig had already hastened General Allenby's Third Army's participation in the proposed Somme offensive. He had also asked the Second Army commander, General Plumer, to study alternative battle sites further north, including the Messines Ridge. In addition, among other tasks charged to him, and prior to his assuming command of the Fourth Army on its formation on 1st March, Rawlinson was instructed to involve himself with Allenby's preparations. Although Haig had hedged his bets by seeking alternative sites on which to do battle, he found himself warming to a

Somme offensive, believing as he did that France was nearing the end of her tether and that the war must be won by the forces of the British Empire.[4]

With respect to Joffre's letter, Haig could see at a glance that such tactics were militarily unsound and, knowing the feelings at home, politically damning. True, he supported trench raids and wearing out fights, but certainly not in the way and on the time scale envisaged by Joffre. Besides, he did not have sufficient heavy artillery for that sort of commitment.

After much correspondence which climaxed in a conference on the subject, Joffre finally dropped his plan for the April and May preparatory offensives on 14th February. However, it was agreed on that day to mount the combined offensive astride the Somme about 1st July, preceded by a partial British attack in the La Bassée-Ypres area some days before. It was further agreed to try to carry out the Somme offensive even sooner should Russia be attacked in the meantime. Joffre still pressed for the BEF to relieve his Tenth Army. He also wanted adequate ground immediately across the river on the British side for a corps from his Sixth Army — being the army selected for the French assault. He explained that it would allow the Sixth Army more elbow space in which to guard its left. More likely, Joffre's real reason was that of insurance should the British attack fail. Haig conceded to this demand, but refused to take over any more of the Tenth Army line:

> I said that the state of the British Army (75,000 below strength in 39 divisions) and all divisions wanting training, combined with the difficulty of moving so many divisions, made it impossible to carry out the relief of the 10th Army in the near future. General Joffre asked if I would accept the principle of relieving the 10th Army. I said 'Certainly,' and he asked 'When?' I replied 'Next Winter.' The old man laughed, and I remarked we could not do impossibilities; besides he was short of men in the depots and it was much more costly to attack than to hold the line, so the British must now attack and not be detailed to hold passive fronts. I added I had no doubt that under proper arrangements the attack will be a success. General Joffre argued no more.[5]

And so the die was firmly cast for a joint Somme offensive; an

[4] Haig: *The Private Papers of Douglas Haig, 1914-1919*. Ed. Robert Blake. Page 125. (Eyre and Spottiswoode, 1952).
[5] Haig: *op. cit.*, page 129.

offensive conceived by Joffre and, despite various growing pains, matured by the British desire to show co-operation. Yet the fact remains that the chosen· area was deficient in enemy arterial communication lines, nor was there any enemy-held centre of consequence to take for many miles beyond the German front. Indeed, there was no military objective, common or otherwise, behind Joffre's proposal and Haig's acceptance than that of attrition.

Another Commander-in-Chief also had attrition in mind that February, but his name was Falkenhayn. After a series of subsidiary attacks that commenced on the same day as the Allied conference, his *Fifth Army* struck at Verdun on 21st February. Commanding *Fifth Army* was Crown Prince Wilhelm, and his basic task was to break the back of the French military resolve. The offensive, aptly code-named *Gericht* and meaning the 'place of execution', began with an intensive bombardment on a French front that was no more than seven miles long. The aim was to pulverise the front line troops before pushing through German infantry to exploit the gap created by the artillery. The plan would have succeeded but for the grim tenacity of surviving French units, buttressed by the endeavours of a new commander for the Verdun sector: General Pétain.

The Verdun crisis relit Joffre's fuse on the vexing question of his Tenth Army. This time Haig agreed to do something about it. He divided its sector into two and made the First Army, commanded by General Monro, responsible for the top half. The southern half was filled by sliding Allenby's Third Army to the left, except for three corps which remained in place. These three corps formed the nucleus of Rawlinson's Fourth Army and were, from south to north, XIII (Lt-General W.N. Congreve, X (Lt-General Sir T.L.N. Morland) and VIII Corps (Lt-General Sir A.G. Hunter-Weston). On 24th March, the headquarters of Lt-General Pulteney's III Corps with one infantry division moved into Fourth Army's area. About six weeks later, the 19th and 34th Divisions were assigned to Pulteney.

Meanwhile, Germany's offensive at Verdun was meeting with increased opposition. By the end of February, Wilhelm's *Fifth Army* had suffered 25,000 casualties to Pétain's 30,000. Wilhelm's renewed assault of 5th March did not greatly enhance his situation, but merely pushed up the casualty figures on both sides. The element of artillery surprise had withered away and Verdun became a bloody slogging match. As March bowed out, losses were calculated at around 81,000 Germans as against 89,000 Frenchmen. To put it succinctly, not quite what Falkenhayn and Wilhelm originally had in mind. Although reducing France's striking capacity, Verdun was far from crippling her will to fight. As for the enemy, Verdun increasingly made it less likely for Germany to strike in strength elsewhere along the Western Front in 1916.

For the Allies, Verdun had other significant factors. It stopped Joffre's schemes for preliminary attacks near to the time of the joint Somme offensive. It also reduced the number of French divisions that were earmarked for the proposed French assault south of the Somme. Just as critically, it threw the date of the offensive into the air again. Concerned about the enemy's latest attack at Verdun in early April, Joffre was keen to bring the date forward. He asked Haig to ensure that all British preparations were completed by 1st June. To his credit, Haig agreed with the proviso that only military necessity would justify a June offensive, stating to Joffre that the longer the postponement, the better the opportunity to have more British divisions available for it.

In candid terms, Joffre did not rate highly in Haig's book as a military thinker. This was evident when Joffre visited him on Friday afternoon, 7th April, so that Haig could settle three main points of the Somme offensive, namely the objective, the dividing line between British and French forces and the timing of their attacks.

I explained my views . . . but Joffre did not seem capable of seeing beyond the left of the French Army (which the French propose should be at Maricourt) or indeed of realising the effect of the shape of the ground on the operation proposed. He said that I must attack Northwards to take Montauban ridge while the French troops attacked Eastwards from Maricourt. I at once pointed to the heights away to the North East of Maricourt and showed that his proposed movement was impossible until the aforesaid heights were either in our possession or closely attacked *from the West*.

The old man saw, I think, that he was talking about details which he did not really understand. Whereas I had been studying this particular problem since last January and both knew the map thoroughly and had reconnoitred the ground. The conclusion I arrived at was that Joffre was talking about a tactical operation which he did not understand, and that it was a waste of my time to continue with him. So I took him off to tea. I gather that he signs anything which is put in front of him now and is really past his work, if indeed he ever knew anything practical about tactics as distinct from strategy. Joffre was an engineer.

Whatever he thought of Joffre, Haig still needed to square the proposed joint offensive with the British Government. He arrived in London and motored to the War Office on the morning of 14th April. There, he met with Lord Kitchener and Lt-General Robertson. After Kitchener had complained of the politicians who never consistently held the same view for more than two days and were forever back-stabbing each other, Haig asked outright whether the Government approved of his combining with the French for a summer general offensive. The fudged answer he received was that all Cabinet ministers had reached the conclusion that the war could only be ended by fighting, and that several of them were keen for a definite victory. It was sufficient for Haig. He accepted their reply as confirmation to forge ahead with his preparations.

He called at 10 Downing Street where he saw Asquith extremely agitated:

He was angry because the War Office had filled up certain new Divisions (some still at home) instead of employing the men as drafts to bring Divisions at the front up to War Establishment. In reply, I stated that I agreed that the Divisions at the front ought to have been made up to full strength before this, but at the same time, the extra Divisions were equally necessary to enable me to hold the increased front. He told me how M. Ribot on behalf of the French Government had come across to arrange for us to give them a big loan, and that unless they had received the money they would have had to make terms with the enemy, or at any rate the French Govt. would have been defeated. I was with the Prime Minister for over an hour.

In common with Haig, General Joffre too had his political burdens. In particular the fiery French senator, Georges Clemenceau, who headed up the Military Committee of the Senate. Despite his 75 years, Clemenceau had an exceptionally active mind and was destined to become Prime Minister of France. For some time, he had disagreed with Joffre's motives. In pursuance of his thinking, he arranged to meet Haig at Aire on 4th May. His object was to persuade the British Commander-in-Chief to use his influence in restraining Joffre from making any large scale offensive until all was ready.

'If we attack and fail,' warned Clemenceau, 'then there will be a number of people in France who will say that the time has arrived to make terms.' He was of the opinion that there was nothing to lose by delaying the offensive. Clemenceau added that the French people were in good heart, but the mood could change if there was a failure after a big effort.

Haig tried to assure him that he had no intention of participating in a premature battle unless a catastrophe occurred at Verdun. Then he certainly would come to the aid of the French forces, although it appeared to Haig that such a situation was unlikely to arise. As far as he was concerned, the German offensive there had been contained. His main worry lay in the danger that the French could ultimately leave the Somme assault to the British. Though Haig surmised that he and Clemenceau had parted on the best of terms, it soon transpired that the French senator was far from satisfied with the outcome. The very next morning, he visited Lt-General Henry Wilson's IV Corps headquarters where he and Wilson had a lengthy conversation. Clemenceau spoke frankly, saying that he thought that an early offensive in the West would be sheer madness. Wilson, always one for political intrigue, jotted in his diary that night:

> He told Haig so. He thought Haig was impressed. He asked Haig if he was under Joffre. The reply was No – though nearly, as Clemenceau gathered ... on the whole I had never seen Clemenceau so anxious about the future. He fully realizes about Asquith and the terrible danger we run from keeping him as Prime Minister. He begged me to work hard at home to make them realize the dangerous position into which we are drifting, and the crying danger and madness of another unsuccessful attack.

Wilson, a great Francophile who later admitted that he was probably 'more responsible for England joining the war than any other man',[6] was disliked by Haig as a person who could not be trusted. Indeed, during the period when Haig was about to become Commander-in-Chief, the question arose of what to do with Wilson. Knowing that Wilson had never even been a company commander in the field,[7] Haig justifiably considered that he should first find his feet with a division, preferably in Britain, before being given a corps command to befit his rank. Robertson demurred. He thought Wilson

---

[6] Major-General Sir C.E. Callwell: *Field-Marshal Sir Henry Wilson Bart., GCB, DSO; His Life & Diaries.* Vol 1, p. 189.

[7] Wilson's career path was via the post of Commandant of the Staff College (1907) and Director of Military Operations (1910).

would do less harm in France away from the political scene. On that note and as Rawlinson moved on as temporary GOC First Army, so Wilson took command of Rawlinson's IV Corps.

When Rawlinson assumed command of the Fourth Army on 1st March, he was instructed by Haig to devote his whole attention to the coming Somme offensive. On 3rd April, he submitted a thirty-six point plan to Haig. In it and with an eye to the divisions which Rawlinson understood would be available for the offensive, he proposed to attack along a 20,000-yard front. With the prospect that the offensive might continue for at least a fortnight, he calculated that this frontage would give him eight to nine men per yard – just adequate for his needs. Equally important, he judged that he would only have sufficient heavy artillery for a 20,000-yard front.

Drawing deeply on the lessons learnt at Loos, when a small penetration was made through the enemy lines at a heavy cost to British life and limb, Rawlinson wished to employ four corps comprising ten divisions for the attack; plus two divisions remaining on the defensive, three divisions in corps reserve, and two divisions with one cavalry division in Fourth Army reserve. Realising the importance of Congreve's XIII Corps, being on the British right flank and next to General Balfourier's XX Corps of Fayolle's Sixth Army, Rawlinson intended giving him five divisions compared with three each for III and X Corps, and four for VIII Corps.

Congreve, a dedicated officer who held the Victoria Cross, landed in France as a brigadier-general in September of 1914. Although the war was just over a month old, it was enough to retard his career in favour of less senior brigade commanders who were there before him. Finally, after ten of his contemporaries had attained the rank of major-general, Congreve was given command of 6th Division in May 1915. In the following November, he became GOC of the newly-formed XIII Corps.

His promotion was well-deserved. With a reputation of being a 'front line' general from his 18th Brigade and 6th Division days, Congreve was instrumental in making the British infantryman and his rifle an even deadlier combination during his time as commandant of the School of Musketry at Hythe. When he arrived there in 1909, each infantry battalion in the British Army had two machine-guns. Congreve knew that machine-guns were essential for the prosecution of any future war, and so the School advocated six machine-guns to a battalion. His foresight met with a blank wall, mainly due to public expenditure cuts that had plagued the pre-war

annual Army Estimates and Vote. Subsequently, Congreve decided
to increase the rate of fire of each rifle by giving the men special
training. It worked. Every Regular soldier worth his salt and an
extra sixpence a day, could fire at least 15 rounds a minute at the
target before him. Moreover, it was not unknown for some
infantrymen to exceed 25 rounds a minute. Congreve left Hythe in
1911 to take command of 18th Brigade, but his good work was
continued and displayed itself at Mons, Le Cateau and at 'First
Ypres' – much to the enemy's cost who thought his troops were
facing automatic fire.

At the time of Rawlinson submitting his plan of attack, Congreve
had under command one Regular (7th Division) and three New
Army divisions (18th, 21st and 30th) with the prospect of an
additional one. Since the inception of his corps, Congreve had
instilled in his subordinates the necessity for their men to respond to
battle conditions, which included the need to shoot quickly and well.
Certainly a basic requirement, but unlike the men of the old
peacetime Regular Army and Territorial Force who had the luxury
of time, New Army recruits had flooded in and made proper training
difficult if not impossible. The result of which meant that very few
New Army men were capable of firing more than 10 rounds a minute
with their rifles. Fortunately, what they lacked in training and
experience, they made up with enthusiasm. With the majority of his
New Army battalions still untried in battle, Congreve was doing his
level best to see that they would be ready for the approaching
offensive. Equally important and in conjunction with his divisional
commanders, he and his staff continued to formulate the corps plan
of attack.

Rawlinson, having submitted his Fourth Army proposals on 3rd
April, was keen to see Haig personally about them. His desire
stemmed from the fact that he had planned the offensive with limited
objectives in mind which was not characteristic of Haig's way of
thinking. Rawlinson, therefore, firmly believed that the
Commander-in-Chief would not agree with his proposals unless he
was present himself to convince Haig verbally. He had hoped that
the meeting could take place on the afternoon of Wednesday, 5th
April, but a telephone call from Lt-General L.E. Kiggell, Haig's
right-hand man, modified Rawlinson's schedule. Kiggell suggested
instead that it would be better if he came later in the afternoon and
stayed the night. This would give the Commander-in-Chief more
time in which to study the scheme. Kiggell's suggestion increased

Rawlinson's suspicions that Haig favoured an offensive with unlimited objectives, and so he prepared himself for a long and uncomfortable meeting.

Before going to see Haig, Rawlinson held a conference of his corps commanders at his headquarters in Querrieu on Wednesday morning. The conference began at 10 a.m. and, after speaking on several aspects of training and discipline, Rawlinson asked each corps commander in turn to give a brief account of his own corps plan of attack. Everything went well until Congreve was asked to speak.

Although a courteous man, Lt-General Congreve was not the type of commander to tell a superior what he would like to hear in the hope that all would come right on the day. Boxed in by the French on his right and with Joffre toying with the idea of attacking later than the British, Congreve's problems extended beyond just attacking the German line. As well as the known enemy strongpoints, which to a greater or lesser extent faced all four corps commanders, Congreve's divisions would ultimately have to contend with wooded areas – geographical features absent along his colleagues' fronts. In this respect, not only did Congreve summarise XIII Corps' plan of attack, but studiously pointed out the potential hazards that needed to be surmounted. Rawlinson was not impressed:

> Hunter-Weston, Morland and Hudson[8] all showed by their descriptions that they realised the problem before them and that they were working on the right lines. Congreve, I was less satisfied with. I therefore called him and Bob Greenly up into my room afterwards and gave them a talking to, pointing out that they saw too many difficulties and anticipated unnecessarily many adverse contingencies.

In short, Congreve's plan was not dashing enough for Rawlinson.

After lunch the Fourth Army commander travelled to Montreuil with his senior staff officer, Major-General Montgomery. Haig met them and, as Rawlinson feared, altered the format of the Fourth Army's proposed scheme. The Commander-in-Chief wanted the eventual line of Fourth Army's advance to be south-eastwards towards the high ground around Ginchy, yet making a protective

[8] Although he was a divisional commander, Hudson represented Lt-General Pulteney. Brig-Gen Greenly was XIII Corps' senior staff officer.

flank north of Pozières. To Haig, Rawlinson's intention was merely to take the enemy's first and second system of trenches and kill as many Germans as possible, whereas his instinct was to aim at getting as large a combined force of French and British across the Somme and fight the enemy in the open. He also wanted to employ Britain's secret weapon – the tank – to capture the high ground at Serre and hold it, so that cavalry and machine-guns could be sent on to occupy Miraumont and Grandcourt, after which to hit the Thiepval stronghold from the rear. Whilst Rawlinson inwardly took note, Haig added that the French were anxious to take over the Fourth Army line in front of Maricourt village – part of Congreve's sector. He asked Rawlinson whether the move would interfere with his operations. Rawlinson responded by requesting some time in which to consider the matter.

Rawlinson stayed overnight at Haig's château. By breakfast he felt that he had solved a number of problems troubling him. He informed Haig that he could accommodate the French at Maricourt, thereby saving a division, but then the Fourth Army Commander immediately asked for another corps under Lt-General Horne's command to take over the attack on Fricourt and Mametz. In this way, he could reduce Congreve's XIII Corps to two divisions. Enough, thought Rawlinson, to attack the German trench system in front of Montauban.

Haig at once agreed, and Rawlinson left Montreuil in a contented mood. A day later, he sent for Congreve and bluntly told him that he did not consider him fit to command five divisions in the coming offensive. Rawlinson further informed him that he had spoken to the Commander-in-Chief, who was sending Lt-General H.S. Horne to take over 7th and 21st Divisions. They would carry out the left attack under Horne's new corps. With that, Congreve knew he had lost the northern part of his sector. He was then told by Rawlinson that he would retain 18th and 30th Divisions for the attack on what remained of his front. What he was not told about was the arrangement which Rawlinson intended to execute with the French on his right. When that was effected, Congreve would find himself even more cramped for room and without essential roads. That evening, Congreve wrote in his diary: 'I had expected something of the sort from the combination of Rawly and Haig, both of whom consider nothing and no one of use unless from First Army. A severe slap in the face all the same. . .'

His only consolation in the past three days was news about his eldest son, Billy. A brigade-major with 3rd Division's 76th Brigade in General Plumer's Second Army, he had been recommended for the Victoria Cross[9] for capturing practically single-handed over 70 Prussians during an attack at St Eloi. One high-ranking officer had even told Congreve that he would be proud to serve under his son, who had celebrated his 25th birthday on 22nd March 1916. Belatedly realising that he had tarnished his career when he gave Rawlinson some home truths, Lt-General Congreve sought a degree of comfort in his son's success. A few hours after Rawlinson's admonishment on 5th April, which Congreve considered to be totally unjustified, he wrote to his son:

My very dear old Son,
   I am prouder of you than I can say, for yesterday I had a letter from Arthur Alan saying all sorts of nice things of you. Today I met Uniacke, who said you had run both the Bluff and St Eloi battles and he considered you had done them admirably and, tonight, I have a line from Plumer, saying 'Billy has again done splendidly. He is really 1st rate.' It is delightful and makes me feel very happy and thankful – and now I have your letter and hope you will get a VC, for you seem to have earned it. I do send you my most hearty congratulations. You have every right to be proud of yourself, but I know you can bear it without having a swelled head. I sympathise greatly with you in the loss of so many good fellows – it is heart-breaking work. I don't feel I can ever make a general, for I cannot face having men killed in the ruthless way generals must do. . .

Whatever the future held for him, at least he had the satisfaction of knowing that his son's personal star was in the ascendant.

A week later, Rawlinson received Haig's written reply to his Fourth Army plan. Having, as he thought, won on points, he now discovered that Haig had poured cold water on important aspects of his plan and required changes. The biggest change concerned Rawlinson's limited objectives which were earmarked for capture in the initial phase. The Commander-in-Chief wanted more ground gained during the initial phase. 'The first advance, therefore,' stated Haig, 'should be pushed as far as the furthest objectives of tactical value which we can reasonably hope by forethought and tactical skill to retain after capturing.'

[9] In the event, his son was awarded the DSO.

Again the ghost of Loos manifested itself. Haig asked Rawlinson to consider a comparatively short intensive bombardment immediately preceding the assault, so as to surprise the enemy and to lower his morale. According to Haig, such a scheme gave rise to better results than to spread out the bombardment over a longer period. It was in complete contrast to Rawlinson's detailed proposal of a long artillery bombardment, followed by the infantry walking in and taking over what remained of the enemy positions.

What also jolted Rawlinson was Haig's requirement to extend the frontal attack northward from opposite the German-held village of Serre to about Hébuterne, plus a simultaneous attack against the Gommecourt salient above Hébuterne as a major diversion. Considering the limited supply of heavy artillery at his disposal, Rawlinson thought that this extension to his front of attack was over-ambitious. Nevertheless, he and his staff set about modifying his original plan.

The amended Fourth Army plan was completed on 19th April and re-submitted. Because Haig wanted the fortified village of Montauban captured in the first advance and not just the trench system in front of it, and also the capture of a heavily defended brickworks a quarter of a mile south-east of Montauban during the initial phase, Rawlinson was forced to reappraise the role of XIII Corps. He recommended that Congreve should receive an additional infantry division.

Among other modifications, Rawlinson tried to grapple with the Gommecourt salient question. It was a tough nut to crack if he was to keep sufficient troops in reserve to maintain a sustained offensive over a lengthy period, as he hoped he could. Finally, fully realising that even a small independent operation there would divert the enemy's attention to some extent from his main front of attack, Rawlinson suggested that, as far as his Army was concerned, activity against Gommecourt should be limited to a demonstration that would include the discharge of gas and smoke.

Haig read between the lines and informed the Fourth Army commander that a simultaneous attack on the Gommecourt salient would be carried out by Third Army troops under the orders of Lt-General Sir Hubert Gough. With regard to Fourth Army, it was now agreed that the Serre-Miramont spur, Pozières, Contalmaison and Montauban would be the first day's objectives. Montauban, however, was dependent on the degree of co-operation that Rawlinson received from the French on his right flank, as well as the amount of assistance he could receive from the French artillery.

Congreve, meanwhile, took it upon himself to reconnoitre his sector and that of the German front from the air. With Captain Robeson RFC as his pilot, Congreve flew from an airfield at Allonville. After experiencing turbulent air over Albert, the biplane flew steadily along as Congreve surveyed the country. He instantly recognised many landmarks and, just as he settled down to enjoy the novelty, a sudden explosion occurred nearby. Captain Robeson immediately jinked the aircraft on to a new tack, since the cause of the explosion was that of a howitzer shell which had been fired directly below them, narrowly missing the aircraft. After flying for two hours and having seen as much as he could in that time, Robeson brought the aircraft in to land without further incident. Congreve peeled off his borrowed leather flying coat, thanked the pilot, and returned in his car to his headquarters at Corbie.

As the days passed into weeks, so the Fourth Army plan was massaged into shape. Yet zero day continually fluctuated on the calendar as external forces influenced the state of play. Italy came under pressure when the Austrians launched their Trentino offensive on 14th May. Startled, Italy cried out for help. It was answered three weeks later. Commencing their last great campaign of the war, General Aleksei Brusilov's South-West Army Group smashed through two hundred miles of Austrian front from the Russian side. In France, Joffre repeatedly beamed the spotlight on the plight of his troops at Verdun, making Haig promise that the Fourth Army would be ready if required by 20th June. Haig still preferred to have a much later date, probably mindful of the tanks being produced in England under a shroud of secrecy. At least he had at last ensured that the Somme offensive would stay a combined operation, even though the haggling over the ultimate date went on. Again, thinking of Verdun, Joffre insisted that 1st July should be the latest date for the attack.

Haig stone-walled, knowing that the later the date the more chance the Fourth Army would have of succeeding. He tendered four options: 1st and 15th July, 1st and 15th August. At the mention of 15th August, Joffre panicked and shouted that the French Army would cease to exist if nothing was done before then. With that, Haig calmed Joffre by agreeing to commence operations around 1st July.

No matter what occurred elsewhere, there was the continuing awesome logistical problem in the Fourth Army of sustaining 400,000 men[10] and 100,000 horses – not to mention other military

---

[10] Total strength of the Fourth Army on the day of the assault was 511,676 men.

requirements such as the movement and the stockpiling of artillery and infantry munitions. Railways had improved considerably to serve both the Third Army and Fourth Army theatres, but still not enough to satisfy all contingencies. Because of increased rail usage and the introduction of many new railway lines and sidings, Rawlinson's Fourth Army would have to rely on road transport in the event of a breakthrough in depth, since only ten miles of railway track remained in store. Whether the Somme country roads could withstand the massive transportation forward should a huge gap open up was another problem, especially if the weather turned wet.

Finalising the plan of attack between the French and the British had proved a difficult task. Agreement was finally reached that General Balfourier's XX Corps, on the north of the River Somme, would attack at the same time as the British. The two other corps in Fayolle's Sixth Army would attack two hours later on the south side.

By 14th June, Rawlinson had his formal operation order prepared, in spite of the actual date of the attack refusing to settle on a specific day. Because the date kept varying, it meant modifications at corps level which, in turn, affected divisions, brigades and battalions. 'A fresh change of plans thrown at me,' wrote Congreve on 21st June. 'This is the second in two days and, seeing battle is supposed to begin on the 25th, it is getting late for so many.'

Even though corps commanders were bemused by these last minute changes, Rawlinson's operation order stood rock-firm and crystal-clear, particularly on the overall objectives:

> The first day's operations will include the capture and consolidation of Montauban, Contalmaison, Pozières and Serre.
>
> As soon as this line has been gained and consolidated, preparations will immediately be undertaken to commence the second phase of the operations.
>
> The Army commander wishes to impress on all commanders that the success of the operations as a whole largely depends on the consolidation of the definite objectives which have been allotted to each corps. Beyond these objectives no serious advance is to be made until preparations have been completed for entering on the next phase of the operations.

Rawlinson's cautionary approach was to have a significant bearing on Congreve's tactics on the day when it finally arrived. In the meantime, he and a chosen XIII Corps staff moved from Corbie on

23rd June to his battle headquarters at Chipilly, by which time the date had been changed again. Four days later, Sir Douglas Haig transferred to his advanced headquarters at Château Valvion, Beauquesne, just twelve miles east-north-east of Albert and ten miles north of Rawlinson's headquarters at Querrieu.

On 1st July at 7.30 in the morning, their lives and the enemy before them, the first wave of British infantrymen rose from the earth and walked into the sun.

CHAPTER TWO

Result and Reflection

Despite the tremendous bombardment, despite the numerous acts of unsung heroism, only one corps in the British assault managed to achieve all its first phase objectives. That corps was commanded by Lt-General Congreve and it was 18th and 30th Divisions that succeeded in doing it.[1] With artillery assistance from the French on the north side of the Somme, giving XIII Corps a 4 to 1 ratio of heavies over its adversary, enemy forward positions had crumbled. Even so, isolated pockets of resistance caused anxiety, especially in the 18th Division's path which affected its time schedule.

The infantrymen of Major-General John Shea's 30th Division were more fortunate. The division's two assault brigades (21st and 89th Brigades) quickly crossed the 500-yard stretch of No Man's Land with little difficulty. They had deliberately started out some minutes before zero hour and subsequently missed the bulk of the incoming shells directed on to their recently vacated positions. On their right, French troops of Balfourier's XX Corps' 39th Division accompanied them over No Man's Land. To accentuate Allied comradeship and co-operation, the CO of the battalion extending 30th Division's right flank, Lt-Colonel Fairfax of the 17th King's, strode arm-in-arm with his French counterpart, Commandant Le Petit, who led the 3rd Battalion of the 153rd Regiment on the far left of the French attack.

Much to their relief, foremost units of 30th Division found the enemy wire well cut and most of the surviving Germans in the firing line too dazed to fight. After neutralising a machine-gun post that had inflicted damage among the attackers, troops swept on to take the fortified village of Montauban, situated less than half a mile behind the German front line trenches. The place was smashed to pieces. An infantry officer of the 17th Manchesters 2/Lt Dick Macardle, witnessed its capture. Granted that his battalion – one of

[1] Congreve's XIII Corps had three divisions by this time. The third one was Major-General W.T. Furse's 9th (Scottish) Division, comprising the 26th and 27th Brigades, also the South African Brigade. The 9th Division was in corps reserve two miles behind the line and hidden from the enemy's view.

three comprising the 90th Brigade – had an easier passage than most, but 90th Brigade's advance had been no cake walk:

At zero the 89th and 21st Brigades went over and took the Boche first and support lines, including Glatz Redoubt and Dublin Trench. At 8.30 we went through them to take Montauban. 'A' Company was in front of us, advancing in sections with about 20 paces between 'blobs' in perfect order at a slow walk. A carrying party of Scots came next and then our Company. Montauban was a mile and a quarter away. Every inch of ground between us and the village was churned up and pitted with shell holes. It was impossible to locate the German front line, and his support trench was a great irregular ditch full of craters and fresh earth.

We advanced in artillery formation at a slow walk, leading our sections in and out of the stricken men who were beyond help or whom we could not stop to help. It seemed callous, but it was splendid war. Men, crawling back, smiled ruefully or tried to keep back blood with leaky fingers. We would call a cheery word or fix our eyes on Montauban – some were not good to see.

German shells littered the battlefield with dead and wounded. All around us and in front, men dropped or staggered about. A shrapnel shell would burst high up and a tidy little section in two-deep formation would crumple up and be gone. The ground was rough and broken, yet we had advanced too quickly although we had done it at the slowest walk; so we lay down for 40 minutes under the flight of shells, waiting. Waiting is hard. We were to rush the village at 9.56 a.m.

The time came and I watched for 'A' Company to rise, but the seconds ticked on. I hailed a sergeant and shouted a question to him on where his officers were. 'All gone, sir,' he shouted back. I caught a glimpse of young Wain, his face haggard with pain and a leg soaked with blood. He was smoking a cigarette and pushing himself forward with a stick. His voice was full of sobs and there were tears of pain and rage. 'Get up, get up, you bastards! Blast your souls – get up!' I waved to him. He smiled and dropped – he knew it was not absolutely up to him any longer. We of 'B' Company took over, for he was the last of 'A' Company's officers and their sergeant-major was killed.

We were enfiladed by machine-gun and rifle fire, but we took the village from a fleeing and terror-stricken enemy. All was wreck and ruin – a monstrous garbage heap stinking of dead men and high explosive.

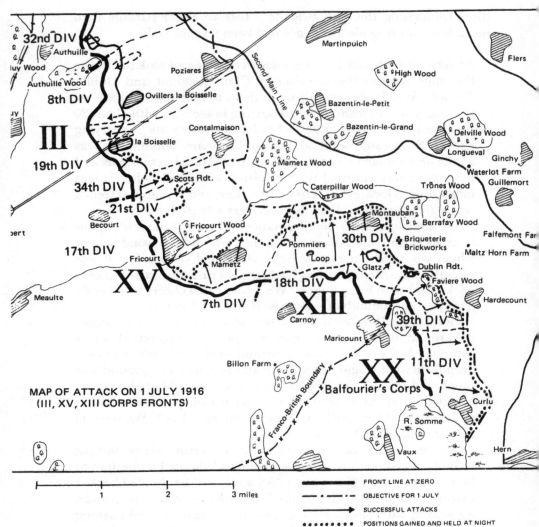

MAP OF ATTACK ON 1 JULY 1916
(III, XV, XIII CORPS FRONTS)

```
|———————|———————|———————|
         1       2       3 miles
```

————————— FRONT LINE AT ZERO

— · — · — OBJECTIVE FOR 1 JULY

————► SUCCESSFUL ATTACKS

········· POSITIONS GAINED AND HELD AT NIGHT

They pressed on to their furthest goal of the first phase; an enemy-occupied assembly trench, code-named Montauban Alley, and situated about 200 yards beyond the village. That section of the trench behind Montauban was entered an hour before noon. The Germans in it, a few hundred, surrendered with scarcely a fight.

From this vantage point the victors could see the enemy fleeing in disorder across a wide but shallow dip in the landscape, known as Caterpillar Valley. Also due north of Montauban, groups of stragglers were seen retreating on a narrow dirt road which disappeared over the far slope of Caterpillar Valley towards a hidden village called Bazentin-le-Grand. The British troops at Montauban Alley, all from two New Army battalions (16th and 17th Manchesters[2]), but soon joined by the 2nd Royal Scots Fusiliers, shot merrily away at the retreating Germans. Meanwhile, forward observation officers began calling up artillery fire to pound the far slope and the road.

Some German troops were very reluctant to leave. They were field artillerymen and their guns were positioned in the valley. Enthusiastically shot at by rather inaccurate small-arms fire, and attacked from the air by RFC pilots who flew their aircraft within 150 feet of the ground, they were eventually driven away by a small party of 16th Manchesters who rushed the nearest field guns. Three were brought back in triumph – the first guns to be captured in the Somme campaign.

With 30th Division capturing Montauban, the opportunity presented itself to take the brickworks which had been by-passed. The brickworks had one feature that had been a passive threat and, much to everyone's disgust, was still standing. It was the tall chimney stack, utilised by the Germans as an observation point.

Already bombarded continuously by French 240-mm heavy mortars during the past seven days, the brickworks was subjected to an additional bombardment by divisional artillery from 11.30 a.m. to 12.30 p.m. As pre-arranged, a company of the 20th King's[3] advanced under the cover of the barrage and stormed the wrecked buildings immediately the last shell fell. Midst acrid fumes and swirling clouds of red brick dust, they hastily wended their way through the debris that abounded with enemy dead. Only on nearing the far side did they find themselves under fire from a machine-gun that had been scrambled to the surface from a nearby dugout. A few casualties were suffered prior to despatching the machine-gun crew to their Maker.

As the dust settled, a group of German officers and men staggered weaponless from an adjacent dugout. Tired and unkempt, they willingly surrendered. The dugout, a deep one, was searched. Two machine-guns and sheaves of official-looking papers and documents came to light. It later transpired that some of the prisoners were members of the *62nd Regiment* headquarters staff and, numbered

[2] Known on their formation as the 1st and 2nd Manchester Pals.
[3] The 20th King's were also a Pals battalion, originally called the 4th Liverpool Pals.

among them, was the regiment's colonel and adjutant. To complete
the bag, a commander and observer of a field artillery regiment had
also surrendered from the dugout.

The German officers taken captive at the brickworks were not the
only key enemy personnel to suffer from the effects of the mammoth
bombardment along XIII Corps front.

A fact overlooked at the time of capture, but verified when the
ruins of Montauban were subjected to a more thorough search,
showed that XIII Corps had much to thank for the help given to its
troops by French heavy artillery. Reinforced cellars were discovered
along with exceptionally deep dugouts, yet a French 240-mm mortar
bomb had penetrated an important dugout with devastating effect.
The dugout had been a central artillery command post and every
occupant was killed in the explosion, thereby substantially
disorganising the control of enemy artillery fire in that area.
Congreve was especially pleased when he heard the news. For days,
he had 18th and 30th Divisions stuffed cheek to jowl in the Carnoy
Valley awaiting the big moment. As he admitted afterwards, any
incoming shell would have found a target, but none came.

It could not be said that the late occupants of that dugout were
unlucky to be hit by such a blockbuster. For the whole of the seven
days, one French 240-mm mortar battery had constantly pounded
the village into rubble. Not unnaturally, another large dugout had
received a direct hit. Packed solid with enemy dead, their putrefying
bodies had to stay unburied due to the intensity of the Allied
bombardment.

It was gratifying to Congreve that Shea's 30th Division had
successfully achieved all its objectives in the allotted time span.
Gratifying, because Rawlinson had wanted to replace 30th Division
before the attack with the 9th (Scottish) Division. Finally, he
directed Congreve to sack its commander, Major-General Fry, who
had been with the division since its inception in November 1914.
Promoted to major-general, Shea superseded Fry six weeks before
the offensive.

While 30th Division was busily accomplishing its objectives,
brigade battalions of 18th Division were desperately attempting to
match its progress. Commanded by Major-General Ivor Maxse and
on 30th Division's left flank, 18th Division had first to capture two
trenches, known as Train Alley and Pommiers Trench, after
breaking through the German firing line. The division's three
brigades – 54th Brigade on the left, 53rd in the centre and 55th

Brigade on the right – were then to proceed and subdue the second objective; being the remaining length of Montauban Alley that ran roughly east of Montauban to an enemy strongpoint, Pommiers Redoubt, on the Montauban-Mametz road. If all went according to plan, total advance would be nearly 2,000 yards once the third objective was reached, namely a vantage point on Montauban Ridge that overlooked a narrow winding wood, aptly called Caterpillar Wood.

Very much the exception along the British assault front, but in keeping with 30th Division's findings, infantrymen of 18th Division discovered that much of the barbed wire facing them had been chopped up. But unlike the enemy firing line in 30th Division's path, leading waves met more pockets of determined resistance. Much of this resistance resulted from a mass of small craters no more than 150 yards wide in area near the Carnoy-Montauban road. There, battalions of 55th Brigade were badly mauled and held up by machine-gun and rifle fire.

The 53rd Brigade in the centre of 18th Division's frontal attack had made good progress, despite valiant efforts to contain them which included a fanatical last-ditch stand by a Bavarian chained to his machine-gun who was only overpowered when wounded. The 55th Brigade on the left wing had done even better, but still the enemy's tactics in and behind the cratered zone created untold havoc among the leading battalions.

Fortuitously, 30th Division's successes elsewhere, coupled with the gains of 18th Division's 54th and 53rd Brigades, began to exert pressure on the defenders in front of 55th Brigade's depleted formations. A number of Germans started slipping back through what remained of their communication trenches. British bombing parties moved into the part-vacuum, hurling grenades before them under covering fire from Lewis machine-gun teams.

Shea's 30th Division infantrymen, having cleared the enemy off a frontage of 1,500 yards to a depth of 2,000 yards by 2 p.m., gazed over the shallow depression of Caterpillar Valley from their forward positions north of Montauban. Ahead lay undulating countryside that presented them with a panoramic view of the Bazentin Ridge on the skyline, not more than 3,000 yards away. Yellowing corn, interspersed with the bright red smudges of the poppy, carpeted its forward slopes. To the east, the ridge sloped gently down to the untouched village of Longueval which snuggled up to Delville Wood. Back along the ridge and less than a mile from Longueval, situated in solitary splendour on top of the crest in full leaf, virtually due north of the victors, stood High Wood.

Away to the victors' left, Mametz Wood sun-bathed midst the din of battle. A few hundred yards to their extreme right was Bernafay Wood, behind which and for the most part hidden was Trônes Wood, just 400 yards further east.

Over the far side of Caterpillar Valley was an even shallower depression in the landscape, which deprived observers at Montauban of viewing the village of Bazentin-le-Grand that was located in the dead ground. Scarcely a shell had dropped on it, but a little to the south of the village and becoming increasingly full of breathless and panicky German infantrymen, field artillerymen, cooks and clerks, lay the enemy main second line.

No more than a handshake away to 30th Division's right, French infantrymen of 39th Division had won all their initial objectives save for a tiny wood by late morning. Their sister division in Balfourier's XX Corps had met with stiffer opposition, but its troops continued to move forward and take ground. Below the River Somme and comprising three divisions between them, both I Colonial Corps and XXXV Corps of Fayolle's Sixth Army were also making satisfactory progress.

Along a six-mile attacking front, two miles of the enemy's front line positions were captured above the Somme and four miles below it – all due to a more systematic bombardment, greater artillery involvement and a more imaginative infantry deployment through departure saps dug forward of the firing line. Added to that was the *élan* of the French infantry who no longer believed in parade ground tactics when crossing No Man's Land, instead preferring short rushes in groups which offered a higher survival rate. Even more telling, particularly south of the Somme where the assault began two hours later, they were not expected by the enemy.

Its right flank secured through 39th Division's accomplishments, Shea's 30th Division was poised for another advance – should the order come. Not since Loos had such an opportunity presented itself. With a thoroughly disorganised enemy ahead, it was a situation worthy of exploitation. A moment to be grasped, and there were on hand ample troops to do it.

As the Official History stated[4] 'The French XX Corps on the right, there being eight hours more of daylight left, was prepared to

[4] Edmonds, Sir J.E.: *Military Operations in France and Belgium, 1916.* Vol 1, p 337.

go on; the men of the 30th Division were not tired, nor had the losses been heavy; and the XIII Corps reserve, the 9th Division, was available, besides the higher reserves.'

Those higher reserves included 2nd Indian Cavalry Division, saddled up three miles behind XIII Corps' jumping-off point.

The 2nd Cavalry Division was one of three cavalry divisions comprising Lt-General Sir Hubert Gough's Reserve Army. Primarily formed for the expected break-out, Gough's Reserve Army came into being at Haig's behest so that Rawlinson could focus his attention on creating the gap through which Gough's cavalry divisions could pass.

Strategically, should enemy resistance crumble during the first phase of operations, it was planned to feed the cavalry along three pre-ordained routes (one for each cavalry division) that would eventually bring them astride the Albert-Bapaume road, thence to Bapaume. For this to occur, a gap would need to be created in the centre of the Fourth Army's front of attack; namely on III and X Corps fronts. It was also planned that the cavalry would only advance when the reserve divisions of III and X Corps had moved forward to clear their line of advance. Even then the three cavalry divisions were strictly forbidden to leave their places of assembly until it was certain that their three specified routes had been made practicable; not just to the old front line, but all the way to the boundary line that encompassed the final objectives of the first phase.

Plans were also drawn up for the protection of both flanks of the committed reserve infantry divisions. The VIII Corps on the left of X Corps would assist in guarding the left flank of X Corps reserve division (49th Division). On the other side of the gap, Horne's XV Corps was to hold its reserve division (17th Division) in readiness for a simultaneous advance on the right of III Corps reserve division (19th Division). The 17th Division would then be directed on to the village of Bazentin-le-Petit and High Wood, its own right flank covered by the remainder of XV Corps and XIII Corps.

Clockwork conformity was the essence of Rawlinson's operational planning, and heavily based on a successful artillery bombardment. So much for the theory. In reality, only Shea's 30th Division had kept to its schedule and Rawlinson had left no room for local initiative, even at corps commander level. Congreve's hands were tied as much as Shea's.

There was no cavalry earmarked for Congreve's XIII Corps

should German resistance give way on his front and, as it was not accommodated in the Fourth Army's overall scheme, it would not be forthcoming. Nor could Congreve do anything about Bazentin Ridge and High Wood which beckoned Shea's infantry. The next phase of operations for 30th Division, once Montauban was firmly consolidated, lay through Bernafay and Trônes Woods to Guillemont. Since no other division was up with the victorious 30th, Shea was instructed to help 18th Division on his left. All the same, patrols were sent into Bernafay Wood where a few stragglers were rounded up and brought in. While this was happening, some battalions of Maxse's 18th Division arrived on the Mametz-Montauban road by 3 p.m. An hour later and the division had secured its part of Montauban Ridge, as well as occupying its share of Montauban Alley.

Macardle's men were active in clearing Montauban's few deep dugouts that had survived the heavy shelling. One dugout was fitted with electric light and sported a push-bell, and all contained cowering and unkempt men in filthy field-grey uniforms. They were pushed up to the sunlight where realisation struck them that they had survived:

> Large parties, laughing and dancing like demented things full of mad joy, streamed unguarded back to Maricourt – holding their hands up and calling, 'Mercy, *Kamerad*.' The village was full of the terrors and horrors of war; dying Germans among the brick dust and rubble, horrible wounds and reeking. We began at once to consolidate, working like demons.
>
> Rumours trickled through. Vandrey was killed, Ford was killed, Kenworthy was wounded, the Colonel was down – seen last in a shell hole with the doctor. We were almost too busy to heed, but the messages stabbed just the same.

At long last, good news came from Horne's XV Corps. Its 7th Division on 18th Division's left had captured Mametz village about 4 p.m. It was the second village to capitulate and when a vital trench was occupied to the north of it, an opportunity arose for 7th Division to take Mametz Wood while the enemy was still punch-drunk. Doubtless the other XV Corps division failing to take Fricourt and Fricourt Wood adjacent to 7th Division's line of advance, coupled with the fact that Mametz Wood lay outside 7th Division's operational sphere, thereby making the XV Corps staff cautious about infringing Rawlinson's rigid plan, ensured the passing up of the opportunity to capture Mametz Wood at that vital moment – something that would be regretted in the days to follow.

Save for the occasional long-range German shell, all resistance appeared to have temporarily ended along the newly connected front of 7th, 18th and 30th Divisions. Balfourier's XX Corps troops on XIII Corps' right flank were experiencing the same phenomenon. Eagerly wanting to press home the advantage, but requiring a simultaneous advance by XIII Corps to cover his left flank, Balfourier sought Congreve's assistance. With a good deal of regret, Congreve had to refuse the request. Congreve's negative reply, its origin deep in Rawlinson's explicit instructions to capture and to consolidate the first phase objectives, signalled the beginnings of a rift between the Allies on the Somme.

As far as cavalry involvement was concerned, the prospect withered on the vine. Rawlinson had ordered the Reserve Army cavalry divisions to stand down at 3 p.m. With set-backs in the centre and in the northern part of the front, he had judged that cavalry would again be surplus to requirements.

There was little else for 30th Division to do, but to strengthen its newly-won positions and await the inevitable counter-attacks. The 18th Division did likewise. To all intents and purposes, other Fourth Army divisions engaged in the day's assault had either gained a few bloody yards of enemy line or nothing at all. Chiefly due to XIII Corps' attention to detail throughout its rehearsals, battle planning and artillery programme, at least something of the day's hopes was salvaged.

Whilst Shea's and Maxse's divisions went about their defensive tasks, and pioneer battalions slaved at making good the road from Maricourt to Montauban, reformed groups of Germans started trickling back to the woods around Montauban, scarcely believing that the advance had stopped where it did. Their return was synonymous with the increasing thunder of the enemy's large calibre guns, many of which were re-registered on Montauban.

The 30th Division's success at Montauban turned sour under the hostile bombardment as the evening wore on. The Germans were shooting on a known target and shooting well. Macardle was in Montauban Alley to the north-east of the village and very much on the receiving end of the shelling:

It was rather terrific and we lost heavily. Sproat was killed, blown to bits. A great many men were buried in the trenches we had dug; one shell killed Sgt Butterworth and more or less destroyed five others in my platoon. My platoon dwindled down to four men and no NCO – and still I was not touched. There was no dugout in 'B' Company's side of the village and Humphreys, who was left in command when Vandrey was killed, had his HQ in a shell hole. We made our men dig holes for themselves under the parapet, for the Alley was about eight feet wide, but first they had to dig fire steps.

The trench became littered with dead and wounded. The dying called for water, but there was none. Those in agony asked pitiably for stretchers, but eight stretcher-bearers had been killed and three of the four stretchers destroyed; the doctor was overwhelmed with work. It was impossible to spare a sound man to help along a broken one. We were standing to for a counter-attack.

The first counter-attack on Montauban came at 9.30 p.m. from a mixed party of Germans who had hidden in a small quarry in Caterpillar Valley, not more than a few hundred yards from the British defences. The attempt died under the vigorous fire from the officers and men on Montauban Ridge.

Confused reports on progress were still reaching Rawlinson at his headquarters in Querrieu. Some gave him false hopes and a sense of misplaced optimism. The casualty figures were a case in point. He was under the impression that losses were 16,000 when, in truth, they were nearer 60,000. However, having decided to place his two most northern corps, X and VIII Corps, under Gough's command with Haig's agreement, he gave instructions that the enemy's resistance should be worn down by pressing home the assault. The object was to secure a line from which to launch an attack on the German main second position. Orders to this effect were issued at ten in the evening. With regard to XIII Corps, Congreve received a directive to consolidate all its gains and to prepare an attack on Mametz Wood in consort with Horne's XV Corps.

About the same time as Fourth Army HQ staff despatched Rawlinson's orders, Congreve began his inspection of XIII Corps' dressing stations where he was surprised to find such a huge number of walking wounded. Badly wounded himself when winning his VC at Colenso, and being an asthmatic person who had constantly to fight his own ill-health, Congreve was somewhat bemused at the sight. He finally attributed it to the clerk classes of his New Army troops 'who thought a scratch a serious wound, having never before met a more lethal weapon than a table knife'.

All the same, his corps casualties were on the 6,000 mark with 55th Brigade of Maxse's 18th Division suffering the most. Certainly such a casualty figure could not be lightly tossed aside, but it was still the lowest of the day. Hunter-Weston's VIII Corps, which tried to take Beaumont Hamel and Serre, headed the corps' casualty list. His corps suffered 14,591 losses without achieving anything.

On the credit side, Congreve's troops had taken the most prisoners. He estimated XIII Corps' 'bag' to be about 1,000 Germans captured plus six machine-guns, as well as the three field-guns from Caterpillar Valley. On the question of artillery ammunition, Congreve believed that 80,000 tons were expended on his front alone prior to the infantry assault that morning.

Arguably, after Rawlinson had cut his sector in two with the advent of XV Corps, Congreve had a simpler task than his colleague, Horne. One wonders whether he could have achieved more with 7th and 21st Divisions if Rawlinson had let him keep the whole of his original front. As it was, Congreve could rest on his laurels. His 18th and 30th Divisions had done what was expected of them, and had done it splendidly.

He went to bed at 1 a.m., but was rudely awakened when the Germans again counter-attacked at Montauban in greater strength, also against the brickworks. The fighting raged from 3.15 to 4 a.m. At one stage the enemy even effected an entry into Montauban Alley. It was to no avail, because Shea's 30th Division's artillery laid down a heavy barrage and the machine-guns defending Montauban and the brickworks did the rest. The enemy losses were high, especially at Montauban where the Germans advanced in close formation. It had been a desperate attempt by the enemy, so desperate that the defenders thought from the German troops' behaviour that they were actually drunk.

The fury of the last counter-attack, although repulsed, told on the dwindling defenders. They had gone without sleep and with very little to eat and drink since the evening of 30th June and, when they were not being counter-attacked, they were shelled. Macardle:

The shriek of shells was like a hurricane among telephone wires and in narrow streets; the last scream and then the all-powerful thud, and the rending crash of them went on ceaselessly. We got tired of the shock of their explosions, making us reel and feel dizzy and numb. We got sick of the reek of high explosives which meant dead and broken men, and our cheery triumphant treatment of this most unpleasant situation changed.

When the first day and night were gone, when the second night began we were silent and grim and – yes – a little afraid. At least we had got to longing for a relief – to hating the endless shattering of the shells – to receiving news of more casualties among our dwindling force (no longer very much of a force) with a weary shrug. Of course we knew Montauban was safe – we would keep Montauban – but every time a pallid runner came down the trench, or over the top and handed one a note, one wondered was it to say that Lt Humphreys was killed and that I am in command of the Company, or the enemy was in Montauban.

Except for the shelling along Montauban Ridge, the remainder of Sunday was fairly quiet in the back areas of Congreve's sector. Reinforcements and supplies began to flow up to the new front line, yet there was a period in XIII Corps sector that day when something different in the war was tried: Bernafay Wood received the first thermite bombardment ever.[5] A total of 500 thermite shells were fired by 30th Division's field howitzers in an attempt to set the wood alight, but the result was disappointing. One consolation was that infantry patrols from the brickworks found German corpses in the still smouldering undergrowth. Certainly the number of enemy dead indicated that the Germans were returning and therefore recovering from their ordeal.

Congreve paid a visit to 18th Division's new front on Sunday morning from his battle headquarters at Chipilly. One reason was to see for himself the results of the seven-day artillery bombardment, knowing that in places the German barbed wire had been some 15-20 yards thick.

I went up to Carnoy and our new position and walked over the German lines. I was surprised how completely the wire was demolished and how little the trenches. A good many dead Germans were lying about in the usual debris of a battle. No shooting except on to Montauban. Everyone walking about in the

[5] Incendiary shells, containing a composition of finely powdered aluminium and oxide of iron.

open as though the Germans were miles away instead of being on the next ridge. Their trenches were very wide and not so good as I expected, nor were the dugouts in evidence, in the back lines anyway; the front one being too much destroyed to tell.

Satisfied that his artillery, which had been augmented by French large calibre firing, had done a good job, he returned to Chipilly where General Sir William Robertson[6] arrived minutes later to congratulate him on his success. Robertson had come to France the previous day for one of his periodic visits in his capacity as the CIGS. After the wretched turmoil of the past weeks when he was in bad odour with his superiors, Congreve accepted Robertson's compliments with deserved pleasure. Since no other corps had achieved so much, he suggested to Robertson that it would be better to capitalise on his XIII Corps achievements and advance north rather than to the east as originally planned. This meant assaulting the Contalmaison-Longueval line, interlinked by the woods and villages of Bazentin-le-Petit and Bazentin-le-Grand. On breaking through the German main second position there, to sweep up on to the crest of Bazentin Ridge and take the high ground, including High Wood.

The prospect beckoned Robertson's imagination. At its highest point where the 75 acres of High Wood proudly straddled its waist, Bazentin Ridge was a shade over 500 feet above sea level and about 50 feet higher than the Montauban Ridge, not to mention the intermediate rise on the far side of Caterpillar Valley. From the wood, the ground tabled westwards to Pozières and north-west to Courcelette via Martinpuich village. Without question, from its exalted position, High Wood held the key to more than all-round visibility. Capture it, and the rear areas behind Longueval and Delville Wood (as far back as the Flers-Gueudecourt-Lesboeufs triangle) would be exposed to accurate artillery registration. It would also give fine observation to many of the German positions away to Bapaume. Better still, if it could be captured quickly before the enemy regained his balance, the chances of a breakthrough would increase enormously if the French co-operated whole-heartedly on Congreve's right.

For a nervous enemy looking balefully at his second main line of defence, High Wood and the ridge offered him a natural contour on which to establish another line of defence more potent than the one in

[6] Robertson was promoted to full general in June 1916.

front. Indeed, there was no reason to doubt that the enemy was busily girding his loins to do just that as Congreve and Robertson talked. With High Wood being the best vantage point for miles around, large tracts of the countryside between it and Montauban Ridge could be observed to Fourth Army's detriment. Moreover, even if Longueval fell, an entrenched enemy in and alongside High Wood could continue to make his presence felt in a fearful manner.

Roughly diamond shaped with the angles to the cardinal points, High Wood's south-western face bounded the Martinpuich-Longueval road. Its other three sides were flanked by chalky lanes. The lane bordering its north-western edge was partly sunken after leaving the wood on its winding route to Flers. The wood's interior was divided by grassy rides and the majority of the trees were of the sweet chestnut variety, whose branches were anciently used for making wooden pitchforks – hence the wood's traditional name of Bois des Fourcaux, but mis-spelt on the maps of the day as Bois de Foureaux.

Nothing could have been further from Robertson's mind than the origin of its Gallic place-name that Sunday as he listened to Congreve's proposal. It certainly seemed the best way to retrieve the situation and he agreed to have a word with Haig.

In the meantime, Rawlinson had Haig pressurising him to move through Bernafay Wood and capture Trônes Wood, but it required Balfourier's co-operation to do it. By early afternoon, Rawlinson heard that Fricourt and Fricourt Wood had both fallen with scarcely any resistance to 21st Division of XV Corps. The news heartened him, especially as Haig was anxious to exploit the successes in the south of the Fourth Army line. Haig was in a hurry and Rawlinson keenly felt his impatience. Mametz Wood had yet to be taken and Haig was eager for its capture too. Unlike Saturday the Fourth Army commander was plagued with doubts by Sunday evening, including whether Foch would consent to Balfourier's XX Corps advancing on Congreve's right in order for XIII Corps to secure Trônes Wood.

He had cause to wonder. Due to XIII Corps not being allowed to advance beyond its first phase objectives, contrary to the French Sixth Army's wishes, Balfourier's XX Corps was instructed to stand fast that Sunday morning.

Painfully aware of Haig's attitude, it did not materially assist Rawlinson's composure to learn of Robertson reporting to Haig on Congreve's proposal – a proposal that slotted in well with the Commander-in-Chief's feelings. If carried out, Rawlinson could see that the change in direction could only place a further strain on Anglo-French relations. It was difficult to believe that Joffre or Foch would countenance such a major modification in strategy, since they expected the British to press forward eastwards as planned. Besides, Congreve could be wrong about the state of play in his sector.

Rawlinson retired for the night a worried man. Before going to sleep, he wrote up his private journal and ended the day's summary with: 'Wullie, who saw Congreve tonight, has been telling D.H. fairy tales about the situation at Montauban.'

Fairy tales? Or the only feasible option left to rescue something from Saturday's sacrificial efforts? Even as Rawlinson laid down his pen, the opportunity on Congreve's front was ebbing away.

During Sunday night, 9th Division's 27th Brigade relieved 90th Brigade at Montauban under shell fire. Macardle's turn came at three in the morning:

We trailed out wearily and crossed the battlefield down trenches choked with the dead of ourselves and of the enemy. There were arms and things on the parapets and in trees, and bodies heaped in shell holes. The dawn came up as we reached again the assembly trenches in Cambridge Copse; from there we looked back on Montauban, the scene of our triumph. . . On the Péronne Road we met McGregor Whitton of the Royal Scots Fusiliers. He had been wounded in the hand early in the push, but had carried on. He was looking for a lost company and was very fed up. I asked after young Victor Godfrey. Young Victor was killed – his problem of marriage to a woman six years his senior finally settled. Towers Clark too was dead, so was Captain Law of County Down, and others I did not know so well.

The 17th Manchesters trudged on with other 90th Brigade battalions, stopping briefly for water from artillerymen at Billon Wood before coming to their destination in the divisional reserve area near Bronfay Farm. On reaching it and although very tired, Macardle was glad to see that they were to have breakfast:

Our reception was enthusiastic. The Brigadier had wired General Shea that '90th Brigade had taken Montauban in drill formation' – the highest possible praise. We were flattered and praised and our hands were crushed in welcoming hand-shakes; and the sun kissed away the ravages of our ordeal.

They were to stay there for the next three days, their euphoria transforming to disenchantment as the weather changed to rain and the ground to mud. Living on half-rations, Macardle gloomily jotted his private thoughts in a small note book: 'None of us have had anything like a square meal, or a bath, or a bed or a moment of comfort – and Shea has wired, "Well done 90th Brigade. You will attack again soon." We are about 400 strong today – we who went in 800.'

Macardle was killed on 9th July when 90th Brigade went back into action; only his brief diary from 30th June to 6th July survived him.

The same Monday morning that had seen the change-over at Montauban, Congreve received word that Bernafay Wood was still virtually undefended. Unable to contain himself any longer, he sought Rawlinson's permission to secure it. Approval was given and Congreve put into motion the necessary orders. After a short bombardment, Bernafay Wood was occupied by two Scottish battalions of 27th Brigade with little loss of life. Three field guns, three machine-guns and 17 Germans were captured in the process. From the cover of the wood, patrols were sent against Trônes Wood who found it defended by a considerable number of machine-gun teams.

Front line activity also began to hum in Horne's sector on 3rd July. With Bottom Wood and Shelter Wood taken surprisingly quickly, patrols started investigating Mametz Wood and a nearby German trench code-named the Quadrangle. Nothing could be seen of the enemy. This was reported at 3 p.m., two vital hours were allowed to pass before Horne gave his consent for the occupation of Quadrangle Trench and two other positions along the southern edge of Mametz Wood after dark. The 1st Royal Welch Fusiliers and the 2nd Royal Irish were ordered forward for the task. Due to a series of unfortunate delays, daylight was on them before they were ready to move off. The collective time lag was to have serious consequences.

Also on Monday morning, just before dawn, troops of 18th Division's 53rd Brigade swarmed into Caterpillar Wood after the RFC had reported it empty. They discovered five abandoned field guns. As Caterpillar Wood fell in Congreve's operational area, its capture added another feather to his cap. Three machine-guns were also found in the wood, which gladdened Congreve. He had visited his front again and, not for the first time, he saw the havoc they could inflict:

Much struck by the difficulties which were overcome, especially by the left of 18th Division. There is a labyrinth of trenches, many still intact despite the bombardment; also a series of little valleys running out from the big Talus Brisé valley that could not be seen from the front, making ideal positions for machine-guns of which the Boche had made the fullest use – judging from the masses of cartridge cases left. Many of our men are lying dead, in some cases a whole platoon together, evidently taken in enfilade by one of these infernal guns.

His information that Trônes Wood positively bristled with machine-guns, was the prime reason that he did not feel justified in ordering infantry to seize it without a preliminary bombardment.

Haig had every intention of launching an assault northwards to Bazentin Ridge, regardless of French opinion. He visited Rawlinson around mid-day, Tuesday, to discuss the necessity of protecting both flanks of the assault:

I impressed on him the importance of getting Trônes Wood to cover right flank, and Mametz Wood and Contalmaison to cover left flank of our attack against the Longueval front. I told him that Joffre would not attack Guillemont when we attacked Longueval, so it might be necessary for us to cover our own right flank.

After lunch at Corbie, Haig went on to Chipilly to see Congreve. Although he urged greater rapidity and the importance of gaining Trônes Wood before the enemy could wire it up, he was very complimentary and Congreve heard about his recent meeting with Joffre:

He told me he had a fine breeze with Joffre the day before, owing to our change of plans i.e. a push north in front of my Corps on Bazentin and Longueval rather than on Pozières. That the old man went off like a soda water bottle and was for a long time quite impossible. Haig waited till it was over and then continued his plans. Eventually, Joffre calmed down and finally bestowed the Legion on two of H's staff! I had thought him of the placid old person type. Haig also said that Joffre is not very good at reading a map.

Congreve listened intently to Haig. With the French on his right, it was crucial to keep on amicable terms for the good of the campaign. As for greater rapidity, he knew that Rawlinson was loath to move without their co-operation on the north side of the Somme. Meanwhile the universal feeling among regimental officers in both XIII and XV Corps was that they were still dealing with punch-drunk Germans. They were eager to deny the enemy the luxury of time to recover.

Along the centre and north of the line, however, enemy resistance continued to stay strong. True that the village of La Boisselle had just fallen to III Corps that Tuesday afternoon, but it had been a prolonged fight that was by no means over. The X and VIII Corps above III Corps' front, both under Gough's command and constituted as the Reserve Army (eventually to become the Fifth Army), made microscopic headway. Around Thiepval and Beaumont Hamel, British casualty figures were taking on the appearance of a computer print-out.

Limited movement continued on XIII Corps' front as night closed in. Elements of 18th Division crept up the slope 500 yards beyond Caterpillar Wood and into Marlborough Wood. It was undefended and a further confirmation that enemy resistance along that part of the front was still soggy.

Congreve received Major-General Haldane's 3rd Division into his corps that Tuesday. He placed the division in corps reserve for the eventual relief of Maxse's 18th Division. Already, changes had been made in his and Horne's corps at the front. In XV Corps, a battered 21st Division with losses of 4,663 officers and men was withdrawn to a rest area during the Monday night. Before dawn on Wednesday 7th Division of XV Corps was relieved by the 38th (Welsh) Division and, in XIII Corps, Major-General Furse's 9th Division took over the whole of 30th Division's front. Rest was much needed by both divisions. The 7th Division had suffered 3,824 casualties since that Saturday and, in the same period, Shea's 30th Division had sustained losses amounting to 3,360 officers and men. Within three days and imbued with fresh blood, 30th Division would be back in action.

Wednesday saw Haldane and his staff busying themselves in moving the three divisional brigades forward in preparation for relieving Maxse's 18th Division on 8th July. Haldane had already seen Congreve the day before when he was told that his division would be employed to help capture the German main second line. His division's objectives were Bazentin-le-Grand and Bazentin-le-

Grand Wood. Furse's 9th Division was earmarked to advance on his right and Watts' 7th Division (XV Corps) on his left. It was hoped that the French would attack on the right of 9th Division. After his meeting with Congreve, Haldane motored to Maxse's headquarters which was in a dugout beyond Bray-sur-Somme. He then drove on to Carnoy and walked up to the line captured on 1st July.

Like Congreve, he too was mildly surprised to see men moving about in the open, albeit in dead ground, but so different from Flanders where a man only had to show his nose to draw fire. He went on to 18th Division's front line trench and looked across Caterpillar Valley to the enemy main second line. On his left the enemy were shelling near Mametz Wood whilst XV Corps artillery was saturating the wood itself in readiness for an infantry attack. Haldane knew about the plan, since Mametz Wood enfiladed his front and had to be neutralised prior to the general attack on the enemy main second line. In Haldane's case, this meant passing over 1,500 yards of ground at night to reach the German positions. He thought he might have to employ his 8th and 9th Brigades in the front line of attack with his third and best brigade – 76th Brigade – in reserve. Having appraised the situation, Haldane made his way back to Corbie where his headquarters was temporarily situated in a château that belonged to an old lady who owned a nearby boot factory. The same château was Congreve's base headquarters, but he was allowed its use whilst his corps commander roughed it in Chipilly and until the time came for him and his staff to move closer to the front.

During his activities on Wednesday, Haldane arranged for observers with telescopes to watch the enemy line from the sector his division was due to take over in case new machine-gun emplacements were made. He also arranged for 48 Vickers machine-guns, as well as those of 18th Division, to fire around the clock on the enemy's line. He had good reason for these moves. An enemy map had come into British possession which showed German machine-gun emplacements along the front of the impending attack.

Except for a conference at Fourth Army HQ, Congreve devoted much of Wednesday liaising with his French colleague, Balfourier. With Haig requiring an attack on Friday, 7th July, on the German main second line between Longueval and Bazentin-le-Petit, it was imperative that any advance would not expose the French left flank on XIII Corps' right. To avoid the possibility, Congreve was directed to attack Trônes Wood and a farm called Maltz Horn Farm that lay north of Hardecourt. As Hardecourt faced Balfourier's front, it was expected that his troops would attack Hardecourt at the same time. Such co-operation, if conducted successfully, should offer mutual protection to both corps.

His dealings with the French proved very difficult, and Congreve needed all his tact and diplomacy. The one consolation of the day was that his and Horne's corps were taking a lot of prisoners. A touch of light relief came when Congreve heard that one German had exclaimed in English: 'I am damned well sick of this war. I will never leave London again!'

On Thursday morning, Congreve rode to Balfourier's headquarters for another session. He descended the steps of the deep dugout which served as XX Corps headquarters and was politely greeted by Balfourier, dressed as was his habit in the blue and red uniform of the old Second Empire. In common with Congreve, who preferred the 'choker' type of tunic to a collar and tie, so the ageing XX Corps commander refused to compromise on dress with the recently introduced regulation issue 'horizon-blue' uniform. As they sat down, Joffre arrived and Congreve was introduced to him. He found Joffre not as big and fat as he had envisaged, but thought he looked very ill and somewhat bloodless.

That very same morning, Rawlinson was discussing the broader aspects of the combined Hardecourt-Trônes Wood attack with General Fayolle. The meeting was tinged with acrimony and Rawlinson made little headway, owing to a dispute about the planned attack on Trônes Wood. Finally, he was told that Balfourier's corps could not possibly undertake the Hardecourt attack on the morrow due to the enemy counter-attacking at Bois Favière, being the same tiny wood on the Anglo-French boundary that had eluded capture on 1st July. A postponement was requested until the day after to allow XX Corps to take possession of the wood. Reluctantly, Rawlinson agreed.

The days of comparative inaction had been used by the enemy to good effect. The German *Second Army* commander, General Fritz von Below, whose task it was to stabilise the whole of his Somme front and to regain lost ground, had already organised his long front into three groups under three corps commanders. With 40 fresh battalions close at hand and with batteries of heavy artillery reaching him (including fifteen from the *Fifth Army* before Verdun), together with three extra flights of aircraft, Below was in a position to tell Falkenhayn on 5th July that he was strengthening his defences and would hold on. This was unknown to Rawlinson and his corps commanders, nor did he realise that Allied Intelligence had sadly underestimated the enemy's divisional strength as far back as 1st July. With Below's recent additions, Intelligence still estimated a Fourth Army numerical superiority of roughly four to one when the actual figure was a shade more than two to one.

The French were also continuing to give Congreve an uncomfortable time. As well as hearing Balfourier's explanation for himself on why XX Corps could not attack Hardecourt as planned, Congreve was told that the French had not overcome their disgust in the Fourth Army pursuing its new plan of breaking through to the north. They badly wanted their ally to assist them in exploiting their success south of the Somme. His thoughts on the subject were philosophical, wishing as he did that the Fourth Army had enough troops to do both. On that note, Congreve returned to his battle headquarters.

There to greet him was his eldest son, Billy, brigade-major to 3rd Division's 76th Brigade. After lunch and with his son new to the area, Congreve sent him to Carnoy to explore XIII Corps' positions there.

Billy Congreve's divisional commander, Major-General Haldane, having gone to the front on Wednesday, felt that another visit was in order before his division officially took over 18th Division's lines. Already the pioneer battalion of 3rd Division was hard at work on a new communication trench and, soon, infantry battalions from his division's brigades would move up to swop places with the tired troops of 18th Division. Haldane realised that Maxse's infantrymen were prone to lethargy from their extended stay at the front; a fact that worried him enough to ask Maxse to put night patrols into No Man's Land. His reasoning was based on keeping the enemy away from the British front. In effect, blindfolding the Germans and so preventing them from discovering anything that could be detrimental to the advance.

With his GSO1 and the 9th Brigade commander, Brigadier-General Potter, Haldane reached the firing line and stepped cautiously down into Caterpillar Valley. The officers made their way to the valley bottom and began to climb the far slope towards the German front line trenches. They entered Marlborough Wood that was no more than an acre and which had been turned into a forward position, held only by a platoon and a machine-gun team. From there, Haldane's tiny party crept as near as they dared without showing themselves to the enemy. Through his field-glasses, Haldane thought that he could discern two bands of barbed wire although thick grass all but masked his view. He resolved to send out scouts at the earliest opportunity. On lowering his field-glasses and turning for home with his colleagues, he thought it strange and slightly eerie to be walking about between the lines in broad daylight, just 600 yards from the enemy and 1,100 yards from 18th Division's line which would shortly become his responsibility. Certainly, Flanders was never like this.

CHAPTER THREE

Preparation

Haldane received news about the nature of the enemy's wire the next day. There were two bands with the first band 100 yards forward of the German trenches. The second band zigzagged close to it. He ordered observers to go out by night and to lie up for daylight, then to report back by field telephone on the effectiveness of the artillery cutting the wire.

Except for the XIII Corps front, which awaited the French to secure Bois Favière, both the Fourth Army and Gough's Reserve Army were aggressively active in spite of rain squalls that transformed roads and trenches into quagmires. The intention was to move up to the main German second position by occupying Ovillers village, Mametz Wood and Contalmaison. Despite gaining a foothold in Ovillers, at a cost of 1,400 killed and wounded to the three attacking battalions, nothing much was accomplished. A two-pronged attack on Mametz Wood by XV Corps' 17th and 38th (Welsh) Divisions turned out to be an expensive failure in terms of lives and reputations. At Contalmaison, British troops fought their way into the village and were subsequently shelled out. On his front, Rawlinson sought solace in the fact that some vital enemy trenches were captured and prisoners taken. What they had to say hardened his thinking:

Prisoners tell us that the Boches are in a state of chaos, but their machine-gunners seem to go on fighting all right. . . We must go on pressing the Boches now they are getting tired, as fresh troops may be brought up. They all complain of want of food and water – I shall undertake the attack of Bazentin-le-Petit and Longueval at all costs on the 10th.

To the Fourth Army commander's consternation, he heard that the French wanted to postpone the combined Hardecourt-Trônes Wood attack yet again. Rawlinson pointedly refused. Time was slipping by, and he and Haig wanted the wood captured before the main assault on 10th July. Haig especially was keen to see Mametz Wood neutralised quickly and was annoyed to find it still firmly in German hands at the day's end. In the evening, Haig took measures to reinforce the battle front. Among the formations ordered to the Fourth Army area were 33rd Division from the First Army, and 51st (Highland) Division.

During the night, Haldane started moving his brigades into the line in readiness for the official change over on 18th Division's front the following day. The rain never ceased. That night he scribbled in his diary:

> Shall have my own guns and a battery of the 18th Division cutting wire on 8th and 9th, and rest of 18th Division's guns for defence and attack on the 10th. The French, it is said, want us to push south with them, but Haig is sticking to his plan of pushing north. He thinks the French, if we take Longueval, will be forced into pushing north with us.

As Haldane completed his diary entry, a brigade of 38th Division prepared to attack Mametz Wood again. The order to attack was radically modified at the last moment by Lt-General Horne. He telephoned 38th Division headquarters to tell its GOC, Major-General Philipps, that he just wanted a small probe of the wood's southern defences. Thereafter everything fizzled out. The attack, due to begin at two hours after midnight, failed to materialise. The new orders arrived too late and the trenches leading to the departure point were too congested for the selected battalion to arrive there on time.

Saturday was warm and sunny, but the ground was a sea of mud churned up by thousands of marching feet, horses' hooves and all manner of wheeled vehicles. There was much battle activity, but little difference from the previous Saturday's turmoil. Good progress was made in the morning at Contalmaison, but evening saw the attackers back on their original line. On XV Corps' front, Major-General Pilcher's 17th Division mounted two full-scale attacks on trenches situated on the south-west perimeter of Mametz Wood, but failed to break through to the wood. On Congreve's front, Shea's 30th Division launched the long-awaited attack on Trônes Wood and the trenches south of it to join up with the French. The attack was repulsed. Balfourier sent in his 39th Division to assault Hardecourt village about the same time and succeeded. The French, having gained their objective, were most anxious about their exposed left flank. So was Congreve. He ordered a second attack on Trônes Wood. At 1 p.m., Shea's men attacked again and took the whole of the lower half, except for a heavily defended trench in its south-east corner. Maltz Horn Farm, XIII Corps' other important objective, was reduced to a shell-swept heap in the middle of disputed territory and held by neither side. On the whole and considering how the day had begun, Congreve was fairly satisfied with his troops' efforts.

Not so Haig. He arrived at Fourth Army headquarters and told Rawlinson to defer the assault on the German main second position until Contalmaison, Mametz Wood and Trônes Wood were secured. His departure left Rawlinson in a sombre mood that was not helped by the letter he received from Haig's chief of staff, Kiggell, on Sunday. In it, Kiggell had written that Haig 'did not consider the withdrawal from Contalmaison on the 7th and the failure of the 38th Division to capture Mametz Wood were creditable performances'.

Rawlinson was inclined to agree. The only aspect of Kiggell's letter on which he had doubts concerned the confirmation of not attacking the main German second position until after the capture of Mametz Wood. The Fourth Army commander thought that it could be unwise to wait around.

Horne was another unhappy man. He felt that both Pilcher and Philipps had let him down, especially in the case of Philipps. Unfortunately for Philipps, his appointment as GOC of 38th Division owed more to his political prowess than to his military experience. A Liberal MP since 1906, his meteoric elevation to major-general was almost certainly assisted by Lloyd George, whose son, Gwilym, became Philipps's ADC before the division left Wales.

Philipps's political connections did not cut any ice with his corps commander. Horne removed him from his command that Sunday morning. Philipps returned home under a cloud with his ADC, Lieutenant Gwilym Lloyd George. Pilcher followed a few days later.

At the suggestion of Fourth Army headquarters, Horne immediately placed 38th Division under the temporary command of Major-General Watts, GOC of 7th Division, then in reserve. Due to this change, XV Corps decided to postpone an attack by 38th Division on Mametz Wood from 4 p.m. Sunday to early Monday morning.

Haldane and his staff moved into their headquarters near Bray-sur-Somme on Saturday afternoon. The headquarters were in deep chalk dugouts that gave him a sense of claustrophobia, having never been inside any deep dugout until he came south to the Somme. It was there that he heard about the deferment of the assault on the German main second position. At the same time he heard that the Germans were shaky. The 3rd Division commander took it with a pinch of salt, but the news of the postponement was greeted by him in silent relief. On taking over Maxse's front, Haldane had belatedly discovered that the road his division was to use to bring up essential supplies was so bad and over-crowded, it would have proved an impossible task to move sufficient ammunition up front in time for the attack.

Even though the attack had been indefinitely postponed until Contalmaison, Mametz Wood and Trônes Wood were in British hands, Haldane was delegated to suggest the hour for the attack. He dutifully rose at 3.20 on Sunday morning to study the light, by which time he had a battalion from each of his three brigades in the line. By this arrangement, if the attack was postponed long enough, all ranks would have the chance of seeing the nature of the ground ahead.

The 30th Division commander, Major-General John Shea, had even less sleep. Ordered by Congreve to complete the capture of Trônes Wood, he reinforced the men already there with troops of Brigadier-General Steavenson's 90th Brigade. Following a forty minute bombardment on the northern half of the wood, 30th Division infantrymen renewed their attempts at 3 a.m. to drive the enemy totally from the wood. They did it by daybreak when, to their horror, they found that Trônes Wood was a virtual death trap.

No one could ask for better artillery observation than the Germans enjoyed from their vantage points along the Bazentin Ridge, especially that part from Longueval to High Wood which was excellent for directing artillery on to Trônes Wood.

The enemy began a systematic shelling of the wood and its western approaches with devastating results. German infantry advanced under the cover of the concentrated artillery fire. Frantically resisted, they still managed to plunge into the wood from its western edge. For good measure, Bernafay Wood was also shelled, causing considerable losses to the 30th Division troops assembled there after withdrawing from Trônes Wood.

Shea ordered a counter-attack from a sunken road east of the brickworks at 6.40 p.m. A flanking action, it succeeded in getting one of 90th Brigade's battalions alongside the wood. The men dug in to await nightfall.

It had been another anxious day for Congreve, nor was it over in terms of fighting. With much of the coming attack's fortunes resting on XIII Corps' right flank, Congreve realised too well the importance of securing Trônes Wood. So far, he had received piecemeal help from his French neighbours, as he and Balfourier tried to forge an unbreakable link between their fronts. On Sunday, however, General Foch, whose command included Fayolle's Sixth Army[1], instructed Fayolle to put Balfourier's XX Corps on the defensive until the British had broken through the German main second position. In truth, Foch had grown disenchanted with the British efforts to capture Contalmaison, Mametz Wood and Trônes Wood. Until these were taken, he could see no possibility of an Anglo-French advance.

Thankfully, supremacy of the air lay with the Allies. It was necessary that it continued to stay in that vein, so as to reduce the enemy's chances of seeing too much of the build-up for the attack behind the lines. Even so, the odd hostile aircraft still slipped through on occasions. Early on Sunday evening, one crossed high over the Allied lines and set fire to a French observation balloon. A trail of smoke traced the burning balloon's descent. Congreve witnessed the action and saw the aircraft escape unharmed. It disturbed him that no Allied aircraft was in the vicinity at the time. What with Trônes Wood and the planning of the attack, he had enough on his plate without the additional worry of German airmen reporting back on the activity taking place on his and Horne's fronts.

Because if a breakthrough in the German main second position should occur, it would happen on XIII Corps' and XV Corps' fronts. Already there had been discussions of cavalry involvement. Horne's senior staff officer had come to see him that afternoon about putting the cavalry through the gap which the infantry hoped to make. Congreve's impression was that any cavalry action was far into the future. Besides, there were more urgent questions to consider, such as recapturing Trônes Wood.

Moving forward in groups of twenty men and assisted by a company from 9th Division's South African Brigade, a battalion of Steavenson's 90th Brigade won their way to the northern apex of Trônes Wood during the early hours of Monday morning. By ten in the morning, they had lost it again. After visiting Shea, Congreve went on to see Steavenson at 90th Brigade's headquarters in the

[1] As *Commandant le Groupe des Armées du Nord*, Foch commanded the French Sixth, Tenth and Third Armies.

brickworks. He discovered that the brigade had lost nearly 800 officers and men, mainly through enemy shell fire in the wood. 'So sickening to lose brave men in this way after they had captured the place,' Congreve recorded later.

Horne's XV Corps enjoyed better luck with Mametz Wood on Monday. With Horne's words uppermost in his mind that he could dispose of 38th Division as he wished, keeping any brigades he wanted, or using them as required, 38th Division's new temporary commander, Major-General Watts, committed the whole division in taking Mametz Wood. Supported by a creeping artillery barrage, nearly all the wood was in 38th Division's hands by late evening.

While Rawlinson waited for the outcome of the Mametz Wood fight, good news flowed in to his headquarters from Lt-General Pulteney's III Corps on XV Corps' left. Its 17th Division had taken Contalmaison. After hearing about Mametz Wood, Rawlinson made up his mind not to delay any longer:

> In these circumstances I have decided to begin the bombardment of the second line tomorrow and to attack it on the 13th at dawn, weather permitting.

Realising how the state of the light can vary according to the clearness of the morning, Haldane had again risen early to view the light. This time at 2.15 on Monday morning. He then went to see Watts whose 7th Division would be on his left for the attack. He, too, was in favour of attacking as soon as there was sufficient light to see one hundred yards away, but not enough for the enemy machine-gunners to establish themselves in time.

Again, Haldane heard reports that the enemy's morale was weakening, also that the German main second position was not fully manned along its entire length. He thought that it was best to keep the reports to himself, having generally found them untrustworthy in the past. As for the state of the enemy's morale, all he need do was to glance to his right where the enemy had wrested Trônes Wood back that morning. He judged that the occupants were probably suffering from a temporary drop in morale, due to Congreve ordering another long bout of artillery fire on it with a view to retaking the wood early Tuesday morning. Other than that, Haldane preferred to wait for his brigade commanders' reports rather than what emanated from Fourth Army headquarters.

The Fourth Army's scheme was to seize the German main second position from Longueval to Bazentin-le-Petit Wood with a surprise assault, unlike the slow build-up for the 1st July assault. In the hope that the assault's momentum would carry through to High Wood and Delville Wood, it was planned for 9th and 3rd Divisions of Congreve's XIII Corps to pounce on the German front line from Longueval to Bazentin-le-Grand village inclusive, whilst 7th and 21st Divisions of Horne's XV Corps struck along the line which embraced Bazentin-le-Grand Wood to Bazentin-le-Petit Wood. In order to form a protective left flank, one of III Corps' divisions would attack Contalmaison Villa that lay some 1,000 yards ahead in a north-easterly direction to the village itself.

Owing to the efficacy of enemy artillery and machine-gun fire, a daylight assault over open ground was discarded in favour of a night advance to assembly positions in No Man's Land for a frontal attack at the first streak of dawn. Never before had such a night operation of this magnitude been attempted, entailing as it would a night advance by four divisions on a 6,000 yard front to a depth that varied from 1,500 yards on the right above Bernafay Wood to about 300 yards on the left above Mametz Wood. It was a daring concept. So daring, in fact, that the French refused to have anything to do with it, except to render assistance with artillery fire.

In their opinion, on learning about the plan, the whole operation smacked of foolhardiness and was doomed to fail, especially as the large majority of the units involved were composed of officers and men who enlisted after the war had begun. In addition, a huge proportion of the staffs of formations were comparatively young and inexperienced.

Rawlinson and his corps commanders accepted the risks – and there were many. With Trônes Wood covering a suitable position in which the enemy could collect and concentrate for a counter-attack against the British flank, any advance from Bernafay Wood was liable to be taken in the flank unless Trônes Wood was in British possession. Equally, Mametz Wood was situated within 300 yards of the enemy's main second position. There was the risk that it could become available as a collection point for the Germans to counter-attack against the British left flank.

Moreover, if the enemy discovered Fourth Army's intentions while the divisions were deploying towards their jumping-off positions, a devastating artillery bombardment would catch the troops in the open with dreadful results. Should the Germans follow up with a counter-attack on the right flank from Trônes Wood direction, the disaster could be compounded with the possible loss of Montauban and other positions. Such an outcome would undoubtedly reverberate around the Cabinet room in 10 Downing Street and in both Houses of Parliament.

It was a bold plan and, because of its uniqueness, one that required careful attention to detail. Above all, it required the utmost secrecy if it was to succeed. Unless secrecy was preserved up to the time of the assault, Rawlinson realised that all could end in disaster. Yet, because of the gains that could ensue from it, he felt totally justified in accepting the risks.

Unfortunately for Rawlinson, Haig's opinion differed. Haig, having questioned the Fourth Army commander about the plan of attack on Monday, revisited Rawlinson on Tuesday morning with Kiggell, as he considered the plan to be 'a manoeuvre which one cannot do successfully against flags in time of peace'.

With everything prepared to the last possible detail, Rawlinson was thunder-struck when Haig ordered him to radically alter the plan. Haig's scheme was to let XV Corps attack first against the line Contalmaison Villa – Bazentin-le-Grand Wood from Mametz Wood at about two hours after dark on the 12th. Montgomery, Rawlinson's chief of staff who was present at the meeting, implored Haig to reconsider – with good reason. Haig's changes meant losing the element of surprise and, worse, it would give the Germans the chance to concentrate artillery and infantry reserves against a very narrow frontage of attack. It also presented Horne's XV Corps with the invidious task of changing directions in the dark between two phases of the operation.

Haig refused to reconsider and declined to discuss the matter further. With that, he returned to his GHQ at Valvion for lunch, leaving two very frustrated senior officers in his wake.

Oblivious to what the future held in store, Haldane and his GS01, Lt-Colonel De Brett, had risen at 2.50 that morning and studied the sky until 3.40 a.m. with an eye to finding a suitable time for zero. They agreed on 3.20 a.m. Mid-morning, both officers went to XIII Corps' battle headquarters where Congreve – equally as ignorant – confirmed Haldane's suggested time for the assault on 13th July, but to be preceded by five minutes of intense shelling. First there would be a preliminary two-day bombardment – already underway – with twice the amount of ammunition used on XIII Corps' front for the run up to the 1st July operation. All reports indicated that the German main second position was inferior to their old front line. If this was the case then having an artillery piece to every six yards, compared with the ratio of one to every twenty yards on 1st July, should create untold damage.

At the mid-morning conference, Haldane was notified that he was being given the use of a regiment of 2nd Indian Cavalry Division. It would be his decision when it should be ordered through if a breach was made. The news was unexpected. He had intended employing his best infantry brigade, Brigadier-General Kentish's 76th Brigade, for hot pursuit should the occasion arise.

An hour after their departure, Congreve was requested to attend a meeting at Querrieu at 2 p.m. Horne received the same message. Both corps commanders arrived at the appointed time, Congreve in a happier frame of mind in the knowledge that a brigade of 30th Division was back in Trônes Wood, although the thought still nagged him on how long he could keep it this time. His precarious well-being was soon dispersed along with that of Horne's when Rawlinson dropped the bomb-shell. They were aghast, and Horne could hardly believe his ears when told that Haig wanted his corps to attack without the support of XIII Corps on his right.

Try as they might with Haig's scheme, they could not transform it into something better than the one rejected by him. At 3 p.m., they decided to bite on the bullet. Rawlinson telephoned GHQ and spoke to Kiggell, informing him that it was their unanimous opinion that the original plan was still the best. Kiggell referred Rawlinson to Haig who would not give way. The Commander-in-Chief was insistent, telling Rawlinson that he personally felt that the experience of war, as well as the teachings of peace, were against the use of large masses in night operations, especially with inexperienced staff officers and young troops.

He accordingly ordered Rawlinson to attack the line from Contalmaison village to Bazentin-le-Grand Wood with XV Corps, reinforced by a brigade or division as Horne might desire and, if it should prove necessary, for Rawlinson to be prepared to further reinforce him. Once the breakthrough was effected, Horne was to establish a strong flank on the west of Bazentin-le-Petit Wood, then wheel his troops to the right and begin to work eastwards – rolling up the enemy trench system facing XIII Corps' front, taking Longueval, Ginchy, Guillemont and any other strongholds in his path, yet missing the actual crest of Bazentin Ridge and, with it, High Wood.

As for Congreve, Haig directed that his corps should construct

strongpoints in the form of trenches or earthworks along the spurs
north of Montauban for jumping-off places, and to be prepared to
attack at dawn on Friday, 14th July. Wrote Congreve afterwards:

> It seems to me to invite defeat in detail and to advertise our
> intentions by my digging. However, orders are orders and one
> always likes one's own plans best, but all having been settled and
> agreed (and by himself too!), it is trying to alter all for what I am
> sure is worse. I am disappointed too in Haig himself.[2]

In compliance with orders from XIII Corps, Haldane motored to
Furse's divisional headquarters where he met Congreve's senior staff
officer, Greenly; at 6 p.m. Greenly told him about Haig's change of
mind.

'Unsound and contrary to the principle of economy of force,' was
Haldane's immediate reaction, imagining how the Germans could
concentrate their guns on Horne's XV Corps. The idea of XV Corps
attacking in the early hours on the 13th and, if successful, followed by
XIII Corps' attack on the 14th, made no sense to Haldane – nor did
Greenly's next comment to him:

[2] By no means was it the first or last time that Haig disappointed Congreve. Just
before the German offensive in March 1918, Congreve made the following diary
entry on 9th March: 'Met Haig and Lawrence at Tyke Dump at 11 and walked with
him to Metz. Found him as difficult as –, but quite friendly and genial as far as he
can be. I asked what he thought of the French opinion that the Boche will accept our
terms and so force us to make peace, as he has got all he wants in the East and can
afford to give up Alsace and Lorraine, France and Belgium. I was astounded to find
that Haig is a Landsdowne-ite and for making peace, considering that we cannot
attack on the West this year and that America will not be worth considering before
1920; therefore, we had better make peace and take steps to secure Persia and
Afghanistan before the Boche gets at them. He thinks submarines will be well in
hand by August. He has no plans for a future war, because the Boche will have had
enough of it for a very long time to come, and because our Empire will be greatly
strengthened by the War. All I can say is that he is amazingly optimistic. I can't see
what Persia and Afghanistan matter if we are going in 10 years hence to be beaten in
Europe, and beaten we shall be if we don't beat the Boche now. He says we can't. I
don't believe a word of it.'
    In fairness to Haig, among other pressures, he had fought and lost an important
political battle earlier that year against Lloyd George and the Cabinet Committee,
who denied Haig the men to bring the BEF up to its proper established strength at
the very moment that Germany was actively preparing for the greatest battle of the
war. To compound his troubles, the Cabinet Committee insisted that the BEF
should be radically reorganised to hide this deficiency – much to the detriment of
morale and fighting efficiency.

Sir D. Haig also ordered assembly trenches to be made with communication trenches to them all along the front. As this would spoil the plan of attack, which is based on surprise, he was induced to modify his wishes. I told Rawlinson when he came to me that I was strongly in favour of having no assembly trenches and that I would guarantee to get my brigades across the open unknown to the Germans and surprise them, but, with assembly trenches, that would be impossible. We have also to make strongpoints all along the front which must, of course, be as inconspicuous as possible.

Greenly listened sympathetically as Haldane promised to arrange for their construction to commence that night, each one large enough to take a machine-gun and its team.

Haig's proverbial spanner had thrown everything out of gear. There was much to do and time was critically short. With the artillery programme already under way, Rawlinson's first move was to rearrange it, which inevitably caused confusion through the various levels of command. Leaving his staff to grapple with the problem, he assembled the commanders of the three cavalry divisions and gave them his views on their future employment should a gap present itself in the enemy's line. He then saw Pulteney at III Corps headquarters, briefing him to make a subsidiary attack (timed with Horne's assault) on Contalmaison Villa – a fortified place near Bazentin-le-Petit. Assailed with foreboding, Rawlinson returned to Querrieu. After dinner, he received a message from Horne who was doubtful about the enemy wire being cut along his front of attack in time for his assault. The Fourth Army commander promptly telephoned GHQ:

I called up Kig and told him this, suggesting that if Horne had to postpone his attack till the 14th, and if Congreve had by that time constructed the strongpoints on the opposite hill, I was strongly of the opinion that both attacks should go in together at dawn on the 14th.

The delay is to be regretted, because the enemy is bringing up more guns and working hard at his second and third lines of defence – putting up more wire and digging hard about Martinpuich, Flers, Morval and High Wood. Moreover, he is bringing up fresh troops from all the Western front.

Quite willing to accept the attendant risks of the former night attack plan, Rawlinson suspected that Haig's refusal to sanction it stemmed from political considerations. Another long casualty list would be looked upon with serious misgivings in London to Haig's detriment. On contemplating the matter, Rawlinson put pen to paper and wrote a letter of reassurance to his Commander-in-Chief, yet echoing the suggestions he made to Kiggell on the telephone.

The same evening found Congreve mentally wrestling with his continuing problem of Trônes Wood:

> At 10 p.m., heard we are again ejected from Trônes Wood. I am at my wits' end on what to do there, for it is essential to any advance to my front that I should hold it to cover my right. I am wasting a fearful lot of good troops on it and getting no further towards keeping it.

It was not long before he reached a compromise:

> Decided to let the Boche keep the damned wood until I want it; meanwhile making it hell for him with gun fire.

Problems were certainly not a British monopoly. The German commander in the West, Falkenhayn, was experiencing his own – on the Somme and before Verdun. On 11th July, he travelled south to his Verdun front and arrived at *Fifth Army* headquarters during the afternoon. His arrival coincided with the news of an attack which had failed just a mile north of the French-held city. Because of the critical situation on the Somme, Falkenhayn immediately issued the order for a strict defensive operation to be put into effect without delay. He then ordered numerous artillery units to be withdrawn at once for deployment on the Somme, joining other artillery units already sent there from the Verdun front. Falkenhayn's orders made 11th July an historic date. Although his Verdun campaign would bleed on to the end of the year, it was now, in truth, completely finished in terms of an offensive operation.

Regardless of which night attack plan might be chosen, the activity of shifting supplies and ammunition to the front continued. The night of 11th/12th July was no exception, and dumps of all kinds of battle stores were built up in Caterpillar Valley under cover of darkness. Approximately three miles west of Montauban, men of 21st Division relieved the tired survivors of the badly mauled 38th (Welsh) Division in Mametz Wood by 6.30 a.m. The bitter wood fighting had cost the plucky Welshmen nearly 4,000 casualties in their five-day period at the front. It was thought that the northern edge of Mametz Wood had still to be taken, but the Germans had chosen that night to evacuate the wood. They left behind hundreds of their dead and 13 heavy artillery pieces.

The night of 11th/12th July saw also the 7th Division move up on the right of 21st Division. In XV Corps reserve, during the previous five days for rest, 7th Division's depleted ranks had been force-fed with drafts of men from many different regiments in an attempt to bring the division quickly up to war strength again. Because of the urgency (its 20th Brigade received 1,400 reinforcements on the march up to the front), there was no time in which to properly absorb the newcomers. Haig, on the other hand, was pleased to hear that reinforcements from England were arriving satisfactorily and grandly noted that 7th Division was '23 men over war strength!'

On 7th Division's right in XIII Corps' sector was Haldane's 3rd Division. He had arranged for his 8th and 9th Brigades to be in the front line with 76th Brigade in divisional reserve, but very close to hand: two of its battalions in Caterpillar Valley, one in Montauban Alley and the other in trenches just behind Montauban.

Alongside Haldane's 3rd Division was Furse's 9th Division with part of his sector incorporating the western half of Bernafay Wood. He also had two brigades in line (26th and 27th Brigades) with one in reserve. The eastern half of Bernafay Wood and the ground between it and Trônes Wood was still Shea's 30th Division's responsibility until relieved by Maxse's 18th Division during 12th July. Having suffered a further 2,300 casualties since returning to the front to take Trônes Wood, Shea's men badly needed a rest.

Maxse's task was to establish a defensive flank along the eastern edge of Trônes Wood (currently being heavily bombarded), linking up with 9th Division on the left and with the French near the ruined Maltz Horn Farm on the right. Even though the French refused to commit any infantrymen, Rawlinson was promised the use of Balfourier's artillery to help in holding the flank, as well as to bombard any worthwhile enemy target within range of XX Corps' guns.

Wednesday, 12th July, made its appearance. With it came Haig's agreement in response to Rawlinson's last minute appeal. On Haig's instructions, Kiggell visited Rawlinson in the morning to discuss a few details and to emphasise the necessity for constructing good supporting points on the front of XIII Corps. Still nervous about the whole scheme, Haig wanted insurance should the attack fail. If it did occur, he wished Rawlinson to know that the supporting points must be held regardless of cost – hence the machine-gun nests. Kiggell also made it clear that Haig wanted Mametz Wood and Trônes Wood to be firmly held so that both flanks were covered. Kiggell eventually departed, leaving the Fourth Army commander in a much happier frame of mind:

> All is well and we may carry out the attacks simultaneously with the XV and XIII Corps. Kig says it will be one of the 16 decisive battles of the world and certainly, if we are wholly successful, it will have very far-reaching results – especially if I can get the Cavalry through to catch the guns and break up the commands. The 14th is an auspicious day: the Anniversary of the Bastille. I have hopes therefore of bringing off a big success. . . We can only pray that God may be on our side in this titanic struggle for liberty.

Haig was more direct. Whatever he felt personally, he wished the troops to be informed that success in the forthcoming battle would probably end the war by Christmas. Congreve conveyed the emotive message to his divisional commanders without comment. Haldane chose to forget it. 'I have found that such prophecies are invariably wrong and do harm,' he opined.

Every person of consequence now knew that the assault would begin on 14th July at 3.25 a.m., but preceded by only five minutes of intense shell fire to achieve maximum surprise; during which time the infantry would commence their advance from their assembly areas in No Man's Land. Other tactical lessons had been absorbed from the holocaust of 1st July. Instead of artillery 'lifts' from one specified enemy position to another, an artillery barrage would 'creep' forward in front of the advancing infantry.

Through this method – an innovation – very few pockets of resistance would escape unscathed. For a creeping barrage to be really effective, infantry would have to follow close behind it. In addition, having at last acknowledged that shrapnel shells had little impact on an entrenched enemy, it was decided to use only high-explosive shells for the five minute bombardment and the subsequent creeping barrage. However, since there was a very real danger of some HE shells hitting buildings and trees, thereby spraying the advancing troops with lethal slivers of metal, it was also decided that all HE shells would have delay-action fuses.

Time was of the essence now. The enemy's defences were becoming stronger by the day as guns and men were brought into the threatened area. Reports flowed into Fourth Army's headquarters about the abysmal state of the enemy's morale. The reports held substance, because British patrols continued to dominate No Man's Land. It was imperative to jealously guard that supremacy right up to the moment of the attack.

In order to hoodwink the enemy about the true nature of the five-minute intense bombardment, a slow bombardment of the German main second position began on the morning of 12th July, but interspersed with periods of intense fire that were intended to disguise the true purpose of the final one before the actual attack. Enemy artillery barked in reply, for the most part dropping shells on Bernafay Wood, Montauban, Maricourt, Mametz Wood and on Contalmaison. Casualties were sustained, but the secret stayed safe.

With feedback from RFC daylight reconnaissance sorties and from forward observation officers, XV and XIII Corps artillery repeatedly pounded the back areas during the night, disrupting and retarding any attempt by the enemy to reinforce his front with men and material.

The morning of 13th July was dull, cold and fairly windy. A little rain had fallen earlier, but had ceased by breakfast time. Deaf to the frantic telephone calls from the French, imploring him to give up the 'foolish' idea of a night assault ('. . . an attack organised for amateurs by amateurs'), Rawlinson visited each of his divisional commanders and found them in good heart and confident of success. He saw Haldane at 11 a.m., telling him that he wanted to push cavalry to High Wood. He added the titbit that Intelligence reports suggested that 3rd Division might meet with a counter-attack at Delville and Bazentin Woods. With the cavalry appointed to be the first through any gap, Haldane thereupon earmarked his 76th Brigade to deal with the problem should it occur.

Rawlinson expected great things from the three cavalry divisions in his army if a breakthrough was achieved. He had placed 2nd Indian Cavalry Division under XIII Corps' jurisdiction for action at High Wood, but preferred to keep his own hand on the other two for the time being. Should the moment arise, he intended sending one cavalry division through to Leuze Wood (about 1,000 yards east of Guillemont) and the other to Martinpuich.

With the 2nd Indian Cavalry Division going under corps command and not under his own, Haldane was no longer responsible for the decision to order it forward. However, Major-General MacAndrew who commanded the cavalry division would await his instructions at Haldane's battle headquarters.

As Rawlinson made his rounds, his chief of staff, Montgomery, found himself with a visitor from General Balfourier's headquarters. He was Captain E.L. Spears, the British liaison officer attached to XX Corps. Balfourier had sent him to Querrieu to restate the telephone messages about abandoning the night operation. Montgomery listened patiently and then he spoke. 'Tell General Balfourier, with my compliments, that if we're not on Longueval Ridge by eight o'clock tomorrow morning, I'll eat my hat.'

On his return to Balfourier's headquarters, Spears translated Montgomery's announcement word for word. It was greeted with disbelief.

Inwardly, Haig was still experiencing qualms about the scheme. On the 13th, he had his staff arrange the transfer of another division (Major-General Stephens' 5th Division) to the Fourth Army area as a reserve. He felt that it might be needed, as the enemy was busily milking his own line in other sectors to reinforce his Somme front. Haig also sent his deputy chief of staff, Major-General Butler, north to the First and Second Army area with a message to bombard the enemy front adjacent to where the two British armies met and, for good measure, to throw in an infantry assault involving at least two divisions.[3] GHQ had estimated that enemy troops, equivalent to nine battalions, had journeyed down to the Somme from that sector. Haig wanted the Germans to know that they could not thin their line with impunity.

After lunch, Haig visited Fourth Army headquarters where Rawlinson did his best to convince him that the risks were not as great as he had anticipated. For his part, Haig clarified the assault's objectives. Firstly, occupy and consolidate the Longueval-Bazentin-le-Petit Wood length of the enemy main second line. Secondly, take High Wood and establish a right flank on Ginchy and Guillemont and if possible to extend left and take Pozières Ridge and the village of Martinpuich.

[3] Known as the Action of Fromelles, involving the 61st Division (First Army) and the 5th Australian Division (Second Army), the attack was ill-conceived and ended in disaster. Allied casualties were 257 officers and 6,823 men. The enemy, mostly Bavarian troops, lost fewer than 2,000.

Haig then brought up the subject of cavalry commitment. He made it quite plain that, except for a few squadrons from the 2nd Indian Cavalry Division to take High Wood, no cavalry division was to go forward until the infantry had broken through in strength.

It was not difficult for Rawlinson to understand Haig's reasoning. Even one hostile machine-gun could create mayhem amongst a cavalry formation. At least Haig had sanctioned the seizure of High Wood by cavalry, although his approval was tinged with reservation. It was sufficient to satisfy Rawlinson's enthusiasm, but what compelled him to consider deploying cavalry at all?

Perhaps it was due to the shorter distance that 2nd Indian Cavalry Division needed to travel when compared with the other two cavalry divisions. Certainly the ground to High Wood could have once entered the category of good cavalry country, but two weeks of shelling from both sides had brought about cratered zones. No matter that there was less ground to cover, could High Wood be reasonably left for that critical period of time which the cavalry would require to reach it? Admittedly High Wood was marked down as the first cavalry objective, but why was it not part and parcel of the first infantry objective? Indeed, why should its capture be left to cavalry, when infantrymen in hot pursuit could comfortably reach it within twenty minutes of passing through the enemy's main second position? All senior commanders were aware of High Wood's importance, but the method adopted to achieve its capture rang of fanciful optimism.

After his discussion with Rawlinson, Haig visited Congreve at Chipilly and Horne at XV Corps headquarters in Heilly. Finally, he saw the III Corps commander, Pulteney, at Montigny. He found them all full of confidence.

Nevertheless, Congreve still had to complete the capture of Trônes Wood. With zero hour at 3.25 a.m. the next day, there was precious time in which to do it. A little headway had been made that day, but it was a fleabite to the task facing Maxse's 18th Division. Rawlinson had ordered Congreve to complete its capture 'at all costs' by midnight. The XIII Corps commander ensured that Maxse was under no illusion about the importance of the operation. Maxse thereupon moved forward one of his brigades (Brigadier-General Sir T.D. Jackson's 55th Brigade) in readiness to attack at 7 p.m.

A two-hour artillery bombardment preceded the attack, after which two battalions of the 55th Brigade tried to gain possession. The conditions in the wood were almost indescribable. Shelled continuously for five days by both sides, trees had fallen in every direction which impeded progress. The undergrowth was very thick too. The result was that units in the wood found it nigh impossible to locate their own bearings or keep direction. Adding greatly to their discomfort, groups of Germans were missed as the troops struggled through the tangled maze.

Practically every step brought fresh casualties. Many soldiers, realising the futility of their task, withdrew as best they could from the wood. One party of troops, about 100 strong and belonging to 7th Royal West Kents, actually thought that they had reached the wood's northern tip and that the whole of the wood was in British hands. They settled down to defend their position in complete ignorance of the fact that the attack had failed. Unknowingly, they were fated to be shot at and shelled in nightmarish conditions until well into daylight.

Congreve retired to bed at 10 p.m., having been incorrectly informed that most of Trônes Wood was captured. Just as he was beginning to doze off, Maxse telephoned to say that his men had been driven from the wood. Congreve checked his watch and discovered that it was a few minutes past midnight. With his right flank still unsecured and with the main advance about to start in three hours, all hope of sleep vanished. He promptly asked the 18th Division commander what he proposed to do. Maxse replied that he would send in 54th Brigade to renew the attack, promising to take possession of the wood by the time the infantry assault was due to make itself felt.

The 54th Brigade commander, Brigadier-General Shoubridge, received a telephone call at 12.45 a.m., instructing him to bring his brigade forward from where it was in support near Maricourt and to attack Trônes Wood at dawn. On winning the wood, to hold its eastern edge as a defensive flank to 9th Division's attack on Longueval. In minutes, Shoubridge had his troops marching the two miles to the front for the last desperate attempt on Trônes Wood.

Two hours before Shoubridge received his order, an important gain was accomplished on the other flank. The 1st Division of Pulteney's III Corps had seized a wood called Lower Wood, just beyond the north-west corner of Mametz Wood. The action was an integral part of Fourth Army's plan to use the wood and its trench system as a springboard to capture Contalmaison Villa, thereby securing the left flank against envelopment after the main assault had begun.

With much of the enemy's attention diverted to both flanks, preparations went ahead for the assembling of infantry formations in No Man's Land. Selected battalions from a total of six brigades from four divisions,[4] comprising 22,000 officers and men, waited their turn to move beyond friendly wire into No Man's Land under a cloudy night sky. Only one of the leading formations was a Regular Army battalion. The rest were of the New Army. Haldane, for example, had deliberately arranged his two brigades' attack so that four New Army battalions were in front with four Regular ones in support. His philosophy was based on the premise that, being new units, they would be keen to distinguish themselves while the old units behind would act as backstops should anything go wrong.

At first glance, much could go wrong. However, good briefings, accurate timings and a thorough reconnaissance of the line of advance from brigade commanders downwards, helped to reduce the possibility. Where needed, rolls of white tape were run out for 1,000 yards to aid assembly. Even the discovery on the morning of 13th July of enemy telephone tapping was put to advantage. That evening, at 9 p.m., a counterfeit order was transmitted to various front line units, telling them that operations were postponed. Unlike the regrettable telephone message intercepted by the enemy on the eve of the 1st July assault, which sent so many infantrymen to their deaths, this one would actually help to save British lives.

The terrain over which the advance would be conducted was mainly uphill. The exception was on the extreme left and north of Mametz Wood where 21st Division's 110th Brigade was positioned. There, flat ground existed and there, too, the narrowest crossing would take place – 300 yards. The 110th Brigade's right-hand neighbour, 7th Division's 20th Brigade, had 600 yards to cross. The biggest advance fell to the lot of 3rd Division's and 9th Division's assaulting brigades. They had to traverse silently over 1,000 yards of upward sloping ground just to reach their assembly positions.

To avoid the danger of formations remaining in exposed positions for a long time, orders were issued for the night advance to be timed so that troops could reach their assembly positions at 2.55 a.m., just half an hour before the attack was to go in.

Covered by strong patrols and a picquet line, infantrymen steadily made their way in the dark to their appointed places. Behind them,

[4] From left to right, assaulting brigades were the 110th (21st Division, XV Corps), 20th (7th Division, XV Corps), 9th and 8th (3rd Division, XIII Corps), 27th and 26th (9th Division, XIII Corps).

artillery fire purposely kept a fairly low profile for the sake of normality. Now and then a Vickers machine-gun chimed in, adding to the impression that nothing unusual was afoot. To the backdrop of this audio camouflage, their hearts racing and pulses quickening, troops continued to arrive and form up on their markers with scarcely a casualty from the occasional incoming shell.

All the arrangements went without a hitch, but it was still touch and go. A Bavarian sentry at Bazentin-le-Grand thought he saw movement in No Man's Land, and reported his suspicions. At Longueval, four enemy patrols began to roam No Man's Land. One ran into a British patrol, two returned without seeing anything and one simply disappeared. In all, enemy activity was of little consequence. The complex manoeuvring of battalions in No Man's Land continued unabated.

With 76th Brigade in reserve and no longer participating fully in the unfolding drama, Major Billy Congreve watched enviously from the sidelines. As the brigade-major, his influence had dominated his brigade's operational planning when its role was to pursue the enemy in advance of the cavalry. Yet the fruits of his labours were not entirely wasted. It so happened that 9th Division's 27th Brigade was belatedly ordered to a spot in No Man's Land that was originally intended for his brigade. The assembly point was completely devoid of identifiable landmarks, making the laying out of white tape extremely difficult for accurate positioning of battalions. With the problems already solved on paper by 76th Brigade staff, there was only one thing to do. 'It was a bitter feeling having to hand over all our lovely plans,' wrote Congreve to his father. 'A night march and attack is a thing I have long wanted to work.'

Early that night in 7th Division's sector, their battalion in divisional reserve, a small party from the 2nd Royal Irish Regiment climbed a hill above Fricourt for recreation. Among the group of soldiers was Private Anthony Brennan, whose great pal, Frank Waldron, had newly been promoted to lance-corporal. Anthony Brennan wondered whether it would cause their separation.

We had been inseparable since our arrival in France and had shared many a hardship. We always bivouacked together; shared the same section of fours on route marches and, in short, were really tried comrades. Although we did not know it, the hour of our separation was almost at hand, but not in the way that I had thought probable. We stood looking down on the bivouac lights and watching the star-shells away up in the front line. We had all been to Confession in the afternoon, and felt that as far as we were concerned all possible preparations had been made for the morrow. It was an animated scene on that hillside. The atmosphere was more akin to a fair-ground than to an army on the eve of a battle. We were all very gay and excited.

Thirty feet down in one of the four dugouts that constituted his battle headquarters close to Carnoy, Haldane waited for news of the assembly of his two front line brigades. A message came in from the signals unit, housed in an adjacent dugout. Some of the tenseness left Haldane's features as he read it. Both brigades had arrived at their positions at 2.45 a.m. He breathed a little easier as the seconds ticked on to zero.

As arranged by corps headquarters, Major-General MacAndrew of 2nd Indian Cavalry Division was due to make an appearance at Haldane's dugout within the hour. Already the Secunderabad Cavalry Brigade of the division was on its way under the command of Brigadier-General C.L. Gregory. Yesterday his cavalrymen had camped a mile south of Méaulte, near Albert. Now they were well on their journey to Bray-sur-Somme, having vacated their bivouac at 1.30 a.m. When reaching the outskirts of the town, their horses would be fed and watered before proceeding to the vicinity of 3rd Division's battle headquarters. After assembling there, brigade regiments were to await the order to go through to High Wood. On seizing High Wood, they were to cover the advance of the rest of the cavalry and to threaten the enemy's retirement from Delville Wood to Flers.

In its role as the advanced guard of 2nd Indian Cavalry Division, Gregory's Secunderabad Cavalry Brigade travelled with attachments: one Canadian Cavalry Brigade squadron (Fort Garry Horse) with portable bridges, one field troop of Royal Engineers, two armoured cars and 'N' Battery of the RHA. The actual cavalry brigade was composed of the 7th Dragoon Guards, 20th Deccan Horse and the 34th Poona Horse, together with a machine-gun squadron and a veterinary section. While the brigade travelled, the rest of the cavalry division – Ambala and Meerut Cavalry Brigades – remained in their assembly areas near Albert, but ready to move should the call come from XIII Corps. Gregory's situation was somewhat different. Both XIII Corps and XV Corps could legitimately call upon his services.

In No Man's Land and with incredible silent stealth, leading companies started creeping forward with an eye to reducing the gap between them and their adversaries to 100 yards or less. The sky was beginning to lighten as the darkness slowly gave way to misty grey surroundings. Dry of mouth, their dew-damp figures quivering with fearful anticipation, they steeled themselves for the big moment.

It was not long in coming.

II

RENDEZVOUS AT HIGH WOOD

'Ghastly by day, ghostly by night,
The rottenest place on the Somme.'

Corporal H.F. Hooton

CHAPTER FOUR

High Wood: First Contact

With a resounding roar that raked the infant dawn with crimson fingers, the concentrated might of the Fourth Army's artillery burst into action at precisely 3.20 a.m. At the same moment on XIII Corps' right in order to stop the enemy reinforcing Trônes Wood, Balfourier's heavy artillery placed a murderous curtain of shell fire down its eastern side. For the waiting infantry in No Man's Land, it was an unforgettable experience. Over their heads came thousands of shells, screeching and screaming like demented express trains to crash on the German positions before them. Where they stood, crouched or edged forward in the bruised grass and broken earth of No Man's Land, they felt the shock waves massage their bodies and ruffle their uniforms. Beneath their feet, quaking ground tried valiantly to absorb the blasts that rocked the almost indiscernible landscape.

Far from the front at his château outside Beauquesne, ghostly patterns frantically played across Haig's bedroom ceiling; patterns forever changing from the varying reflected light of the orchestrated gun fire. Unable to sleep, there was little for him to do than to stare up from his pillow and listen to the strident sounds saturating his room. Decision time had come and gone, and he was powerless to influence the immediate future. That responsibility had shifted down the command structure to rest on the youthful shoulders of Private Thomas Atkins, his NCO's and officers close to the German main second line.

Just as the barrage lifted on to the enemy's support trench system, storming parties sprang forward to wipe out any survivors with hand-grenades. Hard on their heels came more of the first wave, their rifles with fixed bayonets at the ready. Except for 500 yards of enemy line east of Bazentin-le-Grand, surprise was virtually complete and little resistance was offered initially, although some opposition was later encountered when the first wave of infantry missed a number of deep dugouts as they followed the creeping barrage. The 500 yards of contested territory, however, held the seeds to a problem that would loom larger as each hour passed.

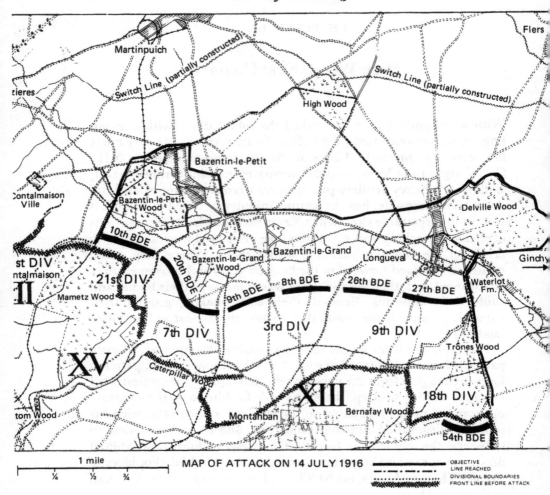

MAP OF ATTACK ON 14 JULY 1916

OBJECTIVE
LINE REACHED
DIVISIONAL BOUNDARIES
FRONT LINE BEFORE ATTACK

The unfortunate check was in 8th Brigade's section of 3rd Division's front. Haldane heard about it at 4.20 a.m., by which time the GOC of the 2nd Indian Cavalry Division, MacAndrew, had joined him. It appeared that the 8th East Yorks had come up against uncut wire and that 8th Brigade's other assaulting battalion, 7th KSLI, found itself stuck in a sunken road and in shell holes near the German trenches. Earlier, Haldane received information that both the assaulting battalions of 9th Brigade (on 8th Brigade's left) were doing well. They were in the enemy's line and were fighting their way through the village of Bazentin-le-Grand. To their left, men of 7th

Division's 20th Brigade had been equally victorious. On finding the wire cut up and the flattened front line trenches full of dead Germans, they moved on to the support trenches where a brief fight resulted in more enemy dead. They then pushed through Flat Iron Copse, being a small scrubby wood situated a few hundred yards south-west of Bazentin-le-Grand Wood. This last advance flushed out large parties of Germans, who retreated up the slope towards High Wood and afforded rifles and Lewis guns with targets reminiscent of a shooting gallery. Few of the enemy reached High Wood's leafy haven or, indeed, the risky shelter of Bazentin-le-Grand Wood. The 20th Brigade's infantrymen, having advanced so fast, were then obliged to wait for the artillery barrage to lift from Bazentin-le-Grand Wood before capturing it.

Further to the left in XV Corps area, men of 21st Division's 110th Brigade had overrun their enemy trench system objective and had managed to link up with 1st Division of III Corps by 4 a.m. On Haldane's immediate right, 9th Division's infantrymen had also crossed the enemy's line and were advancing on the burning village of Longueval. Heartening news, but 9th Division's advance failed to solve the hold-up on 8th Brigade's front. Thereupon, Haldane sent word for the brigade-major to go personally with a company of the 2nd Royal Scots and try to break the deadlock.

Not withstanding 8th Brigade's dilemma, it could be justifiably said that the assault had the hallmarks of a successful outcome. Nothing quite like it had been attempted before on such a scale, and its audacity was starting to pay dividends. The German main second line was breached and many of the objectives accomplished on schedule. By the time Gregory's Secunderabad Cavalry Brigade reached its next position, it was expected that the way would be clear to snatch High Wood and to harass a retiring enemy.

On this assumption and with the 7th Dragoon Guards at its head, the brigade was ordered forward. The 7th Dragoon Guards left Bray-sur-Somme at 4.30 a.m., followed at intervals by the rest of the brigade. A little after five o'clock, they crossed the Albert-Péronne road and were moving up in troop column through sporadic shelling to the far end of Carnoy Valley[1], south-west of Montauban. The regiment halted there, dispersing the troops to lessen the risk of sustaining casualties from shell fire. The dispersal had its desired effect. The only casualties were four horses wounded.

Around 6.30 a.m., 9th Division's battle headquarters received

[1] Also known to Fourth Army personnel as Montauban Valley.

entirely separate reports from its two assaulting brigades that Longueval had fallen. Excellent though it seemed at the time, both reports were to prove incorrect. The true situation was that only the southern half of the village was occupied, but on the strength of these reports a message was flashed to 3rd Division's battle headquarters at 6.58 a.m.: 'Have occupied whole of Longueval and are consolidating.' In anticipation of such successes, with the 7th Dragoon Guards already in Carnoy Valley as the advanced guard, Gregory was instructed to bring the rest of his brigade up to the vicinity of 3rd Division's battle headquarters. They duly arrived by 7.15 a.m.

As eager as ever to commit cavalry, Rawlinson was impatient for the right kind of news to reach his headquarters. Suddenly, among the deluge of incoming signals was the erroneous one that the whole of Longueval had been captured. Already delighted over the reports that the villages and woods of Bazentin-le-Grand and Bazentin-le-Petit were taken, Rawlinson made his decision:

> Things have gone so quickly and so well that I have authorised Congreve to send through the 2nd Indian Cavalry Division. He sent the order to them at 7.40 with High Wood as their objective. If they get possession of this, we shall be on the high road to success.

It is contentious whether the XIII Corps commander sent the order at the time stated by Rawlinson. In his private diary, Congreve clearly put the time at 8.10 a.m. Whatever the difference, one thing was quite apparent that Friday morning of 14th July. Given the opportunity, Rawlinson was determined to make history by employing cavalry in its proper role for the first time since trench warfare began in October 1914. The optimistic reports from the front convinced him that the moment had arrived.

Away to the north-east of the waiting cavalry, Shoubridge's 54th Brigade finally won Trônes Wood by 8.15 a.m. The welcome news was relayed to XIII Corps headquarters as the 7th Dragoon Guards received their orders to attack High Wood. Although it was too early for them to hear about the Trônes Wood victory, information tendered to the 7th Dragoon Guards included reports that Longueval and the Bazentin-le-Grand area were devoid of enemy infantry activity. On that note, two patrols were despatched to reconnoitre the ground.

Both patrols, under Lieutenants Malone and Hastings, rode round the eastern side of Montauban to study the approach to High Wood via Longueval. On nearing Longueval and much to their chagrin, Malone and Hastings discovered that their patrols were increasingly being subjected to hostile machine-gun and rifle fire, much of it coming from the enemy positions where 8th Brigade was still held in check. Recognising that any cavalry advance in that direction would be fraught with peril, they had little option but to turn back and report the unpalatable facts.

It was decided to try another route and two more patrols were sent out at 9.30 a.m., commanded by Lieutenants Adair and Struben. They veered to the western side of Montauban for Bazentin-le-Grand and Bazentin-le-Petit. The torn ground proved so slippery that the horses had difficulty in keeping their balance, and negotiating the trenches required good horsemanship. Moreover, their presence did not go unnoticed by friend and foe alike. Adair's and Struben's patrols, being such a rare sight at the front, were mistakenly identified by some XV Corps infantry as the advanced guard. One message to that effect was relayed back to XV Corps headquarters about cavalrymen trying to advance between Bazentin-le-Grand Wood and Bazentin-le-Grand village, but want of crossings over the trenches was stopping them.

The situation became so obscure at times during the morning that, at one stage, even XIII Corps' battle headquarters formed the impression that the cavalry advance on High Wood had started. As 3rd Division's battle headquarters was the 'nerve centre' for 2nd Indian Cavalry Division's operations, Haldane had earlier received a message from XIII Corps concerning Germans seen to be massing behind High Wood, but artillery was 'not dealing with this for fear of hitting cavalry'. Fortunately a telephone line had been run out from Haldane's headquarters to the Carnoy Valley which now held the whole of the Secunderabad Cavalry Brigade. In no time at all the true status was ascertained and Haldane's signallers conveyed the tidings that 'none of our cavalry had passed through our lines half an hour ago and were not at all likely to be in High Wood'. Within minutes, High Wood was being shelled.

However, progress was being made in preparation for the cavalry taking High Wood. If it happened, 7th Division's 22nd Brigade planned to send forward two battalions to occupy and consolidate the wood and sufficient of the trenches on either side of it. A necessary task, because air reconnaissance had shown that the

Germans were fast constructing a trench – known as the Switch Line – which extended from the Albert-Bapaume road to the Flers defences, via the top section of High Wood. Definitely a daunting obstacle when fully completed, since its line on either side of High Wood was on the reverse slope and hidden from ground observation. Fully aware of High Wood's strategic importance, 7th Division was already moving up a Royal Engineer field company to assist in consolidating the wood.

When surveying the terrain between the village and wood of Bazentin-le-Grand, also the approach to Bazentin-le-Petit Wood, both cavalry patrol officers experienced similar receptions to their predecessors. From the rifle fire, retaliatory shelling and enemy machine-gun activity from the north-western part of Bazentin-le-Petit Wood, they judged that not all was sweetness and light as they were led to believe. To compound matters, a German counter-attack had commenced from the direction of High Wood on to Bazentin-le-Petit village. The officers had seen enough. Adair and Struben returned across Caterpillar Valley with their patrols.

Whilst the first cavalry patrols were in the field on reconnaissance work, Lieutenants Williams and Peacock of 9th Light Armoured Car Battery[2] were in a position of readiness near Bronfay Farm and not far from 3rd Division's battle headquarters. Their two armoured cars – Rolls-Royces – formed part of the Secunderabad Cavalry Brigade's column. At 9 a.m., Williams and Peacock received orders to assist in the attack on High Wood.

At long last, they too were about to participate in some real action – or so they thought. Nervous but cheerful, both officers with their machine-gunners boarded their respective vehicles and headed up the muddy congested road towards Montauban. In spite of the road's awful condition, which resembled a badly rutted track, they managed to get within 300 yards of the smashed village before the mud defeated them. The more the engines protested, the faster the wheels spun, and the deeper the vehicles sunk. Thoroughly frustrated and cursing their ill-luck, they set about the onerous job of digging out the bogged armoured cars from the glutinous muck. Had the officers known, their demoralisation would have taken a further fall. For the rest of July, they and their iron steeds were to be relegated to patrolling the roads in and out of Mametz.

[2] The 9th Light Armoured Car Battery had an establishment of four armoured cars with one towing a 3-pdr gun. Two of these vehicles were serving with the Secunderabad Cavalry Brigade at that time.

Private Brennan of the 2nd Royal Irish would have willingly changed roles with them if he had been gifted with seeing the future. He and his comrades of 'A' Company had risen early that morning. Their objective was the Bazentin-le-Petit cemetery. Since 7th Division's 20th Brigade had carried all its objectives by 5 a.m., which included establishing a line from Bazentin-le-Grand Wood to the northern edge of Bazentin-le-Petit village, it meant that the division's 22nd Brigade would follow through to attack the village itself. The brigade's battalions selected for this work were the 2nd Royal Warwickshires and the 2nd Royal Irish.

Both battalions moved off by five o'clock. The Midlands men who led were detailed to seize a trench called Circus Trench and then cover the 2nd Royal Irish advance on Bazentin-le-Petit. The battalion's 'C' Company would make for the village, 'A' Company for the cemetery east of it, and 'B' Company was to act as left flank guard with 'D' in reserve.

A short walk brought Brennan's company to Mametz Wood. Soon they were threading their way around shell holes and shattered tree stumps to the assembly point for the attack.

This was on the edge of the wood, facing the enemy. A steep incline was just in front of us. At its base was a sunken road going off to the left and round it. As we stood in skirmishing order awaiting zero hour, the battalion's scouts, led by Lt Harrison, moved across our front and took to the sunken road. Dear old George Buckley – a scout and a Kilkenny man – called out to Frank and me as they passed, wishing us in his characteristically hearty fashion the best of luck. As they passed from our sight around the left of the incline, we saw a big black cloud just above that spot. The scouts rejoined us an hour or so after we arrived at the cemetery, but poor George was missing. He had been killed by the shell of which we had seen the smoke, a few seconds after he left us. After Frank Waldron, he was my best pal in the battalion. It was a bad beginning to a day that was to prove disastrous to my friendships.

The actual attack went remarkably well. Circus Trench was taken against light opposition, and Bazentin-le-Petit fell with the help of the 6th Leicestershires from the neighbouring 110th Brigade of 21st Division. Over 150 soldiers of the *16th Bavarian Regiment* with its commander and headquarters staff were captured in the village.

After attacking the cemetery, 'A' Company established a defensive line from the cemetery to the crossroads near the village. As instructed, 'B' Company formed a defensive flank on the left of the village and linked up with 110th Brigade in Bazentin-le-Petit Wood.

Private Brennan was on the extreme right of the line during the attack, the company's boundary marked by the ruins of the village windmill some 50 yards from the small valley that contained the cemetery. When advancing, he had speculated on whether he should break formation to investigate the windmill. He decided not to bother and continued with the others to the cemetery. The apparent disappearance of the enemy instilled a degree of casual confidence in the men. They walked about outside their trenches or stood in groups enjoying the exhilaration of victory. Then, quite without warning, a machine-gun opened fire from the ruined windmill. Suddenly, Brennan was encompassed by sounds which he could only describe as the swishes of a thousand giant canes and the anguished screams of his mates:

> I saw the legs of an old veteran, Tom Shea, completely covered in blood, and I remember thinking that poor old Tom had got it at last. My own escape was little short of miraculous, as men were howling and groaning all around me and yet I wasn't hit. The general effect was most unnerving, but the instinct to survive made everyone dive headlong for the trenches. It must have been at this stage when Lt Dean took a handful of men, including Frank Waldron, and tried to rush the windmill. Dean and Frank Waldron and most of them were killed before the machine-gun was silenced, if indeed it was silenced. At any rate it ceased to trouble my sector of the trench, which was just as well, as we soon had to face trouble from another quarter.

That 'trouble' stemmed from German reinforcements. By coincidence, as the dawn assault went in, an enemy division was on the point of arriving to relieve the *183rd Division* in the Pozières-Bazentin-le-Petit Wood sector. The division's regiments with other units were subsequently fed in to bolster up the fragmented front, including the hurried manning of the partially completed Switch Line west of Longueval and which cut through High Wood. The commander whose immediate responsibility was to rally his men on the new front was General Sixt von Armin. Directed to take over command from the River Ancre to Longueval at nine o'clock that very morning, von Armin found himself plunged into a critical situation. There were no rear positions behind the incomplete Switch Line and his artillery had suffered severely. Fortunately, High Wood offered a good rallying point. It was from there that German troops advanced to counter-attack the village of Bazentin-le-Petit at 11.45 a.m. They were assisted by their comrades holding out in Bazentin-le-Petit Wood. It was this action which the last cavalry patrols had seen.

The enemy advance was reported prior to the Germans reaching the village. In response to an urgent appeal, two platoons from the 2nd Royal Irish 'B' and 'C' Companies rushed to help the troops in the village. Private Brennan saw the Germans moving in groups on his left front. 'They were using the old skirmishing tactics of a short rush of a few yards and then a flop.' Brennan with his 'A' Company comrades fired volley after volley, but with little success. A youngster next to him fell with blood pouring from his mouth. Brennan continued firing, although he doubted that his contribution was altering the course of battle. His doubts multiplied when it became obvious that the Germans had driven outlying troops back into the village. Friendly artillery fire soon intervened to stop the enemy from capitalising on his advance. An hour later, the Germans mounted another attack from High Wood. This time, they entered the east side of the village.

This left us isolated in the cemetery and subject to the enemy's enfilading fire. Our captain, a very cool and capable officer named Hegarty, gave the order to withdraw and we retired down the road towards Mametz. We halted a little way down the road and waited. In the meantime, things began to happen again in the village. Our adjutant had been proceeding from battalion headquarters towards Bazentin-le-Petit when he observed our fellows being driven from the village. He rallied them and, collecting every available man in the vicinity, including some old veterans of a Pioneer battalion who had been grave-digging, he led them in a brilliant and successful counter-attack which sent the enemy flying back. As soon as we became aware of the changed situation, we moved up to the cemetery again.

The enemy's two counter-attacks showed High Wood's tactical importance as well as its noticeable defensive value. Private Brennan's battalion could testify to the wood's potency, being one of the first infantry formations to lay the foundation to its future sanguine reputation. That day the 2nd Royal Irish suffered 334 casualties. A mere drop compared with the days and weeks ahead in the struggle to take High Wood, but a bleak omen nevertheless.

Yet there is evidence to suggest that possession of High Wood was possible before mid-morning, a possibility foreseen by the 7th Division's commander, Major-General Watts, soon after his troops' earlier success at Bazentin-le-Petit. On his right, 3rd Division's 9th Brigade had all but captured the village of Bazentin-le-Grand by 6.30 a.m. As for his own division, only four battalions had been employed to seize the division's objectives. With two-thirds of his infantry still uncommitted, and with his artillery being pushed forward to new positions, Watts proposed to XV Corps headquarters that he should exploit the opening made by his leading battalions. The reply he received was negative. Instead, he was instructed to leave the High Wood operation to the cavalry. Just in case destiny should beckon, Watts ensured that his reserve brigade, the 91st, was ready for action soon after 11 a.m.

Surprising though it may seem, one senior officer actually walked into High Wood, apparently during the artillery lull in expectation of the cavalry advance. He was the GOC 9th Brigade, Brigadier-General Potter:

> I had been very strictly enjoined not to push the advance beyond the final [infantry] objective laid down, which just included Bazentin-le-Grand. Leaving the consolidation proceeding on that line, I walked out alone to examine the ground in front. It was a lovely day; the ground was very open and sloped gently up to a high ridge in front, so I wandered on until I found myself approaching a large wood which continued over the crest of the ridge. There was no sign whatever of the enemy, so I walked into the edge of the wood but saw no sign of a German, nor any defensive works. As I had advanced about a mile, and was quite alone, I considered it time to return. . . . The wood reached by me I afterwards knew as High Wood, and it is a great regret to me that the advance was not pressed that day and the hundreds of thousands of casualties afterwards expended in the capture of the position possibly avoided.[3]

[3] Extracts from a letter sent to Brigadier-General Sir J.E. Edmonds (PRO). Edmonds was the official military historian. Playfair had also written to him.

Playfair, a Royal Engineer officer from 8th Brigade, met with a similar experience:

I accompanied my CRE (Lt-Colonel C.A. Elliott) into Bazentin-le-Grand at about 6.30 a.m. on 14th July in order to examine a large cellar known to have been there. We walked some way beyond, towards High Wood, without a shot being fired. I mention this, because I have always believed that High Wood could have been occupied straight away.

Whether the wood could have been occupied by infantry while the enemy was massing to the north of it is questionable, but the 800-yard stretch along High Wood's south-western edge offered an excellent entry point if the wood itself was undefended. On balance, therefore, it was a risk worth taking despite the pockets of resistance in the fighting front and the threat of the incomplete Switch Line being manned.

Around noon and recognising that the cavalry had not and could not advance, sanction was given by Fourth Army headquarters for XV Corps infantry to push on to High Wood. The cavalry would follow, but only at the request of XV Corps. It was also requested by XV Corps for XIII Corps artillery to shell High Wood until asked to stop. Everything seemed straightforward and Congreve was happy to comply, having not been allowed by Fourth Army to let his 3rd Division commander use 76th Brigade for hot pursuit in the first place. However, there was a snag. The XV Corps commander, Horne, intended only to order the infantry forward when the whole of Longueval was in the hands of XIII Corps.

Since Horne's plan was to advance on High Wood from Bazentin-le-Petit, it made as much sense to await Longueval's capture as Rawlinson's insistence on the cavalry seizing the wood. With High Wood commanding the heights, an early morning occupation would have considerably weakened the enemy's resolve to defend Longueval and Delville Wood. Outflanked and with their supply lines to both village and wood constantly under fire, not to mention the very real threat of envelopment around their Pozières position, the Germans would doubtless have retired to their Flers defences, or expended valuable men in trying to retake High Wood in the face of machine-gun and artillery fire. The burning question was whether the same benefits would apply by the time Longueval fell, or would the delay give the enemy time to draw on his resources?

Part of the answer came as the two corps commanders anxiously waited for news of Longueval's demise from Furse's 9th Division. For the second time that day, Bazentin-le-Petit was subjected to a counter-attack. It was the same counter-attack that had forced Brennan's company to vacate the cemetery. The nearby wood of Bazentin-le-Grand was simultaneously assaulted, but the attack was repulsed by the entrenched troops whose prowess was later recognised by an angry hail of shells.

More positive news filtered from 3rd Division's front, where part of its 8th Brigade was being mauled along 500 yards of enemy-held trenches. The brigade-major, as ordered by Haldane, eventually arrived in the troubled area with a mixed party from the 2nd Royal Scots in reserve. At first he had asked the battalion commander, Lt-Colonel Dyson, for a company of men. On hearing that the company was required for a frontal attack that rang of mass suicide, Dyson refused his request. Instead, the brigade-major had to opt for a composite outfit that consisted of the battalion's bombers, snipers and volunteers. In the event, it proved to be a more satisfactory arrangement. Methodically working from 9th Brigade's section of captured trenches, with another force acting in concert from the right end, they vigorously bombed along the German trenches. By 2.30 p.m., resistance had virtually ceased with minimal casualties to the attackers. Their total bag was 280 prisoners, four machine-guns and a fair proportion of enemy dead.

The oddest episode of the action was the release from captivity of the 7th Shropshires' CO, Lt-Colonel R.E. Negus. He had been wounded during the assault, when his battalion tried valiantly to force a path through the uncut barbed wire. He lay squirming with pain on the trench parapet before being dragged down by the German defenders and heaved into a deep dugout. Just as a bomber was about to throw a grenade down the steps, Negus shouted out and was rescued.

The unavoidable delay in 8th Brigade fulfilling its objectives was, in Haldane's opinion, the prime reason for the cavalry failing to pass through his lines to High Wood. With the fighting for Longueval very much in progress, any cavalry advance through the middle of the two disputed zones could have led to unacceptable losses amongst horses and horsemen. As the 8th Brigade troops consolidated the newly-won stretch of line, a message reached Horne that Longueval had fallen at 3.10 p.m. In reality, 9th Division's Scottish infantrymen with support from its South African Brigade had only temporarily wrested the village from the enemy's tenacious grasp. No sooner were they in the northern end of Longueval than hostile machine-gun fire from the north-west corner of Delville Wood drove them back.

Nothing had changed radically at the top of Bazentin-le-Petit Wood either. A machine-gun nest was repeatedly making its presence felt and causing a great deal of mischief in the process. To a lesser degree, so was Rawlinson from Fourth Army headquarters. Horne was told that it was vitally important to press on and obtain lodgement in High Wood that evening, and a regiment from the Secunderabad Cavalry Brigade was at his disposal. Rawlinson's motivation was stimulated by a recent report that enemy artillery had stopped firing in front of III Corps, and that the Germans were leaving Pozières in droves. He greatly feared that the guns were retiring and was frustrated that no cavalry was through to charge them.

Rawlinson was not alone with troubled thoughts; Horne experienced a few himself earlier that afternoon. A combined attack by his 21st Division and III Corps' 1st Division was scheduled to bring the right of III Corps into the salient, created by the assault. It was not to be. The fighting had taken its toll on 21st Division's three infantry brigades, one of which was down to 1,200 men. When III Corps judged that its 1st Division could not act independently, all thoughts of an offensive movement evaporated.

On the credit side, prisoners from the XV Corps front rose to six officers and 602 men by 3.30 p.m. The first ones to go into captivity came from the XIII Corps front an hour after day-break, when its 9th Division fought through the enemy's main second line on the way to Longueval. As the prisoners drifted back under escort, so too streamed the British wounded – hobbling back as best they could to the advanced dressing stations, occasionally passing the stoical stretcher-bearers with their bloody charges. Among the advanced dressing stations was one set up in a small quarry just north of Montauban. Two weeks previously, it had hidden the group of Germans who tried to retake Montauban in the evening of 1st July.

To the rear of Montauban, back across the crumbling old front line and into the Carnoy Valley, Gregory's Secunderabad Cavalry Brigade continued to champ at the bit. Behind the valley, south of the Albert-Péronne road, 2nd Indian Cavalry Division's two other brigades also waited and wondered whether their long-sought moment of glory was approaching or fading with the westering sun.

For a brief period, Horne waited too, having been in earnest contact with Fourth Army headquarters over the wisdom of using cavalry. In the XV Corps war diary, a staff officer wrote: 'The position now is that either the Cavalry or part of 7th Division are to go for High Wood tonight. The decision of the Army Commander is awaited.'

When it came, Horne responded swiftly. After giving orders for a 7th Division brigade to move up to take High Wood at 5.15 p.m., he arranged with XIII Corps for units of the 2nd Indian Cavalry Division to stand by to cover 7th Division's right flank and go for the high ground between High Wood and Longueval.

Haldane and MacAndrew were notified of XV Corps' intentions through XIII Corps' battle headquarters, Chipilly. Telephoning Gregory, MacAndrew outlined the cavalry's role and asked him to report to 3rd Division's battle headquarters for a more detailed briefing. Before going, Gregory placed his brigade on stand-to. As excitement filled the air, working parties were recalled from levelling shell holes and bridging trenches in readiness for the mounted advance.

During his briefing with MacAndrew, a signal came in that bore the news that the 7th Division's attack was postponed to 6.15 p.m. It was welcomed by all concerned, not least by Brigadier-General Minshull-Ford whose 91st Brigade was the reserve of 7th Division and assembled on the east side of Mametz Wood. It was there that he received the same message, literally minutes after being told that his brigade would be attacking High Wood in conjunction with the cavalry. Happily his divisional commander, Watts, having correctly foreseen the possibility, had verbally ordered Minshull-Ford to concentrate 91st Brigade east of Mametz Wood as early as 8 a.m. The position was actually in a small valley just south of Bazentin-le-Grand Wood, known as Flat Iron Valley and which took its name from one of the two coppices situated there. The valley became a target for periodic bombardments during the afternoon, so Minshull-Ford arranged for part of his brigade to shelter in Mametz Wood. The rest had dug 'funk holes' and hoped for the best. No two battalions were more pleased than the 1st South Staffords and the 2nd Queen's when Minshull-Ford ordered them forward to their positions of deployment. In the meantime, Horne had ordered 33rd Division to move up from its corps reserve area and come in line on 7th Division's left, west of Bazentin-le-Petit village.

On his return to his cavalry brigade, Gregory received amended orders by telephone. He was instructed to send two regiments to

Sabot Copse, being the other coppice in Flat Iron Valley, where they would pass from the command of XIII Corps to that of XV Corps. Gregory was specifically ordered to report to Minshull-Ford's headquarters immediately on his arrival in the valley. The two regiments selected for the advance were the 7th Dragoon Guards and the 20th Deccan Horse. The Secunderabad Cavalry Brigade's remaining regiment – the 34th Poona Horse – was to continue on stand-to and stay under XIII Corps' control. For the other two cavalry brigades, south of the Albert-Péronne road, it proved to be another false dawn. They were directed to return to base where they would come under XV Corps' command.

The updated plan of attack appeared straightforward enough, although the timing was decidedly optimistic. To be at their place of deployment by 6.15 p.m. would require super-human effort and much luck. The officers and men of the 1st South Staffords were to lead, deploying with their left flank on the Bazentin-le-Petit cemetery and with the 2nd Queen's on their right. Minshull-Ford sent up the 21st Manchesters to provide a reserve and a right flank guard. He had been told that the 33rd Division's leading brigade (100th) would support his left by attacking the Switch Line, north-west of High Wood. So far there was no sign of the brigade. He would have been doubly worried if he had known that the 100th Brigade commander, Brigadier-General A.W.F. Baird, had not received any such order.

The cavalry's function was one of co-operation. The 7th Dragoon Guards were to attack the enemy's positions on the east side of High Wood, working on the infantry's right flank. The 20th Deccan Horse would prolong the line to the 7th Dragoon Guards' right and help to take the high ground before wheeling eastwards and raiding Delville Wood. About the same time, Furse's 9th Division would renew its efforts to capture Delville Wood from the south – hindered by the fact that Longueval had yet to fall. Except for the 9th Division's attack, due to start at 6.30 p.m., timing was critical for cavalry and infantry with respect to High Wood. The bombardment of High Wood was due to lift at 6.15 p.m., and the attackers needed to cover the intermediate ground as quickly as possible to gain any benefit from it.

A young cavalry subaltern, 2nd Lieutenant Pope, began to lead his troop from Carnoy Valley and along the Carnoy-Montauban road at 5.40 p.m. A memorable occasion and 2nd Lieutenant Pope was a little awed by it. His troop headed the 7th Dragoon Guards' 'B'

Squadron: the regiment's only squadron armed with lances. Following in column of sections were the rest of the regiment. Further back were the four squadrons of the 20th Deccan Horse and, again, just the first squadron carried lances. Attached to both regiments were sections of the brigade's machine-gun squadron. Following up in the rear, but very much part of the historic scene, rode the 'N' Battery of the RHA.

Tired infantrymen, artillerymen in their gun emplacements and returning wounded stared disbelievingly at the novel sight of the column riding towards the front. Their astonishment gave way to cheers of encouragement which were savoured by British and turbaned Indian horsemen alike. Leaving the battered road to Montauban, they cantered on to enter Flat Iron Valley to the rich accompaniment of jingling harnesses and the melodic thump of hooves. The valley, already a place of desolation, bared her wounds to them, prompting a young Dragoon officer to record:

> There was not a square yard of ground that was not broken up with shell holes. The trees in the woods stood blackened and broken, stripped of all their leaves and branches. Dead and wounded, British and German, lay on every side. Here and there a wrecked German gun, with the mangled remains of a team that had striven in vain to withdraw it. Further on, three or four burnt-out railway trucks stood among the debris of a siding.

Truly, they had arrived at the front and in the area of concentration. The time was 6.25 p.m. Gregory spurred his horse to Minshull-Ford's headquarters and reported his presence. With the hour-glass empty, Minshull-Ford quickly indicated where he wished the cavalry to be deployed, hoping that the 1st South Staffords and the 2nd Queen's were ready to commence the advance on High Wood. In fact, both battalions had experienced very heavy shell fire on their way up and were only deploying in loose order as Gregory left the brigade headquarters. With no more ado, Gregory ordered the two cavalry regiments forward.

With lances unslung, 'B' Squadron again led their regiment with the 20th Deccan Horse advancing on their right. They rode by the wood of Bazentin-le-Grand to debouch in the pasture of a valley south-west of Longueval, by which time the infantry to the left of the 7th Dragoon Guards were also advancing. They were heartened to see cavalry riding for a mounted attack; so too was Anthony Brennan who had volunteered for grave-digging duty in the hope of finding the body of his pal, Frank Waldron. He and the other men in the burial party avidly watched a squadron of cavalry going forward on their right. 'We gave them a cheer as they passed, for we really believed that it was a sign that the break-through had come at last.'

Brennan's party had seen 'B' Squadron with 2nd Lieutenant Pope's troop in the vanguard and nearest to them. Supported by 'C' Squadron with drawn sabres, 'B' Squadron galloped through a cross-fire of machine-gun bullets that did remarkably little damage. Two hundred yards on, Pope's men reached the cover of a bank on top of which ran the Martinpuich-Longueval dirt road. They leaped the bank, crossed the dirt road and into a field of standing corn speckled with poppies. The cornfield sloped up to the plateau adjacent to High Wood. Ploughing through the corn, they wheeled to the right, levelled their lances and charged some German machine-gunners who were sheltering in some of the shell holes among the corn. About 15 of the enemy fell victim to the lances. Faced by this totally alien, albeit archaic form of warfare, another 32 surrendered in fear of being speared.

Hostile machine-gun fire and rifle fire, much of it coming from the Switch Line, finally forced the 7th Dragoon Guards to dismount under the cover of the bank. Owing to the height of the crops, the line of the troublesome trench could not be located. One troop was sent out to reconnoitre, but was checked by heavy machine-gun and rifle fire. Cries of the wounded were heard, motivating Pope to ride three times into the corn and bring in two of the wounded men across his saddle. For this gallantry, he received the immediate award of a Military Cross. He was not the only officer to distinguish himself; a mounted Hotchkiss section braved the murderous fire which resulted in the killing of a gun-horse. The section officer, Lieutenant D.J. Hartley, tried to retrieve the machine-gun but died in the process. Another officer, Lieutenant Anson, took command and managed to reach the dead gun-horse with the body of his fellow officer beside it. Finding the machine-gun to be damaged, he nevertheless succeeded in withdrawing the survivors of the section from their exposed position, being wounded himself during the retirement.

The leading squadron of the 20th Deccan Horse had also galloped into trouble, necessitating another squadron to come up on the squadron's right flank. Everything had gone comparatively well in the beginning. The advanced guard had collected ten petrified prisoners, all from the *16th Bavarian Regiment*, before being fired on

from Delville Wood and from infantry hidden in the crops. With the
landscape littered with dead horses from both cavalry regiments,
help arrived from the air.

Flying a Morane monoplane, an RFC pilot and his observer had
seen their predicament in the evening's fading light. The pilot,
Captain Miller of No 3 Squadron, swooped low to allow his observer
to fire tracer bullets at the Germans concealed in the crops and along
the Switch Line. The holes appearing in the fabric of the aircraft
testified that it was risky work, but the tracer bullets enabled the
cavalry machine-gunners to pin-point the danger spots. Miller made
one more pass without his observer firing his Lewis gun before flying
off to where 'N' Battery had taken up a position, some 700 yards
south of the captured main second line and about 900 yards south-
west of Longueval. Major T. French, commanding 'N' Battery,
glimpsed the observer tossing a bag from the aircraft. On opening it,
French discovered that it contained a rough sketch of the enemy
positions confronting the cavalry. His artillerymen began registering
their guns moments before a salvo of German shells exploded some
distance behind them.

Away to the left, Minshull-Ford's infantry had not been idle
during the cavalry action. After a short delay to let the 1st South
Staffords arrange protection of their left flank, due to the non-arrival
of 33rd Division, infantrymen commenced the 1,600-yard advance to
High Wood. Before 100 yards of ground was covered, machine-gun
fire from the west of the wood started to tell on the South Staffords. In
addition, desultory shooting broke out from Germans in shell holes
and in hollows between the battalion and High Wood. The 1st South
Staffords merely halted and returned rapid fire before pressing on
again.

The South Staffords' discipline was self-evident; equally, so was
their mounting casualty rate. Orders were urgently issued to the 2nd
Queen's to push on hard for High Wood, hoping that the battalion
could reach it and outflank the death-dealing machine-guns. Largely
shielded by the 1st South Staffords, they covered 700 yards of ground
in ten minutes as they went forward in four lines 150 yards apart on a
front of 350 yards. The battalion's two leading companies crossed a
hedge at that point and were rewarded with their first trophies: three
abandoned 77-mm field guns less breech blocks, one limber and piles
of ammunition.

Their exhilaration was short-lived. Beyond the hedge, they
encountered hostile small-arms fire in similar circumstances to their

1st South Staffords' comrades. The 2nd Queen's continued advancing with scarcely a waver, steadily winkling the enemy from cover like beaters on a deadly pheasant shoot. Their courage failing, many Germans turned to flee and a fair proportion were bowled over by the 2nd Queen's firing from the standing position. Those who did not choose to run were either captured or bayoneted. Once more the RFC intervened when a pilot of No 3 Squadron descended to tree-top level, his observer strafing field-grey figures between the two advancing battalions and High Wood.

In the space of half-an-hour from capturing the field guns, both leading companies of the 2nd Queen's were on the south-western fringe of the wood. When compared with the pitted ground outside, High Wood seemed barely touched. It was nearly 8 p.m. with the evening misting up as the 2nd Queen's tried to scan High Wood's leafy interior for signs of hostility as they waited for the 1st South Staffords to come abreast. Nothing could be seen except dense undergrowth and young saplings among the more mature trees. What sounds there were in the wood were lost in the overall din of battle, much of it from the Switch Line. As the leading companies of the 1st South Staffords came up level with them, they plunged into the dark recesses of the wood.

Back in Flat Iron Valley, staff of 91st Brigade watched the foremost battalion of 33rd Division's 100th Brigade march into view at 7.30 p.m. Minshull-Ford was out when Baird visited his headquarters. Instead, Baird saw the brigade-major and asked whether High Wood was yet taken. If it was, his orders were to push forward patrols to the Switch Line west of High Wood and, if the trench was not occupied, to advance further to Martinpuich. On the other hand, if the Switch Line was manned by the enemy, his brigade was to attack it the next day at 9 a.m. Everything, however, was wholly dependent on 7th Division capturing High Wood. On comparing his instructions with those given to 91st Brigade, it became apparent that the misunderstanding stemmed from divisional level. It was soon resolved and the brigade-major stressed that 100th Brigade's support was still being counted on for the good of the operation. Acting on his own initiative, since his orders were in direct conflict with 91st Brigade's, Baird promptly ordered up his two leading battalions – the 1st Queen's and the Glasgow Highlanders (9th HLI) – to co-operate on the left by making good and occupying the road from the north-east end of Bazentin-le-Petit village to the western corner of High Wood.

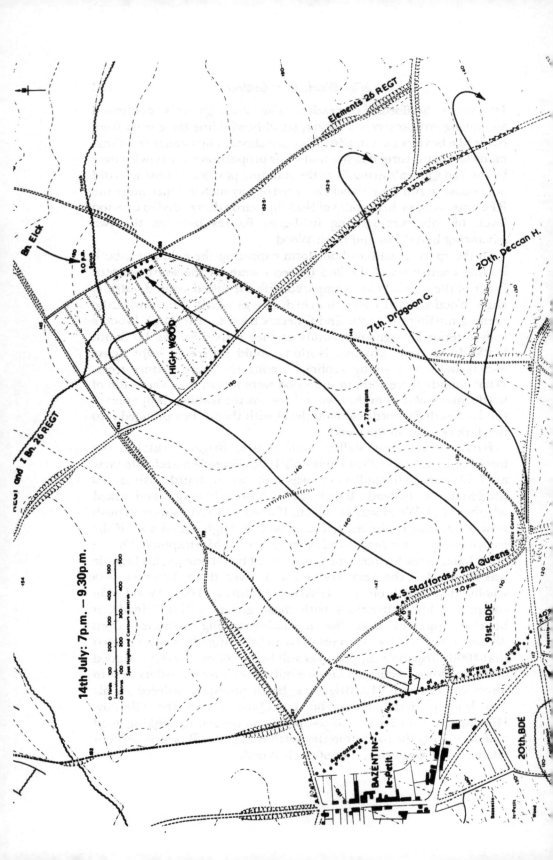

Elements 26 REGT

Bn Eick
9.0 p.m.
gun

HIGH WOOD

REGT and I Bn. 26 REGT

20th. Deccan H.

7th Dragoon G.

77 mm guns

9.30 p.m.

1st. S. Staffords. 2nd Queens
7 p.m.

91st BDE

20th. BDE

Mill

Cemetery

forward

Approximate line

BAZENTIN-le-Petit

Bazentin
le-Petit Wood

14th July: 7p.m. — 9.30p.m.

Spot Heights and Contours in metres

At their place of assembly near Mametz Wood, which seemed to
be full of dead Welshmen from the ill-used 38th Division, word
reached the Glasgow Highlanders that High Wood was taken and
secured by 91st Brigade. Baird was still at Minshull-Ford's
headquarters when he heard the news. There was no reason to query
it. Ordered to form up in two ranks, the Glasgow Highlanders were
told they would be going up to consolidate a newly-won position. At
a respectable distance behind the Glasgow Highlanders, officers and
men of the 1st Queen's prepared to move out. Then, shouldering
arms, both battalions marched off in the direction of High Wood to
the noise of artillery fire and exploding shells.

On entering High Wood at twilight and with the foliage deep in
shadows, both the 2nd Queen's and 1st South Staffords had
difficulty in seeing more than twenty yards ahead. Keeping direction
was an ever-present problem in the thick and thorny undergrowth.
They encountered very few of the enemy at first, but the sniping
played havoc with their nerves as they tugged their way through
impeding brambles and stepped around tree trunks. Now and then
they paused to duel with indistinct muzzle flashes or to fire a volley
immediately to their front. After what appeared to be eternity, but in
reality only about twenty minutes, 'C' and 'D' Companies of the 2nd
Queen's reached the one track that cut diagonally through the centre
of the wood. Green flares were lit there to signal the British position
to friendly aircraft. A number of the 1st South Staffords tried to reach
an intersecting track above the 1st Queen's, but being closer to the
Switch Line that snaked through the northern angle, they were shot
down by machine-gun fire. From the north-east side of the wood,
came the quickening crackle of small-arms fire as the lead squadron
of the 7th Dragoon Guards swept into action with their lances.

The 2nd Queen's continued their passage through the wood
towards its eastern point against increasing opposition. Eventually,
after bombing several deep dugouts and capturing a doctor among
an assortment of prisoners, they occupied the whole of the south-
eastern edge and part of the north-east frontage. They began to dig
in, since the Germans manning the 300-yard stretch of Switch Line
within the wood made it impossible for them to occupy the complete
side. Repeated attempts by the 1st South Staffords in their area of the
wood to breach the Switch Line came to nought. They lost valuable
officers and men in the process, including a gallant young subaltern
named 2nd Lieutenant Potter. Already the holder of the DSO, he
had been strongly recommended a few days previously for the VC.

The absence of such capable officers would be keenly felt as darkness shrouded the wood.

Outside and to the right of the wood's southern point, surviving cavalrymen of the 7th Dragoon Guards and 20th Deccan Horse entrenched themselves on a line below the road to Longueval. For all their derring-do, they had failed to break through the new enemy defences that hinged on the Switch Line. The machine-gun had triumphed again.

One German officer of the *26th Regiment* specially blessed the misty night, regardless of the fact that two-thirds of High Wood was in British possession. He was Major Witte who found himself responsible for the defence of the wood. More than once he had wished for sufficient men to counter-attack, and now the night allowed him to be reinforced with two infantry companies and two machine-guns from Eaucourt Abbey, four miles north of his position. Even as the first company filed into High Wood, so a company from the 22nd Manchesters entered it at the other end to beef up the sorely tried 1st South Staffords. An RE field company from the 3rd Durhams also arrived to assist in the consolidation, but the reinforcing of Witte's position was not yet finished – nor was it on the British side.

Having left Flat Iron Valley and relatively escaping some shelling on the way up, shadowy kilted figures of the Glasgow Highlanders reached a five-lane junction just north of Bazentin-le-Grand, aptly called Crucifix Corner from the sizable crucifix there. Everyone briefly halted as the CO, Lt-Colonel John Stormonth-Darling, studied his map and conferred with his senior officers. Then, leaving 'C' and 'D' to wait in a sunken road, he led 'A' and 'B' Companies along the lane that intersected the Martinpuich-Longueval road at High Wood's southern point. Their objective was to establish strong points on the lane running parallel to the one they were on, which linked High Wood's western corner with the village of Bazentin-le-Petit. To achieve this, Stormonth-Darling intended deploying his troops over the field between the two lanes. The 1st Queen's were meanwhile by-passing Bazentin-le-Petit to reach the same lane, where they hoped to make touch with the Glasgow Highlanders and prolong the line back to the cross-roads north-east of the village.

In the wood, Witte had other plans as his men deepened the trench and made further machine-gun emplacements. At 11 p.m., after braving British artillery, two more companies from another regiment arrived to plug a gap that existed between the *7th Division* and the *3rd Guard Division* boundaries behind High Wood. Thirty minutes later, Witte speedily acted. With bomb, bullet and bayonet, he counter-attacked from the northern apex.

Back at Fourth Army headquarters in Querrieu, as star shells and gun fire illuminated the new front line, Rawlinson was enjoying the accolades befitting a successful army commander. Unlike 1st July, almost everything had gone to plan. Delville Wood had yet to fall, but the latest reports received from the front notified him that High Wood was taken. A much relieved Haig had already visited him to offer his congratulations, and so had Foch whom Haig also met in Querrieu. It pleased Haig to learn that the French were openly admitting that their troops could not have carried out such an attack, not even Balfourier's XX Corps – France's famous *Corps de Fer*.

Overall, it was a tremendous achievement and an audacious one to boot. Arguably at no time in history had so many troops assembled so close to an entrenched and active enemy by night, let alone gone on to win nearly 6,000 yards of main trench system. Including the preliminary bombardment, 492,000 artillery rounds were fired and 2,287 of the enemy taken prisoner. In terms of enemy killed, wounded and missing, the total figure exceeded the 9,000 British losses for the day. The *16th Bavarian Regiment*, for example, which had all its three battalions in the front line, lost nearly 2,300 officers and men.

Rawlinson masterminded the 14th July operation and, being a cavalryman, played no small part in ensuring the cavalry's participation, but who was the architect? Congreve's personal diary entry for the next day presents a principal clue to a perennial enigma:

> Haig came to see me and was very complimentary and grateful for our success yesterday, and indeed it was a good operation. I do not think so great a force was ever before got into position within 300 yards of an active enemy for a dawn attack, and our losses before the advance were very small. Our advance was over 1,400 yards of open ground. The arrangements of the Brigade staffs, the discipline of the battalions and the effectiveness of our artillery are the causes of our success. I think it will be a text book operation. I am told it is the most successful of the war and I planned it!

In High Wood, as the minutes ticked up to midnight on Friday, 14th July, the day's operation was anything but over.

CHAPTER FIVE

Confrontation

Totally unaware of Witte's counter-attack, Stormonth-Darling sent two platoons from each of his 'A' and 'B' Companies to skirt the wood's south-western edge in line abreast. Allowing a short time interval, he ordered the remaining platoons to sweep after them before he returned to his 'C' and 'D' Companies. The sounds of battle bounced and echoed in the night as the forward platoons trudged across the large grassy field, but 150 yards from the wood's western corner and where the lane led off to Bazentin-le-Petit, they were startled by someone shouting sharply in German. A brightly coloured flare zoomed up to throw the landscape into relief. Even as the flare reached its zenith, machine-gun fire and rifle fire broke out in their proximity as the German counter-attack reached the edge of the wood.

Men, notably of 'A' Company who were nearer to the wood, collapsed in dark heaps. Those still on their feet sufficiently recovered their wits to throw themselves at the turf. Urged on by their officers, they bit their entrenching tools into the flinty ground, hardly daring to raise their heads as they dug awkwardly for dear life. The second wave of Glasgow Highlanders, witnessing the commotion ahead, stopped in their tracks and followed suit. A few, who were walking close to the road by the south-western edge, formed a defensive line facing it.

Inside High Wood, Major Witte's storming parties were working with fanatical precision. The onslaught had taken the 1st South Staffords full in the throat and their right reeled back in confusion. This act brought untold pressure on 'D' Company of the 2nd Queen's who, until then, was in touch with the South Staffords. Attacked on their exposed flank and from the front, officers and men of 'D' Company managed to hold their ground for a while before their flank was forced back under a shower of stick-grenades. Casualties were great, but the precious minutes afforded by their heroic stand were employed to good effect. The battalion's 'B' Company was brought up to form a line facing north-west through the wood.

It was a shrewd defensive tactic, since the 1st South Staffords' front was torn apart. Ragged groups fell back, taking many of the 22nd Manchesters with them. The 3rd Durham RE Company, trying to prepare strong-points at the southern and eastern angles of the wood, spent as much time in picking up their rifles to help ward off the frequent attacks than doing what they were sent up to do. Stormonth-Darling found the situation extremely worrying on his return. His second wave had stopped and were digging in 200 yards to the rear of the casualty-stricken first wave – just where he intended to place his 'C' and 'D' Companies in support. He was also perturbed about the condition of his men. Except for a drink of tea at 1 p.m., no one had anything to eat or drink since breakfast. The only good piece of news was that a company of the 16th King's Royal Rifle Corps were on their way up to help his battalion to consolidate. As for the 1st Queen's who had reached the designated lane via Bazentin-le-Petit, they were vexed and puzzled over the non-appearance of the Jocks – having despatched a patrol along the lane towards the wood without finding a single Glasgow Highlander. Another patrol was sent out later. The subaltern in charge reported back at 1.15 a.m., stating that the Glasgow Highlanders were entrenching the side of the wood from the western corner south-eastwards.

The true situation was very different. Except for a small portion held by the 2nd Queen's on the north-east side, all the wood down to and around the western corner – including a section of the south-western face – was in German possession. After mopping up that area of the wood, Witte had concealed a company of men at the western corner to protect his advance southwards. He could afford to keep them positioned on his right flank, as he had again been reinforced with a large body of infantrymen who had come from Flers.

Wholly ignorant of the fact, some reserve Glasgow Highlanders arrived at High Wood from collecting reels of barbed wire at a forward engineer stores dump near Bazentin-le-Petit Wood. Weighed down with wire and stanchions, they stumbled along in the dark towards the western corner when they distinctly heard German voices. Moreover, the owners of the voices were busily entrenching down the south-western face. Quietly placing their loads on the ground, the wiring party slipped away to rejoin their company.

They were but a sample of those soldiers that night who had reached the conclusion that discretion was the better part of valour. A steady flow of 7th Division men left High Wood's claustrophobic

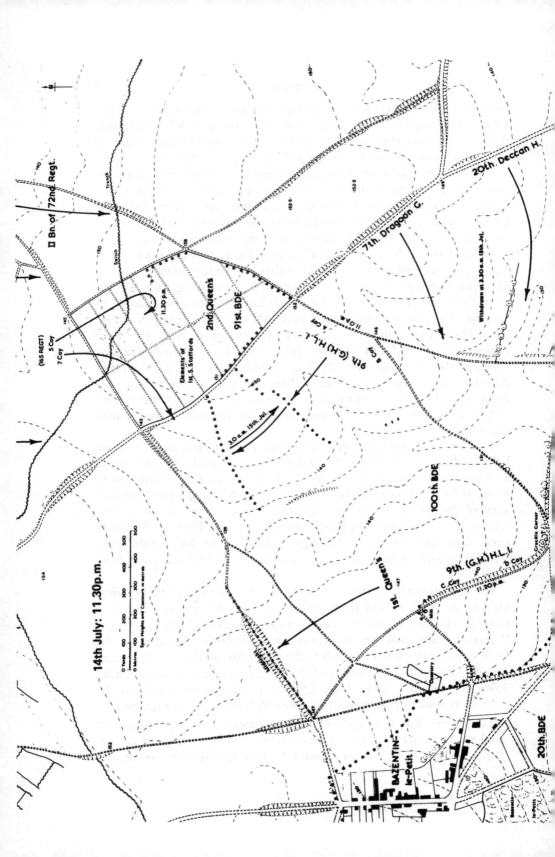

interior as the Germans worked their way downward. Stormonth-Darling knew that something had to be done quickly to stiffen the resolve. He decided to place some of 'C' Company's platoons – the lot if necessary – across High Wood to stem the German advance. Repositioning his own HQ by the three abandoned enemy field guns, he notified the 100th Brigade headquarters of his intentions. His message ended with the words: 'Will hold on at all costs.'

Soon afterwards Stormonth-Darling discovered that only nine men capable of firing a rifle remained in his first line. He had them withdrawn to the second line. This incident, coupled with the disorder in the wood, made him decide to pull back his right flank in case he was attacked from the south-western face. In pursuance of this plan, a platoon of Glasgow Highlanders was sent up to take a line alongside the wood. As the platoon filed along its edge, figures were dimly seen to hurry past in the opposite direction. Not knowing their identity prompted one platoon member to call: 'Who are you?' Back came the reply over a shoulder: 'Manchesters. It's hell up there!'[1]

Strung out below the Martinpuich-Longueval road, Gregory's cavalry were well aware of the deepening crisis and the uplift in the enemy's morale. Having taken appropriate precautions, a three man reconnaissance patrol was seen creeping up to a 20th Deccan Horse listening post. Shots rang out, resulting in the killing of one scout and mortally wounding another. The third man vanished in the waist-high corn midst the glare of a Very light.

The Secunderabad Cavalry Brigade commander was ordered to withdraw his units at 2 a.m., but deemed it inadvisable on account that any sudden retirement would expose the right flank of the 21st Manchesters who were near them. After conversing with that battalion's CO, Gregory instructed the 7th Dragoon Guards and 20th Deccan Horse to 'stand to' at 3.30 a.m. for a gradual withdrawal at 3.40 a.m., by which time the 21st Manchesters should have rearranged their flank.

As dawn slid over an unseen horizon to herald a misty morning, so three platoons of the Glasgow Highlanders' 'C' Company wended their way to High Wood. They had been ordered to move up on Stormonth-Darling's instructions and their ears were still ringing from a shelling they received when waiting to be called from reserve. To their right they noticed the cavalry withdrawing under cover of

---

[1] Aiken, Alex: *Courage Past*, page 54.

the mist from the valley south of the wood.

The evacuation was orderly, though tinged with pathos. Wounded men rode as best they could, their bodies bent or swaying precariously in the saddle. Owing to the absence of proper stretchers, others more seriously hurt were carried away on blankets slung between lances. For them and their bearers, it was an uncomfortable journey due to the blankets sagging and the lances bowing. A number of cavalrymen walked, leading horses lamed by bullets and shrapnel. Undetected by the enemy, they disappeared into the mist and into legend. The whole action had cost the brigade 10 dead, 91 wounded and 3 missing. As for their trusty mounts, 43 horses were killed, 103 were disabled and 15 went missing. Not until late 1918 would the Western Front see mounted cavalry go into action again.

The three platoons of Glasgow Highlanders came to the fringe of High Wood, where the reserve bombers were told to fall out. Captain J.A. Cowie headed the first platoon as the men filed into the wood. Cowie reached a small glade when something made him dodge to the left. The NCO following him, Lance-Sergeant Finlayson, took cover on the right. In next to no time a German soldier casually walked into the glade. His rifle was slung and he was whistling to himself. His pursed lips froze when he saw Cowie's revolver pointing at him. Unofficially, no prisoners were to be taken. In his case, an exception was made. Minus his equipment, he was escorted to the rear under guard. His *pickelhaube* was snatched up by one of the men, Private Martin. Always a highly prized souvenir, Martin stuffed the coveted helmet in the top of his haversack.

Another platoon made contact with the enemy when they were about 60 yards inside the wood. The element of surprise was lost when a corporal inexplicably called out for the Germans to halt. The enemy replied with a fusillade of shots that ripped through the undergrowth, killing and wounding men. A Lewis gun section from 'A' Company was ordered into the wood to give support. About this time the battalion's second-in-command, Major A.H. Menzies, was placed in charge of that area of the Glasgow Highlanders' operations. Outside High Wood and to the left of the battalion's new line in the field, contact with the 1st Queen's was briefly made and lost. It was later discovered that the 1st Queen's had themselves formed a defensive line along an empty German trench that faced the wood.

By 4.30 a.m., with a brightening sky enhancing the ground mist, many felt that the wood's southern half was fairly secure. Three platoons of the Glasgow Highlanders were in position halfway across High Wood with the 2nd Queen's still holding part of the north-eastern edge. Scattered about the wood were elements of the 1st South Staffords and a sprinkling of the 22nd Manchesters, plus sappers of the 3rd Durham RE Company. Shooting flared up whenever a target presented itself, but on the whole the fighting had stabilized. After such a harrowing night, men began to think that they could relax a little.

Private Martin and Lance-Sergeant Finlayson were typical examples of this attitude. Resting beneath a tree, they idly talked of Finlayson's impending departure for home to be commissioned. Their conversation ended abruptly when a sniper's bullet drilled Finlayson's head. Martin ducked behind the tree and tried to crawl out of harm's way, closely pursued by bullets. The angle of the shots suggested that the sniper was concealed in a tree. The thought then occurred to Martin that the *pickelhaube*'s brass eagle adornment was reflecting the light and pinpointing his every movement. He hastily extracted the partially exposed helmet from his haversack and made good his escape.

He joined his platoon and related his experience to his officer, Lieutenant Woodside. The platoon officer thereupon took Martin and another private on patrol to find the source of the enemy activity. On probing the northern half, they found Germans in quantity with many of them standing around talking. The two rankers wanted to shatter the cosy scene with hand-grenades, but Woodside shook his head. It was essential that they report back on what they had seen. The decision found little popularity with Martin and his colleague as they retired from their vantage point.[2]

No one in the vicinity of High Wood could miss the gravity of the situation. Certainly the fighting had temporarily stabilized, but the wood was far from being in British possession. Baird and his 100th Brigade staff were under no illusion. Fully logged and in front of them were the disturbing reports received through the night from Stormonth-Darling and the officer commanding the 1st Queen's. With the 33rd Division assault still planned for 9 a.m. against the Switch Line in front of Martinpuich, which meant the infantry advancing in full view of High Wood, it was imperative that 7th Division completed its capture beforehand. Fearing the dreadful consequences if it was not, 100th Brigade kept 33rd Division fully

[2] Aiken, Alex: *op. cit.*, page 57.

briefed on the situation. An astute tactician, Baird even wrote to divisional headquarters to point out that the success of the morning's attack depended utterly on the wood being clear of Germans. He requested that the importance of the matter should be pressed upon 7th Division, whose 91st Brigade was responsible for its capture.

Hearing that Stormonth-Darling had effectively committed the whole of his 'C' Company to High Wood, Baird's brigade-major placed under Stormonth-Darling's command the company of the 16th King's Royal Rifle Corps which was journeying up to support him. Both companies were to advance through the wood if 91st Brigade failed to clear it by 9 a.m.

Fervently praying that nothing would be allowed to happen until High Wood's capture, Baird issued his orders on how the assault would be conducted. Dividing in half the 1,000 yard frontage allotted to his brigade, he informed the 1st Queen's that they would attack on the left with the Glasgow Highlanders on their right. Both battalions were to commence the attack from the line taken up overnight. Placing the 2nd Worcesters in reserve, Baird instructed the 16th King's Royal Rifle Corps to support the attack along the whole line. In addition to the divisional half-hour artillery bombardment of the Switch Line prior to the advance, he detailed two machine-gun sections to each assaulting battalion. In case the attack went ahead without High Wood's capitulation, Baird left the remaining sections under the brigade's machine-gun company commander, Captain Graham Hutchison. His orders were to support the assault with as much direct and indirect fire as possible whilst paying special attention to the protection of the right flank of the attack.

Unaware of 100th Brigade's repeated representations to divisional headquarters, Stormonth-Darling read his copy of Baird's plan of attack with growing alarm. Bad enough to advance with tired and hurt troops, but to advance with the enemy dug in on his right was tantamount to suicide. 'He absolutely enfilades me up to the road (which I am not holding),' scribbled the battalion commander in reply, desperately adding: 'Could northern edge also be shelled from 8.30 to 9.30 a.m.?'

In total sympathy with the Glasgow Highlanders' plight and knowing that the attack was less than three hours away, Baird immediately responded to Stormonth-Darling's latest message by telephoning 33rd Division's senior staff officer, Lt-Colonel Symons. In brusque tones he told Symons that he wished it to be thoroughly understood that, in his opinion, the impending attack had no hope of being successful as long as the enemy remained in possession of any part of High Wood. While promising to pass on to 7th Division about the necessity of securing it, Symons dustily retorted that although the brigadier-general's opinion would be recorded, the attack was to proceed as planned regardless of whether the wood was held by the enemy. Visually fuming, Baird slammed down the phone.

Again the fog of war had intervened. The 33rd Division's insistence on the attack taking place as timed lay partly rooted in a XV Corps signal that came at ten o'clock the previous evening. It categorically stated that 7th Division had seized High Wood. Accepting the statement at its face value, 33rd Division headquarters thought that Baird's brigade was suffering casualties from a small portion of the wood that was not yet quite cleared. Since the division was committing all three infantry brigades for the attack, it was strongly felt that the attack would fail if the right did not advance. The division's 98th Brigade, currently arriving at Bazentin-le-Petit, had orders to attack on 100th Brigade's left. Should the two brigades capture the Switch Line in front of Martinpuich, then the third infantry brigade (19th) would advance through them to the village itself.

With little faith in the divisional staff, Baird contacted 91st Brigade headquarters direct and made it plain that High Wood must be taken by 9 a.m. A message was then sent to Stormonth-Darling, instructing him to investigate and to report back if any such orders had been issued to the 91st Brigade unit on his right, which happened to be the 21st Manchesters. On receiving the message from a runner, he set out for the Manchesters' position.

With the time nearing 7.30 in the morning, thousands of infantrymen in 33rd Division's brigades began deploying in readiness for the attack. In 100th Brigade, officers and men of the 2nd Worcesters formed up in two lines in the shallow depression south of High Wood. In front of them the 16th King's Royal Rifle Corps extended themselves along the lane leading to the southern corner. The 1st Queen's were forced to reorganise their lines in the open, which brought them to the attention of the Germans in High Wood. They eventually accomplished the manoeuvre under constant small-arms fire and shrapnel bursts. The Glasgow Highlanders did what they could in straightening their lines further back and at right angles to the wood's south-western face. Virtually everyone was in position an hour before the attack, by which time Stormonth-Darling had completed his mission. Grim-faced, he wrote a brief account of his meeting and handed the message to a battalion runner.

Hutchison, less four sections, deployed his machine-gun company behind the Glasgow Highlanders. He had watched the Jocks move into position with good discipline, yet pallid and listless, as if expecting the inevitable. Now they lay half-hidden in the long grass ahead of him, waiting for the start of the bombardment. A little to his left, just beyond a broken hedge, stood the abandoned German field battery surrounded by dead gunners and horses. Near the scene of carnage was a despondent Stormonth-Darling with a few Glasgow Highlanders comprising his headquarters' staff. Hutchison looked up and noticed that the mist was rapidly dissipating.

> The sun peered through, orange and round, topping the trees of High Wood. Then its rays burst through the disappearing mists, and all the landscape, hitherto opaque and flat, assumed its stereoscopic vivid form. The village of Martinpuich, jagged ruins and rafters all askew, broken walls and shattered fruit trees, looked down. Both trees and village appeared Gargantuan, and the men waiting to attack like midgets from Lilliput.[3]

In III Corps' area, on 33rd Division's left, Strickland's 1st Division troops had relieved 21st Division and were waiting to advance on the village of Pozières. Away to the south-east of High Wood, young colonials of 9th Division's South African Brigade vigorously fought for supremacy in Longueval and in Delville Wood. The bombardment, when it came, drowned the distant noise of battle.

It appeared impressive, even sounded impressive, as shells rained down in the vicinity of the Switch Line; yet contrary to Stormonth-Darling's plea for High Wood's northern edge to be hit, and the 1st Queen's commander requesting similar treatment for its western corner, very few shells were sent there. With about ten minutes remaining of the bombardment's duration, Baird was handed Stormonth-Darling's message. Timed at 8.01 a.m., it began: 'I understand orders were issued to 21st Manchesters to retake wood, but their OC said to me it was too big a job for him. Anyway I have arranged to put 3 platoons of my own and the KRR Coy through.' The brigadier-general was temporarily lost for words. Recovering his composure, he felt thankful that at least the Glasgow Highlanders' commander had his wits about him. Then, out of the blue, Baird received a signal from the 33rd Division headquarters:

[3] Hutchison, G.S.: *Pilgrimage* (Rich & Cowan Ltd, 1935).

'7th Division report that the whole of High Wood is in their possession.' Knowing that it was not true, he turned away in disgust.

The bombardment stopped. An uncanny silence descended over High Wood and the vast grassy field with its narrow slope. The Glasgow Highlanders stood up, their bayonets gleaming in the early sunlight. Some looked to their front, others cast glances at the foliage of High Wood on their right. Few knew of their objective. Diagonally ahead of them in two extended lines, infantrymen of the 1st Queen's gazed philosophically up the slope to the invisible Switch Line some 700 yards away. In the forefront of the battalion, instantly recognisable by his tall stature and monocled right eye, was the CO, Major G.B. Parnell, revolver in hand. Roughly 1,200 yards back from the 1st Queens, riflemen of the 16th King's Royal Rifle Corps awaited the word to move in support. Inside High Wood, assorted bodies of troops prepared to advance through its interior. Whistles blew and, dream-like, everyone destined for the attack went forward.

An inferno of rifle and machine-gun fire broke from the edge of High Wood and from the direction of the Switch Line. The lines staggered and men fell limply to the ground. Hutchison saw the Glasgow Highlanders increase their pace to a steady jog-trot, passing their own dead of the previous night. In the distance were the 1st Queen's, their second line starting from the lane going up to High Wood's western corner. The Queen's assembly point had been close to the cross-roads north of Bazentin-le-Petit. Only three men were excluded from the battalion's advance. One of them was the RSM, Dick Mevins. A minute before he had helped a 'D' Company signaller, Private Ernest Collins, to untangle a length of telephone cable as the second wave departed from the lane. Now he gazed after them, wondering whether they would ever make it.

Collins, an old campaigner for his seventeen years, busily reeled out the cable whilst keeping a weather eye on the events ahead. Nearby was his signals sergeant, Sergeant Dabbs, a Boer War veteran who had little time for Collins. The feeling was mutual. On moving up the slope and under fire from High Wood, Collins heard Dabbs yell out. He glanced around and saw the sergeant clasping a bleeding hand. 'I'm hit,' he called. 'Serves you right!' shouted Collins in reply, using an expletive. The signals sergeant stumbled back to the lane. Collins continued reeling out the cable, happily thinking that he had heard the last of his tormentor. Little did he know that Dabbs would report him for insubordination and that he would eventually find himself in six weeks time tied to a field gun wheel, serving two weeks Field Punishment No. 1.

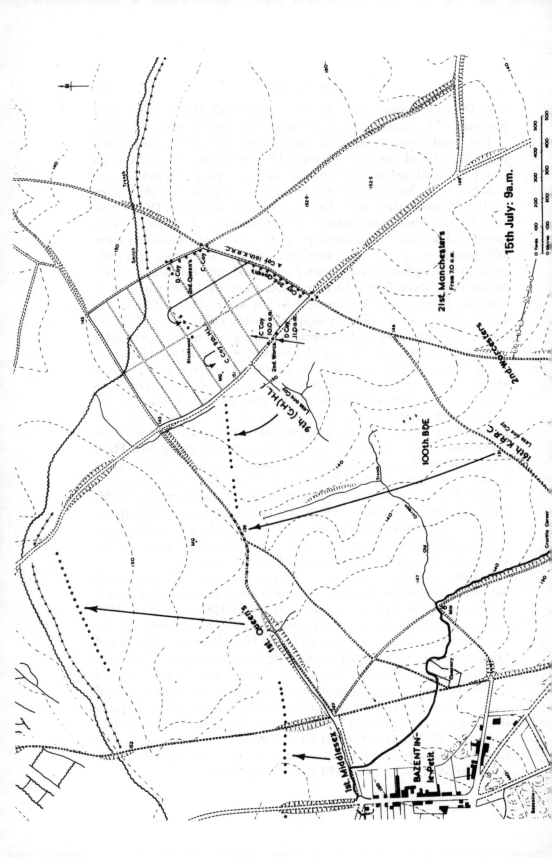

By now the Glasgow Highlanders were in real trouble. A terrific storm of shrapnel added to their misery. In ones and twos they fell in kilted khaki lumps, until the line of attack was thinned out to a few men. Some tried to bound forward in short rushes, but to no avail. The 1st Queen's, being further away from the wood, did better until the leading line came up against a continuous band of barbed wire about 40 yards from the Switch Line. Not a strand had been cut by the bombardment, nor did it seem that the Switch Line was damaged in any way from the shelling.

Major Parnell attempted to climb over it, shouting: 'To Victory!' His body was flung from the wire by a machine-gun burst. Others were scythed to the ground beside him. The Germans in the Switch Line increased their fire and more in the first wave dropped lifelessly. Those in the second line wavered. Collins witnessed the slaughter just as he felt his cable go slack, severed by shrapnel or a HE shell. 'That's it,' he thought, and ducked into a convenient shell hole.

Two companies of the 16th King's Royal Rifle Corps advanced to fill the gap between the 1st Queen's and Glasgow Highlanders. They came on splendidly, their dressing excellent. Topping the slope of the field, they found themselves among the dead and wounded Glasgow Highlanders. There they met the murderous machine-gun fire, which whittled down their numbers in quick succession. So deadly was it that only ten men of the whole right-hand company managed to get within 25 yards of the lane.

Ignorant to the fate of his men with the assaulting battalions, Hutchison ordered the remainder of his machine-gun company to go forward with the 16th King's Royal Rifle Corps:

As we rose to our feet a hail of machine-gun bullets picked here an individual man, there two or three, and swept past us. I raised a rifle to the trees and took deliberate aim, observing my target crash through the foliage and into the undergrowth beneath. On my right, an officer commanding a section had perished with all his men, except for one who came running towards me, the whole of the front of his face shot away. On my left two other sections had been killed almost to a man, and I could see the tripods of the guns with legs waving in the air, and ammunition boxes scattered among the dead.[4]

Hutchison pushed on through the human debris, too concerned even

[4] Hutchison, G.S.: *op. cit.*

to flinch from the bullets smacking the air about him. He noted the small groups of Highlanders and riflemen pinned down by the intense machine-gun fire that was largely coming from the wood. On the road passing the south-western edge, he caught a glimpse of one of his section officers directing fire towards the western corner. He then came to one of his guns mounted for action, its team lying dead beside it. Hutchison seized the rear leg of the tripod and dragged the Vickers to some sparse cover, giving him the opportunity to load the belt through the feed-block. With no more ado, he turned the machine-gun on High Wood and sprayed the tree-tops and undergrowth.

The battle escalated when a German field battery was seen coming into action south of Martinpuich, less than a mile away. The opening rounds were directed at the slope where the Glasgow Highlanders hugged the earth. A Vickers machine-gun team tried to get the correct range as the first salvo of shells exploded on target.

No one inside the wood really knew what was happening to the officers and men advancing through it. It was just as well, because danger lurked behind every tree trunk, root and branch. The Glasgow Highlanders' 'C' Company started the advance with troops spaced out in line every two or three yards. They went no further than 30 paces before a section of the line ran into an enemy patrol of half a dozen men. Some Highlanders fired at them from the standing position, but the echoes of the shots had scarcely faded when they too were assailed by small-arms fire, also by stick-grenades that whirled through the foliage at them. Private F. Middleton was one of the unlucky recipients:

> We immediately took ground cover. George Cunningham on my left had a knee shattered. My other two buddies, Johnnie Aitken and Willie Walker were killed. Another lad close by dropped with a bullet through his stomach, and was crying out in agony. It was only then that I realised we were in a clearing. A few yards to my left there was a shell hole, and another lad and myself managed to pull George Cunningham along to it. We were loosening his equipment when word was passed along to retire left out of the wood. We had to crawl on all fours for perhaps 100 to 150 yards amidst a hail of bullets. It took all our strength to do it.

Middleton's first impression on reaching the south-western edge was that of brilliant sunshine. A lieutenant ordered his party to join other men who were lying along the periphery of the wood. Middleton told him about the wounded inside the wood, but the officer regretted that nothing could be done about them until nightfall.

The first company of the 16th King's Royal Rifle Corps whom 100th Brigade had ordered up to High Wood also came to grief. The troops were machine-gunned from a small concrete emplacement the moment they crossed the first glade. The second company, ordered up at 10.30 a.m. to reinforce the Glasgow Highlanders, fared no better. Private Martin, who was still in the wood, watched them arrive:

> The KRR came up and assured us that they would clear the wood, but it was not long before they came tearing out of it and away from it. One of their officers threatened to shoot us if we moved from our positions, while his own men ran away. Later they were brought back.

Even before the last 16th King's Royal Rifle Corps' company had reached the wood, it was evident that the advance through it had gone terribly wrong. Major N.M. Pardoe, commanding the 2nd Worcesters, despatched one of his companies into the wood to reinforce the Glasgow Highlanders. He prepared to send another company at 10.45 a.m. His remaining companies ('A' and 'B' Companies) were told to extend themselves along the lane that led down to Crucifix Corner. The 2nd Queen's, meanwhile, defiantly held their positions around the eastern corner and for 120 yards up the north-eastern side. Some separated groups of 1st South Staffords and 22nd Manchesters were still in there, but lacked any cohesion to be a real threat to the enemy.

This state of affairs was recognised at 100th Brigade headquarters by 10.30 a.m. Baird once more made strenuous overtures to divisional headquarters about the need for 7th Division to clear the wood. He hammered home the point by repeating the message to 91st Brigade. His insistence partly influenced an arrangement to be made to bombard the Switch Line again from 11.45 to 12.15, after which the two remaining companies of the 2nd Worcesters would advance in the open on the left of the wood. With the pressure mounting, Minshull-Ford ordered up 'B' and 'D' Companies of the 22nd Manchesters, placing them under the officer commanding the 1st South Staffords.

The bombardment proved to be a dismal failure, because the

Switch Line could not be seen. Consequently, most of the shells fell short with some pitching behind the line reached by the 1st Queen's. The enemy's fire stayed as lethal as ever. The 2nd Worcesters' advance was limited too, although Hutchison's surviving machine-gunners and other troops tried to cover their advance. It was the original intention for the 2nd Worcesters to go through the Glasgow Highlanders' positions in the field, but few of the Jocks were aware of the scheme until the first Worcester jumped in the trench beside them. They were subjected to enfilade machine-gun fire like the rest when they attempted to go forward again. The advance ended with one company lying out 50 yards in front of the Glasgow Highlanders' starting trench and the other company in it. As the latest advance tailed off, so a battery of field artillery galloped dramatically on the scene behind the pinned-down infantry. Initially mistaken for British cavalry, they reined their teams of horses near High Wood's southern corner to bring the guns into action. It was a gallant effort, but fruitless. They were blown apart before a round could be fired.

Weak in numbers and with no likelihood of being reinforced with fresh troops, remnants of the 1st Queen's began falling back from their exposed positions to their starting line along the road. RSM Mevins and the reserve platoon gave them as much covering fire as possible during the lengthy retirement. Exhausted men collapsed thankfully in the lane behind a bank, half caring that long-range machine-gun fire still threatened their existence from the wood's western corner.

The Glasgow Highlanders were no exception when the reality of the situation asserted itself. Those who could still move retired to their starting line with other units. They strengthened the trench and held on as the enemy shells continuously transformed the field into a lunar landscape. The pitiful cries of the wounded were occasionally heard, but little could be done about them with hostile machine-guns traversing the slope. At the 1st Queen's position, young Collins peered towards the wood and was surprised to see a kilted soldier painfully hobbling his way. Collins ran towards him and discovered that the figure was a Glasgow Highlanders' subaltern, badly wounded in the leg. It was the first Glasgow Highlander he had seen all day. Supporting the officer with his shoulder, Collins helped him into the sunken lane.

The Germans applied more pressure when one of their forward guns zeroed on to the south-western side of High Wood, levelling trees in the path of its shells. The bombardment caused many casualties and a sudden rush westwards by the Worcesters. A temporary formation slowly built up 200 yards from the wood and, while this was happening, groups of men appeared from the southern end and were observed running along the road to the western corner. A Vickers machine-gun engaged the target and several were seen to fall. Afterwards it was discovered that the men were British.

The bombardment was a prelude to the enemy counter-attacking through the wood, headed by a company of the *3rd Battalion, 72nd Regiment*. The noise compelled some infantry to re-arrange their positions in the field and face the wood. It also induced Hutchison to move three machine-guns to the right and form a defensive flank to the south-western edge. The Glasgow Highlanders still in the wood were expecting a counter-attack after the shelling. Corporal J.H. Bain waited with other survivors of 'C' Company:

> We were warned not to fire until the last possible moment. First we heard commands shouted in German from the depths of the wood, then the noise of twigs breaking; soon heads could be seen moving above the bushes. We waited until the Germans were about 30 yards away before firing. They were shoulder to shoulder, filling the gaps in the undergrowth. We could not miss and had only to aim to the front.

Remnants of the 16th King's Royal Rifle Corps and other groups joined in to ensure that the counter-attack did not develop, but in the space of ten minutes, men were observed fleeing from the wood. It later transpired that they were from the 1st South Staffords and the 22nd Manchesters. Indeed, many unwounded men from 91st Brigade were congregating on the nearby road; among them was the commanding officer of the 1st South Staffords. Hutchison saw Major Pardoe urging him to return.

Their ranks more than ever depleted by the attempted counter-attack, both companies of the 16th King's Royal Rifle Corps in the wood retired to its south-western edge. It coincided with three companies of the 21st Manchesters being absorbed in the struggle. Advancing in extended order under shell fire, they passed the wood's southern corner and up its south-eastern edge. Around the eastern corner, men of the 2nd Queen's continued to hold their positions. As a precaution against further counter-attacks, Hutchison withdrew his machine-guns 400 yards south-west to a line of shell holes. The situation was so critical that Baird's brigade-major had already

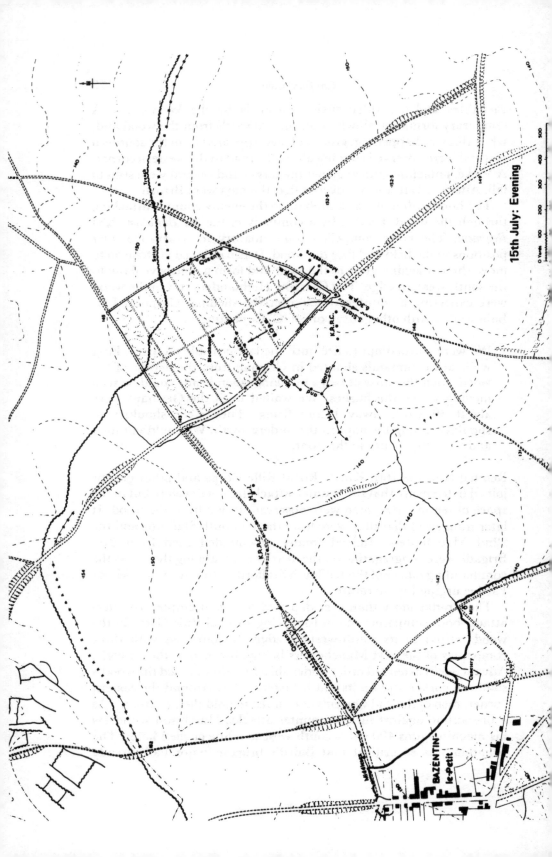

15th July: Evening

proposed to divisional headquarters that artillery should be trained immediately on the wood, since reports had given the impression that the enemy had retaken it.

He was not far wrong, as the enemy had repossessed most of High Wood. The German machine-gunners along the north-western side were also making their presence felt on 98th Brigade's front.

Advancing on the left of 100th Brigade, battalions of Brigadier-General F.M. Carleton's brigade soon experienced machine-gun fire from High Wood's north-western side. Compounding their predicament, the battalions were sniped from Bazentin-le-Petit Wood and bombarded continuously, but the High Wood machine-guns inflicted the heaviest casualties. By 3.55 p.m., Carleton was sufficiently worried to suggest to Baird that 100th Brigade should co-operate with Minshull-Ford's 91st Brigade to take the wood. He even offered the loan of a battalion for the task if co-operation was not forthcoming, not fully realising the help that Baird had already given.

The casualties sustained in the German counter-attack appreciably loosened the hold on the wood. Dirty and unshaven infantrymen fell back to its perimeter in the southern half to join the men who had preceded them. Such was the turmoil that Hutchison found it impossible to understand the situation clearly, so he sat tight with what remained of his machine-gun company. At 100th Brigade headquarters, Baird was notified that the XV Corps heavy artillery would bombard the wood's northern half, also the Switch Line for 100 yards on either side from 4.45 to 5.15 p.m. He received the message with five minutes to spare, leaving no time to tell the commanders on the spot.

Communication was a paramount problem everywhere. No sooner were telephone wires relaid when they were cut again by enemy shell fire. As for runners, their chances of survival when crossing the exposed slopes behind the wood were minimal. Divisional artillery suffered the problem of registering on targets when forward observation officers could not report back, but the problem multiplied for the corps' 'heavies' which were situated further back than the divisional guns. Comprehension of the artillery's dilemma came forcibly home in Private Middleton's small world on the south-western edge of High Wood:

Men were lying along the embankment of the wood to right and left. A shell landed amongst them 100 yards or so to my right.

Seconds later another shell landed 20 or 30 yards nearer us. From the sounds of the shells in the air, they were from our own artillery. A third shell landed, nearer us again – all fair and square on target. We all thought in terms of two more and it is our turn. It was then we saw a solitary British plane flying over our lines and we started waving. We had no observation patches on our backs to distinguish us. Fortunately the shelling stopped.

The aircraft was a Morane monoplane from the trusty No 3 Squadron which arrived over High Wood at the tail end of the barrage. Its pilot and observer were sent to reconnoitre the area at 5 p.m., because no one in the back lines really knew what was happening there. Droning over the wood, they noted that the British were holding a trench to the west and had also collected in large numbers to the south. The observer signalled down and saw what he took to be flags waved in reply from just in the wood on the south-western edge. On the north-eastern side, enemy troops were in strength and opened rapid fire on their fragile aircraft. The Switch Line was a sight to behold. Its whole length was filled with German infantry.

Weary units of 91st Brigade mounted an attack after the bombardment, but counter-shelling and machine-gun fire stopped them. Middleton noticed some 1st South Staffords retiring from the wood until his officer ordered them at pistol point to join their party. 'He certainly had a firm hold on the situation.'

A company of the 22nd Manchesters were sent up as reinforcements. Private T.M. Robertson of the Glasgow Highlanders watched them 'arrive like a mob from a football match'. He warned a few of them not to go any further due to a machine-gun sited to fire through a gap in the trees just forward of his position. The company commander said that they were ordered to establish a post in the wood, telling his sergeant to lead on. The German machine-gun team opened fire at the opportune moment, causing the survivors to turn and flee. Wounded Glasgow Highlanders joined in the movement, painfully dragging themselves back.

A number of 100th Brigade men mistook the company for a complete battalion. Stormonth-Darling made the same error when reporting back to brigade headquarters at 6.10 p.m. that the 'battalion' was 'now in full flight from the southern end of the wood' with the enemy shelling them hard. In his message he let Baird know that he had about 50 men and one Lewis gun with him should the

Germans retaliate. Near him were the 2nd Worcesters standing firm in his battalion's old trenches in the field. On his right was Hutchison, reflecting on his losses (64 officers and men) and the lack of water to cool his remaining machine-guns.

Shelled out of the wood after an unsuccessful attempt to go over to the offensive, the badly mauled men of the 2nd Queen's dug themselves in 50 yards south of High Wood but parallel to its south-western edge. They rallied there at 8 p.m. and returned to the wood to form a defensive flank. With them were stray parties of the 1st South Staffords and 21st and 22nd Manchesters, but the position was far from satisfactory.

Nowhere was there a hint of good news on 91st and 100th Brigades' front, nor was it any different on Carleton's 98th Brigade's 1,000 yard front. His battalions' efforts to take their designated section of the Switch Line had bled into the ground by 5 p.m. Thereupon, Carleton's troops were ordered back to the eastern side of Bazentin-le-Petit Village. The 1st Division's attack on Pozières was also blunted by the enemy's determination. The sum total of these failures meant a drastic rethink at XV Corps headquarters, where the decision was accordingly reached to evacuate High Wood by 3.30 in the morning and smother it with shells.

The 91st and 100th Brigades received short notice, so it was long after 2 a.m. before the battalions in the vicinity of High Wood heard about the plan. There was no time to spare, but the withdrawal from the wood was somehow managed in spite of the Germans constantly sending up flares and rockets, both intermingled with bursts of machine-gun fire that forced the retiring troops to lie down to avoid being hit. As the last detachments made their exits, so the enemy moved forward to take complete possession.

The total butcher's bill for both brigades was in excess of 2,500 officers and men. In round terms the heaviest sufferers in Minshull-Ford's 91st Brigade were the 2nd Queen's and 1st South Staffords with over 300 casualties apiece, followed by the 21st Manchesters with 250 and the 22nd Manchesters on the 200 mark. Battalion casualties were even greater for 100th Brigade and headed by the 16th King's Royal Rifle Corps with 550 and the Glasgow Highlanders at 470. Of the latter battalion's 'C' Company, just one sergeant, a corporal and ten privates mustered for roll call. The third highest casualty figure – over 380 – belonged to the 1st Queen's.

Losses were out of all proportion to the results. Their infantry weak and very shaken, both brigades retired from the immediate area for rest and replenishment. By no means had the Germans escaped lightly, but they were in control of High Wood (albeit experiencing a vicious barrage) and had worked forward to a position 500 yards south of the part of the Switch Line fronting the 98th Brigade. During the night, German artillerymen daringly tried to recover the three field guns; in the process, losing two killed and two wounded (one an officer) and four horses.

Baird attributed his heavy casualties (59 officers, 1,308 men) and the failure to take his allocated section of the Switch Line to the enemy's continuous presence in High Wood. His other reason was that the bombardments of the Switch Line had done no material damage either to the trench itself or to the strong wire entanglements in front of it. Minshull-Ford, whose task it was to capture and secure the wood, placed the blame for his failure squarely on the Switch Line – arguing that effective occupation was impossible until the Switch Line was cleared of the enemy, owing to the heavy enfilade fire coming from it. Their divisional commanders fully concurred with their explanations.

In fairness, both brigade commanders were right. High Wood and the Switch Line complemented each other, as the German engineers intended when siting the trench for a potent main defence line. An attacker's conundrum; the solving of which was further complicated by the fact that the wood's south-eastern side was dangerously exposed to machine-gun fire from Delville Wood's north-western face – and *vice versa*. So far the enemy was holding his own at Delville Wood and in the northern part of Longueval against Furse's 9th Division, and would do for days to come.

Unlike 14th July, what could go wrong had done so on Saturday, 15th July. In Querrieu that night, Rawlinson opened his private journal to chronicle the day's setbacks. Commencing with the phrase, 'Things have not gone so well as I could have wished,' he concluded his entry with a sombre thought:

We evidently have more heavy fighting before us and High Wood is likely to be the source of further bloody combats.

His prophecy would be fulfilled to the hilt.

1. High Wood viewed from Caterpillar Valley Cemetery.
2. Looking back to Montauban Ridge from Caterpillar Valley. Bernafay Wood is on the left. The chimney stack denotes location of the brickworks. Part of Montauban can be seen on extreme right. In the middle ground is the quarry where the Germans mounted their first counter-attack against Montauban at 9.30 p.m. on 1st July. The quarry later served as a British brigade HQ as well as an advanced dressing station. It is a military cemetery today.

3. High Wood with its southern corner nearest to camera. The cavalry charged over the lower road and up the slope towards Wood Lane. The Switch Line was a few hundred yards back from Wood Lane.

4. Entitled 'After the first cavalry charge, July 1916', this photograph was sold as a postcard in Britain with the falsely jovial caption: 'A way-side group of gallant Indian cavalrymen some of whom greatly enjoyed their share in the charge through the cornfields at High Wood on July 14th, 1916, with the Dragoon Guards.'

5. Glasgow Highlanders' route to High Wood on the night of the 14th July. The lane goes from Crucifix Corner to the wood's southern point. A communication trench, called High Alley, was dug parallel to this lane.

6. 1st Queen's position before attacking the Switch Line on 15th July. The lane, leading from Bazentin-le-Petit to High Wood's western corner, was enfiladed by machine-gun fire from High Wood when the battalion, including Pte Ernest Collins, advanced to the Switch Line over the bank on the left.

7. One of the 'rides' through High Wood today – typically illustrating the sort of cover the German defenders enjoyed on the 14th/15th July.

8. A destroyed German block-house a few yards inside High Wood's south-western edge. It would have contained a machine-gun.

9. Route of 33rd Division's pre-dawn advance to High Wood on 20th July. The military and civil cemeteries of Bazentin-le-Petit are in the foreground. The site of 19th Brigade's advanced dressing station is in the chalk-pit a few yards to the right of the civil cemetery. Arrow indicates the site of the mill where Frank Richards was positioned during that day.

10. A chalk-pit near Bazentin-le-Petit civil and military cemeteries, site of 19th Brigade's advanced dressing station on 20th July 1916. Near here on the evening of 14th July, Pte Brennan's party of the 2nd Royal Irish were machine gunned. Robert Graves was brought here after being critically wounded. Photographed by Harold Tyson in 1935.

11. Aerial view of High Wood taken about 18th July 1916. The Switch Line is discernabl⟨e⟩ in the northern apex, also the two trenches dug by the Glasgow Highlanders at right angles to its south-western side. The trench parallel with the south-western side near its southern point was dug by the same battalion during the night of 14th/15th July.

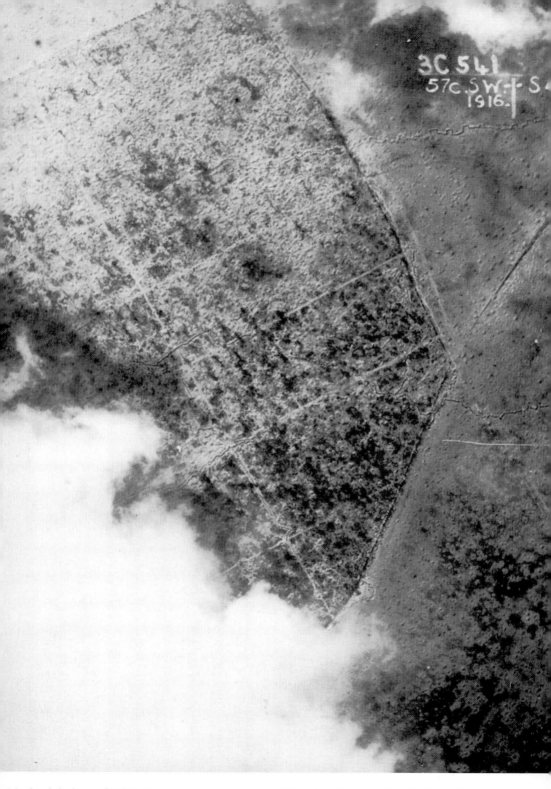

12. Aerial view of High Wood early in August 1916, showing the British front line trenches running through the southern angle. Note the nearness of the German trench system to that of the British close to the wood's eastern corner.

13 and 14. *Left:* Harold Tyson, stretcher-bearer with the 20th Royal Fusiliers in the 20th July attack on High Wood. Photographed here after his commission later in the war, Harold Tyson brought Robert Graves' attention to the fact that the 20th RF more than played its part during the action. *Right:* Pte Walter Nash of the 14th Royal Warwicks. He took part in the High Wood action on 23rd July and was subsequently captured.

15. The track from Quarry Cemetery to High Wood, used by Pte Vincent Lissenden when helping to carry wounded to the quarry in July. The quarry, then an advanced dressing station, is 30 yards to the right of the photograph. It was from this same quarry that Lt-General Congreve's eldest son, Major Billy Congreve VC DSO MC, made his way to the front on 20th July 1916 and to his death by a sniper's bullet.

16. Detail of the original crucifix still in position at the legendary Crucifix Corner in 1983.

17. Evidence of shell holes and old trenches are still visible in Flat Iron Valley, alias Death Valley.

18. 1st Surrey Rifles' Bugle Band at St. Albans in February 1915 on the eve of the battalion's departure to the Western Front. Bandsmen were, and still are, stretcher-bearers in time of war.

19. A German field postcard that was given to a member of the 1st Surrey Rifles by a prisoner.

Die Rattenjagd im Schützengraben.

Die Ratte ist im Schützengraben
Die greulichste von allen Gaben,
Auf Bajonett und Schießgewehr
Spazieren sie vergnügt umher

Und kriechen selbst — o Leser staune —
In Bombardon und in Posaune,
Der Hoboist — es ist zum Rasen —
Kann manchmal kaum zum Angriff blasen.

Doch manchmal läuft die Galle über,
Dann geht es drunter oder drüber,
Dann schließt man einen Angriffsbund
Mit einem schlauen Dackelhund.

Die Ratte rennt mit letzter Kraft
In einen alten Stiefelschaft,
So daß denn auch nach kurzer Frist
Das edle Wild Halali ist.

20. The double-mine crater in High Wood's eastern corner, photographed after the wood's capture. Its size may be gauged by the tiny figure of the officer on its far side.

21. The double-mine crater today – a duck pond.

22. *Right:* Four members of the 140th Trench Mortar Battery, whose hurricane bombardment of High Wood at a crucial moment expedited its capture. Jack Richbell, who later won the MM in 1917, is on the far right.

23. *Below:* High Wood after its capture by the 47th Division on 15th September 1916. In the foreground, a gun team of the 2nd Battery, New Zealand Field Artillery, going forward. Photographed in early October of 1916.

24. A ditched Mk 1 'male' tank astride a trench.

25. An ammunition waggon drawn by a 10 horse team in difficulty on a muddy track leading to High Wood in October, 1916. It was two weeks after the wood's capture before a mule team could negotiate a passage by the wood to the new front line. Until then, all supplies had to be carried forward by the troops.

26. Removing German field artillery pieces from High Wood in October 1916.

27. *Left:* The original 47th Divison's memorial cross at High Wood in December of
    1916. The desolation of the wood at the time can be seen behind the cross.
    Right: The wooden memorial cross to the High Wood dead of the 51st (Highland)
    Division, which was removed from the wood to its present position in front of the
    division's Great War memorial in Newfoundland Memorial Park, Beaumont
    Hamel. The 10 foot bronze figure on top of the permanent memorial was modelled
    on CSM Bob Rowen DCM MBE C of G (Belgian), who was the Glasgow
    Highlanders' 'B' Company CSM at High Wood in July 1916.

28. Unveiling of the 47th Division's memorial cross at High Wood on Sunday, 13th
    September 1925, by Major-General Sir William Thwaites KCMG CB.

29. Memorial to the 1st Cameron Highlanders, which is situated along High Wood's south-eastern edge.

30. The memorial to the 192 Glasgow Highlanders (9th HLI) killed at High Wood. Unveiled on 21st November 1972, each stone on the cairn's facia was brought from Scotland and commemorates one of the dead soldiers.

31. The 1st Surrey Rifles Association church parade at Camberwell in 1983 and in memory to the battalion's fallen at High Wood on 15th September 1916.

32. Wreath-laying ceremony in 1983 at the 1st Surrey Rifles' war memorial, St Giles Church, Camberwell. The standard-bearer is Bill Butler and, next to him, is the Association's president, Dick Stratford. Nearest to the camera is Harold Silvester DCM MM, who was wounded in the 1st Surrey Rifles' advance at High Wood on 15th September 1916.

CHAPTER SIX

If At First You Don't Succeed. . .

Rawlinson had wasted little time when hearing of XV Corps' failure at High Wood and the Switch Line. At two minutes to midnight his chief of staff, Montgomery, issued orders for Horne to secure and consolidate the whole of the wood the next day. High Wood was a fast growing boil that needed prompt lancing before Rawlinson implemented the next phase of the Somme offensive to widen his front. Expecting XV Corps to capture High Wood on 16th July, while wrongly believing that Congreve's XIII Corps had cleared all of Longueval and Delville Wood, Rawlinson also had Montgomery announcing a simultaneous offensive by the three Fourth Army corps for Monday, 17th July. Congreve was to attack Guillemont and Ginchy, Horne's XV Corps against the Switch Line between Martinpuich and High Wood, leaving Pulteney's III Corps to attack the enemy's defences further west, including Pozières. An additional responsibility was given to Horne, whereby his corps' artillery would neutralise the Switch Line for 1,000 yards east of High Wood. To lend more weight to the attack, Rawlinson arranged for Gough's Reserve Army and the French Sixth Army to co-operate on the flanks. Should the elusive moment arrive, he directed the Fourth Army's three cavalry divisions to go on a two hour stand-by.

A neat package perhaps, but flawed before the string was tied. Both Longueval and Delville Wood needed to be secured for Congreve's corps to have any chance of success. Moreover, Rawlinson's 17th July scheme required much preparation. Fortunately, updated reports from the XIII Corps front and a 9.30 a.m. conference with Horne and Pulteney ensured a day's postponement. Hoping that XIII Corps' 9th Division would complete the capture of Longueval and Delville Wood by dawn on 17th July, Rawlinson brought High Wood's proposed capture into the main operation's objectives.

The weather was a factor too. From being fine in the morning, Sunday's weather turned for the worse. Mist and rain set in, preventing all artillery registration. The Germans were not helping either. Caterpillar Valley and Flat Iron Valley were saturated with gas shells on top of their usual quota of HE and shrapnel. The ground and routes through the valleys became muddier and more tainted by the moment, hampering every kind of movement. Yet by the afternoon, 33rd Division's 19th Brigade had completed the relief of Baird's 100th Brigade.

In divisional reserve and for the past three days under the command of Brigadier-General C.F.G. Mayne, battalions of 19th Brigade had marched up to Flat Iron Valley – a place that was fast becoming known as Death Valley, although the cynics were popularising its reputation with the unofficial nomenclature of Happy Valley. Whatever its nickname, Flat Iron Valley was no place in which to tarry. Yet it was there where 19th Brigade congregated on the night of 15th July and where for the first time the brigade's troops encountered gas shells.

The four battalions comprising 19th Brigade's infantry were the 20th Royal Fusiliers (a New Army battalion, raised in Manchester and originally designated as the 3rd Public Schools), 2nd Royal Welch Fusiliers (Regular battalion), 1st Scottish Rifles (a Regular battalion which had gone to France in August, 1914, under the better known name of the 1st Cameronians), and the 5th/6th Scottish Rifles (two Cameronian battalions that were amalgamated on the 29th June 1916).

With the brigade's machine-gun and trench mortar batteries, all four infantry battalions hung around Flat Iron Valley on 15th July as the battle unfolded ahead of them. There was nothing to do except to avoid incoming shell fire and to watch their divisional artillery arriving and positioning the ever-increasing number of guns in the valley. The more adventurous went exploring in Mametz Wood. Among them was a 2nd RWF captain, Robert Graves, who was searching for German greatcoats to serve as blankets. He found the shattered wood thick with Prussian and Welsh dead, including two corpses locked together by their bayonets which had pierced each other's bodies. On his way in and out of the wood, he had to pass a bloated and stinking German corpse whose back was propped against a tree. The dead man created such an impression on Graves, that he made the corpse the subject of a poem, entitled 'Dead Boche'.

The day dragged on and any small talk was largely centred on the rumours about how well 98th and 100th Brigades were faring up front. Hearsay was falsely optimistic at first, but then came a long and uneasy silence. The 2nd RWF's medical officer, Captain Dunn, noticed a runner being asked for news. '"They've got it in the neck," he replied. An understanding look and an unspontaneous smile passed round. "We'll be for it now."'[1]

The 19th Brigade's elevation from reserve to that of support occurred in the dying minutes of Saturday night, which was followed by divisional orders to relieve 100th Brigade. The 1st Cameronians marched off at 1.20 a.m. to take over the line near High Wood. Somewhat earlier the 5/6th Scottish Rifles had gone to Bazentin-le-Petit with instructions to dig in on a line to the east of the village.

Both battalions were in position by daybreak, but not without loss. In the dark a Glasgow Highlanders' guide unwittingly led the Cameronians' 'C' Company on to a German machine-gun in the south-western edge of the wood. The blunder cost the battalion three killed and 46 wounded. The 5/6th Scottish Rifles, ensconced in front of Crucifix Corner with their 'C' Company on the lip of a quarry, suffered a storm of shrapnel which resulted in 70 officers and men being wounded. Altogether, not a pleasant start.

During the afternoon the 1st Cameronians discovered that the defence position was not continuous; troops on their left were echeloned about 1,000 yards to the rear. In danger of being outflanked if attacked, they withdrew to posts about Bazentin-le-Petit which effectively closed the gap.

Like the rain, shelling of High Wood and its surroundings by British artillery never ceased, but the weather eliminated any opportunity to register the heavy howitzers in the back areas. Early in the evening, Rawlinson rode over to Heilly to converse with Horne. The XV Corps commander, an artillery man, was disgusted with the weather. Rawlinson was far from happy too. Unless there was a sudden change, he would have to postpone again. It was an unwelcome prospect. The Germans would utilise the interlude to the full in bringing up more reinforcements and generally strengthening their line.

In the XIII Corps sector, Haldane received his orders from Congreve for 18th July. Unless the attack was postponed, his 3rd Division would push between XV Corps to seize the Martinpuich-Longueval road from the east side of High Wood to Longueval. If the Germans showed any signs of vacating the Switch Line, he was to go through the sloping cornfield and occupy it from High Wood down to the north point of Delville Wood. For this to happen, he knew that 9th Division must complete Delville Wood's capture and clear

[1] Anon: *The War The Infantry Knew* (P.S. King & Son Ltd, 1938).

Longueval. His movements were also dependent on XV Corps taking High Wood. Haldane earmarked the job for the division's 76th Brigade plus two battalions from 9th Brigade, but he wondered whether the two woods could be cleared for his attack to be successful. Equally as worrying, he heard that the enemy was digging in along the lane, called Wood Lane, which led from High Wood's eastern corner to the northern end of Longueval – well in front of the Switch Line. He ordered the lane to be machine-gunned and shelled by field artillery.

The rain and the noise of artillery lasted all night. Captain Dunn of the 2nd RWF spent the night in the battalion headquarters, which was a warren of joined-up shell holes roofed with shell-punctured iron sheets which leaked like a giant sieve. The sun shone briefly before the sky clouded over and drizzle set in. With nothing to do but to avoid if possible the incoming shells, Dunn watched the nearby field artillery in action and the enemy's counter battery work. Time and again he saw the gunners driven to cover and guns disabled. Dunn was impressed and reached the conclusion that the German gunners could not have shot better over open sights. He heard a story next day of an enemy observer with signalling gear being found up a tree in Bazentin-le-Petit Wood. Private Frank Richards, a 2nd RWF signalman, heard a similar tale concerning two men of the 1st Middlesex (98th Brigade) who glimpsed a man dressed in grey and in the act of disappearing in a dugout. Further investigation showed that he was a German officer who had volunteered to stay behind, and the dugout concealed a smaller dugout which held two trench telephones connected to an underground cable.[2] Two days later, when trenching on the right front of Bazentin-le-Petit, Richards and his pals came across the actual cable. He was positive that the cable ran right back to High Wood.

Monday, 17th July, saw Rawlinson in a mood as foul as the weather. He had expected Furse's 9th Division to have cleared the northern part of Longueval by dawn, but Furse had failed him. Congreve, being Furse's corps commander, became the object of Rawlinson's wrath. After telling Congreve to convey his displeasure to Furse, he conferred with his other two corps commanders on the prospects of an 18th July attack. Horne and Pulteney were

[2] Richards, Frank: *Old Soldiers Never Die* (Faber & Faber Ltd, 1933). His story of the German officer is confirmed in Brigadier-General Carleton's operations report of 24th July 1916: PRO W095/2405.

pessimistic. Low clouds, a ground mist and light rain had again put paid to any heavy artillery registration. Travelling to the French sector, Rawlinson sought the views of Foch on the same subject. Foch with Balfourier's support, equally favoured a postponement to 20th July. He also insisted that Guillement and Ginchy should be secured by the Fourth Army before the French assault.

Boxed in by the weather and Foch's attitude, Rawlinson agreed that Congreve's XIII Corps would go for Guillemont and Ginchy on 19th July; likewise with XV Corps operations against High Wood and the Switch Line if weather permitted. Thinking that Pozières could fall fairly easily, Rawlinson instructed Pulteney to adhere to the 18th July assault date.

Haig came in the afternoon and suggested that Gough's Reserve Army should deal with Pozières. The Fourth Army commander could appreciate the value in shortening his front. It would enable him to side-slip his three corps to the right, thereby reducing Congreve's very wide front and allow him to concentrate on clearing Longueval and Delville Wood in time for the Guillemont and Ginchy operations. Meanwhile, Congreve resolved to use 3rd Division to take the northern end of Longueval from the west during the night. Haldane in turn detailed his 76th Brigade to do it. When briefing the brigade commander, Brigadier-General R.J. Kentish, Haldane suggested that he should employ the 1st Gordon Highlanders as, being in kilts, they would be more distinguishable in the dark.

Notified of the 24-hour postponement of the attack on High Wood and his part of the Switch Line, Brigadier-General Mayne of 19th Brigade ordered the 5/6th Scottish Rifles to find 'exactly' where the enemy line was situated and whether it was wired. The CO, Lt-Colonel Kennedy, picked 'C' and 'D' Companies for a patrol from each. His orders were to the point: on finding the enemy line, 'C' Company's patrol to move along it and make contact with 'D' Company's patrol before returning.

The officer responsible for 'C' Company's patrol was 2nd Lieutenant Anderson. Recently commissioned, he wanted an experienced NCO to join him. His choice fell on CSM P. Docherty, whose platoon was entrenched along the lip of a small quarry. At first Anderson intended taking half a dozen men armed to the teeth with rifles, bayonets, boxes of bombs and other military paraphernalia, until Docherty dissuaded him in preference for one private named Thomson from his own platoon. Night was upon them when they set out in a rainstorm, each with a rifle and fixed bayonet plus a bandolier of 50 rounds tied tightly around his body.

They walked forward until the time came for them to start crawling. The three men kept in touch by holding each other's feet until they arrived near the German wire – a hastily thrown-up affair and very different from what Docherty had witnessed in the past. Germans were heard talking in a trench behind the wire. Then their hearts missed a beat as a star shell went up on their right and they saw a wiring party just 15 yards away. The wiring party froze, yet cursed their unknown comrade who had bathed them in brilliant light. More was to follow – brigade artillery opened up as the star shell fell to earth. Anderson, Docherty and Thomson watched with horror as 'friendly' shells erupted between them and their own front. They crawled back about 50 yards and ran the gauntlet of explosions to the safety of the quarry. Scared and angry, they were informed that brigade headquarters had cancelled all patrol work only five minutes after they had started out. Tempers were not cooled by the news that 'D' Company's patrol had never even left their trench.

That night 33rd Division took over the remaining positions of 21st Division at Bazentin-le-Petit. The 2nd RWF moved up at midnight through a light barrage of HE and gas shells between the cemetery and the road to Martinpuich. The hours of darkness were noisy and wet, and daylight revealed to the newcomers the appalling number of British dead strewn over the easy slope west of High Wood. The enemy inside the wood had been reinforced by the whole of the *2nd Battalion/165th Regiment*, plus two companies of the *3rd Battalion/72nd Regiment* with pioneers and machine-guns. All were determined to stay.

The weather continued to side with the Germans, ensuring a further postponement. Handing the Pozières problem to 1st Anzac Corps of Gough's Reserve Army, Rawlinson set in motion the side-slippage of his own three corps. During the day he heard that the 1st Gordon Highlanders had triumphed at Longueval, but were currently under attack in company with the South Africans in Delville Wood. The enemy had also sprung an attack on Trônes Wood. Lodgements were made in all three instances. It was a worrying business.

Rawlinson was visiting the French when Haig called at his headquarters around noon on Wednesday, 19th July. He saw Montgomery and expressed his concern on the very real possibility of the Germans emerging from Longueval and threatening the artillery packed in Caterpillar Valley. He instructed that the salient should be widened without delay, by pushing out to High Wood and joining up the line Bazentin-le-Petit/High Wood/Longueval. His visit prompted Rawlinson on his return to issue orders for XV Corps to attack High Wood at dawn in conjunction with another attempt to clear Longueval and Delville Wood.

Slipping the divisions of the three corps to the right was a slow process and in no way helped by the rain. The 33rd Division carried out the manoeuvre on the night of 18th/19th July, relieving 7th Division of any further responsibility for the actual wood. It was an eerie sensation for some troops of the 2nd RWF when the battalion moved to the right. 'Hordes of rats came over 'D' Company's ground,' remembered an eyewitness. 'They made a noise like wind through corn. It was uncanny.'

The 7th Division's 20th Brigade was to the right of 33rd Division's 19th Brigade and facing the sloping cornfield made famous by the cavalry action. The XV Corps front now extended nearly to Longueval, leaving Haldane's 3rd Division to take over the Longueval/Delville Wood front from Furse's tired 9th Division when it could be managed. Major-General R.B. Stephens' 5th Division moved in between 7th and 3rd Divisions to complete XV Corps' new front.

Mayne's 19th Brigade received orders late in the afternoon for the attack on High Wood, just a matter of hours after the brigade's battalions had withdrawn behind Mametz Wood for a rest. The plan of attack was to advance through the breadth of its 800 yard south-western face and capture the whole of the wood, including the blocking of the Switch Line 50 yards out on either side of it. The 1st Cameronians were chosen to take the north-western half and the Switch Line in the northern apex while the 5/6th Scottish Rifles went up the north-eastern half. Supporting the latter were the 20th Royal Fusiliers, 11th Field Company RE and a pioneer company of the 18th Middlesex.[3] Once inside, troops of the 20th Royal Fusiliers would systematically mop up so that the sappers and pioneers could prepare strongpoints at the western, northern and eastern corners. The 2nd RWF were detailed to wait in reserve at the top of Flat Iron Valley.

Intelligence reported that the enemy had wired the southern corner, also that a machine-gun section was dug in at the western corner. To cover the left flank during the advance, 100th Brigade had loaned the 2nd Worcesters to Mayne for the purpose of establishing

---

[3] Pals battalion: 1st Public Works.

defence line at dusk from Bazentin-le-Petit towards **High Wood's** western corner. On 19th Brigade's right, battalions of 7th Division's 20th Brigade were to sweep over the Martinpuich-Longueval road with 5th Division and capture the lane (Wood Lane) from High Wood's eastern corner to the upper reaches of Longueval.

Light and medium artillery had steadily bombarded the wood since the enemy's reoccupation. Nevertheless a more intense bombardment was scheduled to start at 2.55 a.m. It would include heavy howitzers, regardless of imperfect registration. The bombardment was timed to lift back from the south-western face at 3.35 a.m. for the infantry to go in. Mayne was under no illusions about his divisional commander, Landon, wanting him to wring every advantage from the bombardment. Landon's GSO1, Symons, advised: 'The Major-General wishes me to point out again the urgency to press right on in rear of the barrage, even at the risk of losing a few men from our own fire.'

As for Haig, he left no room for doubt about wanting a successful outcome. Nor did Landon. He made it known to Mayne that 'the C-in-C attaches the greatest importance to the capture and holding of High Wood.' With Haig, Rawlinson and Horne perched on his shoulders, Landon least of all did not relish the prospect of another failure.

'It looks like the goods this time,' thought Dunn at the battalion briefing. His fears were echoed by his CO, Lt-Colonel Crawshay, when summing up. Captain Graves, present also at the briefing, remembered Crawshay finally saying: '". . . so if we're called for, that will be the end of us." He said this with a laugh, and we all laughed.'[4]

CSM Docherty was notified of the impending attack when his temporary company commander, Lieutenant J.S. Coltart, placed him in charge of No 7 Section in a platoon of 'C' Company. He and other section leaders were issued with green ground flares for signalling observing aircraft after securing the objectives. In addition, extra ammunition, bombs, picks and shovels were distributed.

The brigade RC chaplain, Father McShane, made his appearance in the evening and asked for all Roman Catholics. Unlike the majority of the 5/6th Scottish Rifles, Docherty was a Roman Catholic and he joined McShane's small flock. It was the shortest,

[4] Graves, Robert: *Goodbye To All That* (Jonathan Cape, 1929).

yet the most impressive little service that he had ever attended – just 300 troops kneeling on the torn earth and receiving absolution in full view of the brigade. McShane's blessing assumed a deeper meaning against a background of artillery fire and German shells exploding along the road through Flat Iron Valley. Around midnight the participating battalions began the two mile march to the deployment area near Bazentin-le-Petit's shattered windmill.

A sudden flurry of shells checked their progress by Crucifix Corner, searing the ranks of the Scottish battalions. The twelve riflemen in Docherty's section were lucky. They duly arrived with their company at the front line trench unharmed, although battalion strength had sunk to 20 officers and 600 men. Guided by scouts, they moved through the gaps cut in the barbed wire to deploy with the 1st Cameronians on their left. To their right were the 2nd Gordon Highlanders of 7th Division's 20th Brigade. About 1,000 yards ahead, caught up in a gigantic pyrotechnic display of explosions, was High Wood. The battalions advanced to within 60 yards of its edge, where the men laid themselves down to await zero hour. The bombardment in front looked so intensive that it seemed as if nothing could live in it.

The traffic in shell fire was not all one way, as support battalions discovered to their cost when shrapnel flayed amongst them. The barrage encouraged the 20th Royal Fusiliers and 11th Field Company RE to crowd up with the spearhead, thereby eliminating the time gap between waves. One leading platoon of Royal Fusiliers stumbled on to Docherty's position. Not comprehending their motive for moving forward, he peered at his luminous watch and told the RF platoon commander that zero hour was 3.35 – not 3.25 a.m. His words were drowned in the explosions and in the canopy of shells screaming overhead towards the wood. Soon the British fire lifted from the south-western face to crash further back. Leaving the 2nd Gordon Highlanders and 20th Brigade's other assaulting battalion – 8th Devons – to tackle their objective, both the 1st Cameronians and 5/6th Scottish Rifles rushed the burning wood.

In the semi-darkness they found trees uprooted, smoking shell holes and grotesque corpses. A few dazed Germans were even captured in the first minutes from dugouts. One CSM, serving as a private in Docherty's section for the attack, had the satisfaction of capturing 16 Germans single-handed. He took them to the rear and, like all good Scotsmen, obtained a receipt for them. By now, due to the crowding up before zero hour, many units of the assaulting

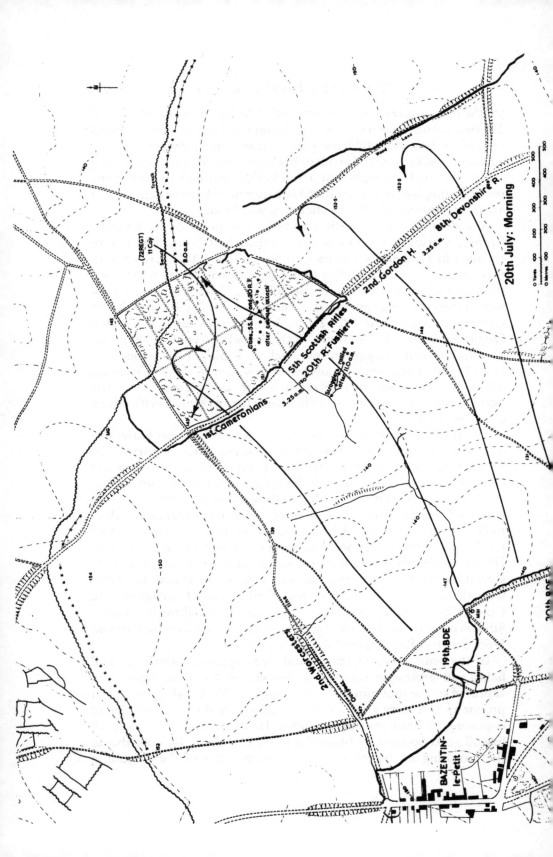

20th July: Morning

battalions were inextricably intermingled. Nothing but light opposition was met in the middle of the wood, but everything changed when the Cameronians came up against the machine-gun at the western corner. Its crew had obviously survived and proved the point by giving a bloody account of themselves. More Cameronians fell when Germans from the Switch Line inside the wood started shooting. They succeeded in keeping the Scotsmen at bay. In other parts of the wood, savage hand-to-hand fighting was in progress.

To the east of High Wood, infantrymen of the 2nd Gordon Highlanders and the 8th Devons had swept over the Martinpuich-Longueval road without much opposition. It was an entirely different experience when they moved up the shell-scarred cornfield that still contained unsightly evidence of the cavalry charge. Here, they encountered riflemen and machine-gunners hidden in the corn and from entrenchments along Wood Lane. Machine-gun fire from the Switch Line behind the lane added to their troubles. Their predicament worsened when other machine-guns chimed in from High Wood to enfilade the advance. The Gordon Highlanders suffered the most, for the very reason that they were closest to the wood; yet one platoon managed to reach Wood Lane through luck and extraordinary bravery, but were wiped out for their pains. Scattered groups of Gordon Highlanders and Devons attempted to dig in near Wood Lane with similar results. Units of 5th Division, prolonging the assault to Longueval from 1,200 yards east of High Wood, were no more successful.

High Wood's lower half was virtually free of the enemy by dawn, but not the nest of machine-guns in a formidable redoubt at the eastern corner. They continued to ravage the Gordon Highlanders. Due to the turmoil, Docherty ended up in the vicinity of the eastern corner with just two men of his original section. Trying to form a new section, he grabbed two more men nearest to him, who happened to be a Cameronian and a 20th RF private, and told everyone to dig, knowing that the Germans were bound to counter-attack. Other soldiers were beginning to entrench themselves along the edge. Not wishing to be surprised, Docherty posted himself as sentry.

To add to our joys, we had overrun some of the Germans and, as dawn broke, some of the men digging were shot in the back by Germans hidden in the undergrowth and a few up the trees. These were soon disposed of, but our artillery were apparently unaware that the right corner of the wood was practically in our hands. Our shells started to land amongst us, killing the Royal Fusilier private, also wounding the 1st Battalion man and the fellow next to me. By this time I was dug in waist deep behind a thick tree that I couldn't span with my arms, and was certainly bullet proof. A contact aeroplane flew over, blowing his klaxon horn, and then I remembered the ground flares. The first one was a dud; I waited till the plane came round again and lit the other flare when the airman honked his horn. He flashed his light down two or three times and then left. The shells, which had still been landing unpleasantly close, then lifted and started going over our heads.

The attack, by 7.30 a.m., had degenerated into a shambles as the enemy continued to harass the attackers from within and outside the wood. The firing, according to one 5/6th Scottish Rifles' officer, 'sounded like hailstones on corrugated iron.' The wood's main ride, already dotted with bodies from the earlier attack, became a veritable death-trap for anyone venturing on it. Sappers of the 11th Field Company lost man after man, including their commander wounded, when preparing strongpoints for machine-gun emplacements. Their pioneers, owing to the confusion in the wood, were diverted to excavating a communication trench outside. Not much was done of it, as hostile shelling made their work almost suicidal.

The assaulting battalions of 7th Division's 20th Brigade were in the same predicament. Sniped at, shelled and under vicious cross-fire from the machine-guns at High Wood's eastern corner, very few could get within 50 yards of Wood Lane and stay alive. Some distance back from the Martinpuich-Longueval road, sheltering under a bank with three stretcher-bearer teams, was the brigade C of E chaplain, Rev E.C. Crosse:

We knew nothing of the situation and the firing was pretty heavy, then I met an 8th Devons' runner who told me. Whereupon I set out with my squads in open order. I reached the nearer road where I found only one officer. He was quite dazed and could hardly answer my questions as to whether there were any wounded and, if so, where they were. At first he said there was no one left. Eventually I found one wounded Devon on the road. I gathered that we had tried to advance to the second road and found it too strongly defended. Another Devon crawled back through the corn as I was there. I still had one empty stretcher, so I went on to the Gordons and took down a wounded Jock. This was about 8 a.m.

It was evident that 20th Brigade's task was hopeless until High Wood was captured in its entirety. Slowly, infantrymen of the 2nd Gordon Highlanders and 8th Devons gave up to retire to their first objective – the Martinpuich-Longueval road. Many of their wounded had to be left behind in shell scrapes or where they fell, but one badly hurt officer close to Wood Lane was dragged back after repeated efforts to reach him by an 8th Devons' youth, Private T. Veale.[1] His bravery was later recognised with the award of the VC. On withdrawing, survivors of both battalions with help from a supporting company of the 9th Devons, started to consolidate their section of the Martinpuich-Longueval road.

Meanwhile little had changed in High Wood; chaos still reigned as the enemy heavily shelled its lower half. At one stage, nothing could be seen of it for black smoke. Casualties had risen alarmingly, none more so than amongst senior officers and NCOs. With their colonel and adjutant seriously wounded, command of the 5/6th Scottish Rifles devolved on to Captain A.S. Crombie, being the next in line and bloody from a light wound.

The 20th Royal Fusiliers' command structure was literally shot to pieces. Their commanding officer, Lt-Colonel Bennett, had already left the wood as one of the walking wounded and nothing much remained in the way of battalion officers. 'From quite early the unfortunate RF men seemed to be getting killed all over the place to no purpose,' noted an eyewitness. 'Bert Wallwork was our last officer casualty,' recorded 22-year-old Private Harold Tyson, a battalion supernumerary stretcher-bearer. 'He was hit taking up a support to the front line under devastating machine-gun fire. He fought bravely and died a hero.' Eventually, RSM Armour who was attached to the 20th Royal Fusiliers, brought some semblance of order to the stricken battalion by organising a party of RF men to dig a new trench line just south of the middle of the wood. The trench was used as a rallying point.

Before long the Germans counter-attacked from the direction of their strongpoint at the western corner. Shouting '*Hoch der Kaiser*', they charged with fixed bayonets and almost overwhelmed the

---

[1] The rescued officer was Lt Eric Savill, who in later years was Warden of Windsor Great Park for Her Majesty the Queen.

Cameronians closest to them. Docherty heard the new battle sounds just prior to units of the enemy's *72nd Regiment* developing their part of the planned pincer movement on his side of the wood:

> There was a terrific howling and shouting away on the left and word passed along that 'Jerry' was attacking. At first there was nothing to be seen from the right side of the wood as there was a slight rise just to our front. Then our Lewis guns and rifles opened up from the front, and the men in my section started to blaze away. I stood up, sheltered to my right and, looking to the dip in front of the wood, saw the old Boche coming on in hundreds. They were big upstanding fellows, with brand new uniforms and had evidently just been flung into the battle. The way they were going was straight across our front and you couldn't miss them – they were only about 150 yards away. I fired as rapidly as I could and must have used about 30 or 40 rounds, but they gained a footing in the wood and drove us back. Every officer with the exception of Lt Coltart had been killed or wounded and practically all the warrant officers and sergeants had gone 'west'.

The shaken survivors of the mingled battalions reorganised themselves at the southern end. Docherty assisted by handing out bandoliers of ammunition to the men who were left. In all respects it had been an unnerving experience and the action had proved too much for some. Preferring to risk the bursting shells outside the wood, rather than the broiling hell inside it, a few dribbled back to Crucifix Corner where Father McShane sympathetically rounded them up. Others like Private Harold Tyson stayed: 'Machine-guns swept us, heavies bashed us, shrapnel lashed us – but we held on.'

Sergeant G. Skelton, also a RF man and defending the new trench line made under RSM Armour's direction, rediscovered an older enemy:

> The heat of the day was intense; water bottles were soon emptied and we suffered much from thirst. The carrying party came up over the open ground, bringing water in petrol tins that had not been cleaned properly. The water was undrinkable, parching the throat if one drank it. This party lost several men through shell fire.

Enemy shell fire was universal. The 2nd RWF, because of their stint in the front line and now waiting in reserve at the head of Flat Iron Valley, lost 10 killed and 53 wounded through it. The battalion's

CO, Crawshay, had heard nothing on 19th Brigade's fortunes at High Wood. Impatient for news, he sent one of his officers and sergeants forward to find out. Brigade headquarters soon afterwards enquired whether he could give them any recent information; failing that to send someone out for it. An hour later the wounded commander of the 20th Royal Fusiliers was seen coming along the road.

> He was intercepted. After summarising the situation he added, in a torrent of ejaculations, that nothing was being done; everything was chaotic; no one was in command; not a message, not an order had been received from Brigade. When the CO recovered his breath he suggested to Colonel Bennett to call at Brigade before going to the dressing station, but this he did not do.[5]

Communication was an ever-present problem. Previous to 19th Brigade's assault on the wood, headquarters had ordered Crawshay to detail a forward liaison officer from his battalion. Lieutenant N.H. Radford was duly selected. He and a brigade signals corporal with eight men, including Private Richards, journeyed in the dark to set up a forward post of a relay system at Bazentin-le-Petit windmill. The partially destroyed windmill was a regular artillery target, but it stood on a rise and gave a superb view of High Wood. Besides the corporal, Richards knew only two of the rankers – a Cameronian who was now a brigade signaller and an RWF man who was a brigade runner. He being an old soldier, wondered how the other five men would conduct themselves should shell fire come their way.

Telephone wires from the mill to the wood were cut by an enemy bombardment at the beginning of the assault. There was a wireless set, but for transmission only to brigade headquarters and there was no way of checking whether the transmitted messages were being received. This closed the options to signalling by flags to and from the wood or by heliograph from the mill, thence to brigade headquarters which was housed in a thinly-roofed trench on the right side of Mametz Wood – over a mile away as the crow flies. At the mill, Richards and the Cameronian set up their heliograph and telescope:

> Shortly after this the enemy began shelling us and, by 10 a.m.,

[5] Anon: *The War The Infantry Knew.*

they had put up one of the worst barrages that I was ever under. . . .
North, south, east and west it was raining shells, and we seemed to
be the dead centre of them all. . . . The ground shook and rocked
and we were continually having to reset the heliograph. When
receiving a message the smoke of the bursting shells and the earth
and dust that was being thrown up constantly obscured our
vision. We could only receive a word now and then. The five men I
didn't know were sheltering in a large shell hole by the side of the
mill; they were absolutely useless and terror-stricken.[6]

Because experience had shown that large actions invariably led to
heavy losses, it had become the practice by 1916 for each battalion to
leave behind a nucleus of officers and NCOs on which to rebuild the
battalion. Such was the case with Major W.G. Macalister, second-
in-command of the 5/6th Scottish Rifles. Despite the bad
communications, he had heard about his CO being wounded and the
dreadful losses among the battalion's officers and men. After calling
into brigade headquarters, he hurried on to High Wood with a
subaltern to take command. Both officers were wounded on route,
but Macalister carried on and entered the wood during the
regrouping period. Lieutenant Coltart was nowhere to be seen; he
was busily retaking the eastern corner after brigade Stokes mortars
had laid out the German machine-gun redoubt.

Macalister swiftly searched around and spotted a familiar face
belonging to a battalion NCO. He dropped down beside him and
spread his map on the ground. 'There's the wood,' said Macalister.
'What is the position?' On being told, Macalister began reorganising
a line of men in shell holes for better defence purposes when he was
killed by a burst of fire.

. More than seven hours of interminable blood-letting had lapsed
before Major Crawshay received orders to move the 2nd RWF up to
High Wood. His officers and men were waiting in their kit in the lee
of a road bank and a third of the battalion were already lost through
shell fire. Among the casualties was Captain Graves. Heavy German
artillery had savagely pounded the low ridge in front of the troops,
menacing the battalion. Everyone was ordered back 50 paces in a
rush. Alas for Graves, an 8-inch shell exploded a few yards behind
him when he was in full stride. Severely wounded, he cried out to
Captain Moody of 'D' Company that he was hit, after which he

[6] Richards, Frank: *op. cit.*

remembered little else. Now the orders which Crawshay had hoped against hope would not arrive had done so. Sorely smitten by shell splinters and shrapnel, his depleted battalion would still have to go and clear High Wood.

All four weakened companies formed up on the cratered road and marched steadily off at 100 yard intervals towards Crucifix Corner, Moody's company leading. Father McShane was there to greet them with a loud cheer, his figure quite dwarfed by the tall iron crucifix that, by some miracle, still stood on a bank of the junction as if immune from shell fire. CSM Docherty met the 2nd RWF as they filtered up the lane to High Wood's southern corner. He had been sent down to collect more ammunition, but he was not alone. Assisted by a slightly wounded man, he carried a badly hurt youth whose foot was blown off. His efforts were to no avail. The lad died as Docherty reached his destination.

Morale was low in High Wood from the rain of shell fire and the loss of comrades. Leaderless men started massing in the open at the southern corner, but Crawshay and his battalion doggedly approached them through the human detritus of previous attacks. For the fatigued infantrymen in the wood who were able to view them marching up, nothing could be more welcome at that moment:

> Looking back through the trees about noon we could see a battalion in platoon formation, at the slope, coming to reinforce us. They were the 2nd Royal Welch Fusiliers. It was a great sight, and many among us heaved a sigh of relief for reinforcements were sorely needed. Their advance was one worthy of their distinguished record and traditions, but we learned afterwards that they lost over 200 men in coming up.

Distinctly unlike the pre-dawn attack which advanced on the wood's south-western face, Crawshay chose the south-eastern face for his battalion's entry with the intention of sweeping through to the north-western edge. Leaving his company outside the wood to await the arrival of the battalion's three other companies, Moody entered the wood with two of his subalterns for a reconnaissance. They pushed their way through discoloured foliage and stepped over broken branches, attempting to avoid fume-laden shell holes as they did so. All around them and, at times under their feet, lay the dead, the dying and some wounded who had not as yet been evacuated. Those who were alive and very much in a dishevelled state, crouched in

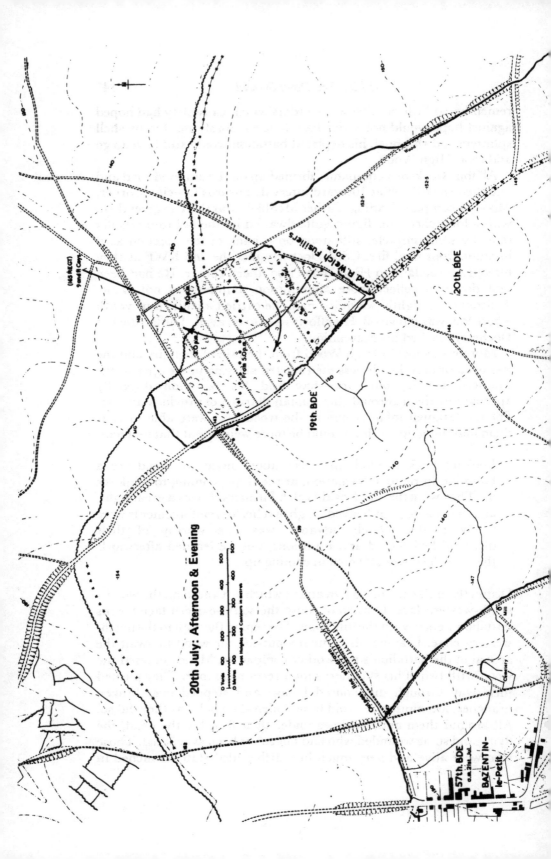

20th July: Afternoon & Evening

shell holes, hastily dug shallow trenches or behind the splintered trunks of trees. Braving the hostile machine-gun and rifle fire, Moody and his two companions went a couple of hundred yards beyond the point where a group of 20th Royal Fusiliers had dug themselves in under their RSM's supervision, just forward of a German gun position that was littered with empty ammunition boxes. They learned nothing of significance from the tangled mess and, at that juncture, Moody was hit in the foot while one of the subalterns received a face wound.

Moody hobbled back in agony to his company, gritting his teeth against the stabs of pain that came with every step. Crawshay had established his headquarters at the southern corner when Moody and his two young officers rejoined 'D' Company. The other companies had arrived and, by 2 p.m., started deploying along the south-eastern face with Moody's men nearest to the eastern corner. The 5/6th Scottish Rifles' sole surviving officer, Coltart, was in close proximity:

> It was the quietest part of the day in my corner of the wood when I heard movement behind me, and saw Moody forming up his company. These Welch Fusiliers were a magnificent sight. They were very weak, their platoons were only the size of sections, but they were out for business. This small controlled force was a most effective contrast to the large loose mass that had been herded into the wood in the morning, when one attacking battalion with one in support, not mixed with it, would have been ample. Immediately after the Welch Fusiliers had all formed up, their CO ordered the advance. They were obviously out for blood, and were most heartening. The platoon sergeant of their right platoon was shepherding his men like a mother, picking up spades, ammunition and anything likely to be useful.

Their arrival was decidedly opportune; even the Gordon Highlanders consolidating the road to the right of the wood's southern corner had been concerned about the wood's defences. Fear that the enemy might storm down it and smash through to his left motivated the Gordon Highlanders to send some of their troops into the wood.

The last uncommitted battalion of 19th Brigade, Crawshay's 2nd RWF advanced relentlessly through the wood. Direction became a problem towards its middle and companies started bunching up, offering better targets for German rifles and machine-guns. The advance developed into quick dashes in the hope of avoiding the ground fire and enemy shells that crashed down through the few standing trees. The strongpoint at the western corner was noticeably active, as were the Switch Line machine-guns in the northern apex. Moody's 'D' Company's ranks were horribly thinned out by them, but Moody was no longer with the company. His wound had proved too much and another officer had succeeded him. When he fell, another officer took over to press the attack home. None of the four companies escaped this dreadful descending order of command.

Through sheer guts and bloody-mindedness, they managed to over-run the western corner strongpoint and then the complete wood. The shelling had also stopped now that the opposing forces were close to each other, but machine-gun fire from the Switch Line outside the wood necessitated the 2nd RWF temporarily to dig in 100 yards from the top of the wood.

The whole attack was over in an hour and every officer who participated in it was a casualty. Brigade had already conferred on Crawshay the title of 'OC High Wood' and, in this capacity, he instructed a battalion signaller to convey the good tidings.

From his vantage point at the mill and still surviving dropping shells and machine-gun bursts, Richards saw the signaller calling him up with a flag. His corporal and the Cameronian were otherwise engaged, so he asked the five soldiers sheltering in the nearby crater for one to come and write the message down as he translated the semaphore. His request met with total refusal. He swore, he shouted, but none was prepared to chance a piece of flying shell or a German bullet. The brigade runner, a mere onlooker, watched Richards damning them and volunteered himself. With signal pad in hand, he wrote down the message of the wood's capture as Richards called out the words.

Splendid news perhaps, but Crawshay's message contained a sting in its tail. He had seen how the attack had crippled his battalion, and he could draw no comfort from the remnants of the other 19th Brigade's battalions. He thereupon made it plain to brigade headquarters that, unless he received immediate reinforcements, he would not be responsible for holding the wood. His men had done wonders. It would be too cruel to see their fine work and sacrifice come to naught through lack of support – and Crawshay thought much of his battalion:

I have never seen such magnificent and wonderful disregard for death as I saw that day. It was almost uncanny it was so great. I once heard an old officer in the Royal Welch say the men would follow you to hell, but these chaps would bring you back and put you in a dugout in heaven.

For something over two hours after the attack the wood was comparatively peaceful, though pervaded with the sickly stench of corpses from the previous actions. The time was usefully employed in generally strengthening positions and in digging a defensive line near the top of the wood, but before its completion an order came to dig and wire a trench running diagonally across the wood to face the Switch Line. Crawshay justifiably queried it, since it meant leaving the western corner and the north-western side open to infiltration. A staff officer eventually arrived and confirmed the order to Crawshay. He explained that this trench was necessary in view of hostile machine-guns being located across the Flers road which bounded the north-western edge. No one on the spot, particularly Crawshay, thought it a valid reason, but orders were orders and work continued on the new trench line.

Evening came and still no reinforcements in the form of infantry. German aircraft were seen in the azure sky and downed a British reconnaissance plane, but vengeance arrived just after eight o'clock when a German Taube tried to shoot down another slow moving plane over High Wood, only to be pounced on in turn by a fighter escort. A dogfight developed and soldiers everywhere in the vicinity craned their necks to watch the aerial battle. The 20th Brigade C of E chaplain, Rev Crosse, was one of them:

> The fight got nearer and nearer until in the full glow of a glorious evening sunset the Boche came lower and lower and fell into Bazentin-le-Petit Wood, bursting into flames. As he neared the earth, every rifle and Lewis gun opened on him and, when he fell, everyone burst into a cheer.

A marvellous spectacle and enjoyed by thousands, but Crawshay had nothing to cheer about in High Wood. The Germans were dribbling back – from the north-west. 'I have 200 men out of a brigade. Am expecting relief brought,' he scribbled, ripping the page from his pad and giving it to a runner to take to brigade headquarters. Signalling by semaphore had long ceased when the last man schooled in the art was hit when sending a message to Richards at the mill. Now there was a series of runner posts between the mill and brigade headquarters.

Firing flared up by the north-western edge and Crawshay heard that the Germans were infiltrating. All his men were exhausted, but the only fresh troops to arrive were a ration party and 98 drafts destined for his battalion. They were all kept. Then two companies of the 18th Middlesex pioneer battalion, navvies in civilian life, arrived as night fell to recommence the task of digging the communication trench. Their appearance coincided with the heaviest bombardment of the day.

Huge shells crashed into the wood, smothering its occupants and their surroundings in volumes of dust and smoke. Men simply vanished in the gargantuan explosions or were flung in disembodied bits to all points of the compass, leaving the still living to hug the quivering ground. The barrage went on for an hour or more, but most of the defenders had lost track of time in their stunned condition.

As Crawshay expected, a counter-attack followed hard on the heels of the barrage. The Switch Line in the wood was retaken, then the western corner. The middle of the wood became No Man's Land as the remnants of 19th Brigade consolidated in its southern portion. Suspense grew with the night as they peered into the inky blackness, which alternated with colourful cascades of light when Very pistols were fired skyward.

Relief finally came at one in the morning with the sudden appearance of two companies of the 1st Queen's and one company of the 16th King's Royal Rifle Corps in 100th Brigade. The intermixed battalions, ravaged beyond words, were glad to go. It had been a harrowing 24 hours since their departure from Flat Iron Valley and none would forget it. They started filing out very tired and shaken, and yet some went defiantly as in the case of Private Harold Tyson. Corresponding with his father afterwards, he wrote:

Men who had been at Mons said that this last fight was worse than anything they had faced before. The enemy ranged their fire so deadly. This wood is nothing now but stumps of trees and shell holes. In fact the whole ground is ploughed up. I am proud of my battalion; every officer and man was a hero and fought as keenly as he ever did on his playing field at school. . . I was very lucky. I found out afterwards that either a bullet or a piece of shell had gone through my gas helmet satchel, inner waterproof cover, through the helmet itself and out again without touching me; also a splinter of shell had gone through my haversack.

Another Royal Fusilier, Sergeant Skelton, was given a job before leaving the wood:

I was ordered to take a machine-gun party of the 16th King's Royal Rifles to the strongpoint at the eastern corner of the wood, which had been made by the 11th Field Company RE. This had been held by a great friend of mine, Sgt Bowers. I found no one to relieve. All were dead and the defences obliterated.

The 11th Field Company RE had lost 11 killed, 53 wounded and 3 missing. Officerless, what remained of the company was brought out by a lance-corporal. Casualties in the 2nd RWF came to 11 officers and 238 rank and file. Having lost all their officers, the 20th Royal Fusiliers ended the day with 397 casualties – 15 more than the 1st Cameronians. The runners who braved the gauntlet of shells and bullets to and from High Wood were all but wiped out. On his way down to bivouac near Mametz Wood in Flat Iron Valley, Captain Dunn chanced across the last runner to be sent; he was lying by the side of the track, crippled by wounds in both legs. The 5/6th Scottish Rifles headed the casualty list for High Wood on 20th July with 18 officers and 389 men; just one officer (Lieutenant J.S. Coltart) and 198 men paraded for roll call in Mametz Wood.

It had a profound affect on CSM Docherty: 'When I looked at the four companies in line, reduced to the strength of four weak platoons, and thought of all the bright lads who had "gone west", I cried like a child.'

Those touched by the savagery of battle on Thursday, 20th July, included no less a personage than Lt-General Congreve. That morning at a position under a mile east of High Wood, his eldest son, Billy, was killed by a sniper's bullet.

Billy Congreve's brigade commander, Brigadier-General Kentish, sent the news by telegram to Haldane at Bray-sur-Somme. He in turn relayed the message to XIII Corps headquarters where Lt-General Congreve was busily planning an attack. Haldane later visited Kentish at Montauban to discuss battle tactics and, on his way back, he met Billy Congreve's servant, Private Cameron. Haldane stopped to talk to him.

He is dreadfully upset about his master's death and had remonstrated with him for risking his life so often, while his Brigadier had not been up to the front line at all. Congreve replied, 'Shut up.' Cameron had gone up himself and had brought back the body. . . . I feel quite bowled over, as Billy meant a very great deal to me. I had hoped that he would rise to the highest rank.

It was a bad day all round for the Fourth Army. Haldane's 3rd Division[7] had failed to clear Longueval and Delville Wood and, further to the right and next to Balfourier's XX Corps, the plucky diminutive Britishers of the 35th (Bantam) Division had come terribly unstuck in a preliminary action to the planned attack on Guillemont. The Bantams went forward to cover the advance of the French left, but the French stayed put in the absence of artillery support.

After dark on 20th July, 7th Division's 20th Brigade was relieved by two battalions belonging to 5th Division's 13th Brigade. The change-over was welcome, because the 2nd Gordon Highlanders and 8th Devons had lost nearly 400 troops between them. Yet this figure would have definitely paled into insignificance if the 20th Brigade commander, Brigadier-General Deverell, had complied with a demand for another attempt on Wood Lane later that day. The youngest brigade commander in the BEF, Deverell pointed out the hopelessness of attacking Wood Lane in daylight until High Wood was captured and the Switch Line beyond Wood Lane neutralised. He thereupon proposed that, unless he received orders to the contrary, his troops would continue consolidating their positions along the Martinpuich-Longueval road. Reason prevailed for once. His proposal met with Horne's approval.

As luck would have it, the Germans made their strong counter-attack when the relief was in progress. The heavy barrage supporting the counter-attack caught the 20th Brigade battalions as they made their exit. Among those killed was Lt-Colonel B.G.R. Gordon, commanding the 2nd Gordon Highlanders. He was the battalion's third CO to be killed in action since the beginning of the war.

Rawlinson had received a mixed bag of reports throughout the day. They tended to be correct, except for High Wood:

[7] The 3rd Division completed the relief of 9th Division, including its South African Brigade, before dawn on 20th July.

The XV Corps established themselves in High Wood and, tonight, I hear they have got the whole of it and joined up with Bazentin-le-Petit to the North and Longueval to the S East. The situation in Longueval and Delville Wood is no better – our attack went wrong this morning and I fear we shot at each other. Anyway, we made no progress and are, if anything, worse off tonight than when we began, having lost a lot of men including young Congreve, Squibby's[8] gallant son. He was only married a month ago to Cyril Maude's daughter. Very sad indeed.

I have been busy all day, arranging the attack on the 22 or 23rd. All things considered I shall, I think, make it on the 23rd. DH came over after lunch; very helpful and nice. The French can't go in till the 23rd. There are many worries and troubles in fighting a battle like this, but I sleep like a top so am always fresh again the next day.

Not many men were asleep in High Wood's enclave and along the Martinpuich-Longueval road. Kept awake by the enemy's barrage of HE, shrapnel and gas shells, they looked to their front and future battleground.

---

[8] 'Squibby' and 'Squibs' were nicknames of Lt-General Congreve – after his great-grandfather who designed the Congreve Rocket.

CHAPTER SEVEN

. . . Try, Try Again

Since 14th July, Caterpillar Valley and Flat Iron Valley had vied with each other on which was the hottest support area on the Somme. Both contained detachments of troops, living like moles in slit trenches that were covered with tarpaulins or corrugated iron sheeting, similarly in shell holes or, for the luckier ones, in old German deep dugouts that were for the most part impervious to anything but the heaviest calibre shell. Located also in each valley was an advanced dressing station, plus the headquarters of the brigade in line and the one in support, not to mention the forward ammunition dumps and Royal Engineer dumps. There were the guns too; divisional artillery of every description, including hundreds of 18-pounders that participated in the continuous racket which bounced and echoed off the shallow slopes. The columns of supply waggons from the transport lines added to the scene, as they brought up rations and war material to nourish the troops and their weapons. Edging among the supply waggons were the motorised ambulances, trying to make headway along the damaged arterial dirt roads in the valleys.

Both valleys were painfully exposed to enemy artillery barrages which were frequent and dreadful, none more so than in the narrow confines of Flat Iron Valley which ran towards the peak of the Fourth Army salient at High Wood. Moreover, Flat Iron Valley was the only line of communication, via its solitary road, and every round of ammunition and every ration had to be funnelled up the valley to the front there. July was now proving to be regularly hot and sunny, and the continual flow of wheeled traffic through the valley's entire length emitted chalky-white clouds of dust which swirled above the transport. Naturally the dust was a good barometer for enemy observers to measure the concentration of traffic during daylight hours. In no time at all they would call down a barrage of air bursts, gas shells and high explosive. Immediately, drivers of horse-drawn waggons and motor vehicles would find their best speeds to vacate the zone involved in the shelling. Conversely, heavily-burdened infantrymen could only trust to luck if they were caught in a bombardment when passing through the valley. Carrying too much kit to run far, there was little else they could do than to keep plodding along at the regulation pace of three miles an hour.

Padded with fresh intakes, it was through Flat Iron Valley that the 1st Queen's and the 16th King's Royal Rifle Corps had marched back to relieve the spent 19th Brigade at High Wood on the night of 20th/21st July. All were in the wood by 3 a.m. and consolidating the southern end. Outside, pioneers of the 18th Middlesex continued extending the communication trench towards Crucifix Corner. The flinty sub-soil and bursting shells made their task a difficult one, but they persevered with equanimity which induced one officer who saw them to comment that 'they worked as though they were opening up Piccadilly, and took as little notice of German shell fire as they would have done of the London traffic.'

Shell fire was having its effects everywhere that night, as Lt-Colonel Dunlop discovered when taking up the 1st Royal West Kents to relieve the 2nd Gordon Highlanders. On arriving at the freshly-dug trenches along their portion of the Martinpuich-Longueval road, he found that his battalion was some 60 men short, mostly from one company which had fallen victim to shrapnel.

The 14th Royal Warwicks had relieved the 8th Devons to Dunlop's right and prolonged the line towards Longueval and the 3rd Division boundary. The Midlands men were one of three Kitchener service battalions recruited in Birmingham and lightly known as Birmingham's 'Pets' from their extra comforts provided by the city. They had been pals at school, in cricket teams and in rugby clubs. They were office workers, shop assistants, teachers, architects, solicitors and accountants. They were 'pals' and proud of it.

The kindred idea of 'pals' battalions came after three Territorial battalions were mobilised in Birmingham on 4th August 1914. When they left the city with the Lord Mayor commanding one of them, it was suggested by the deputy mayor, Alderman W.H. Bowater, that a special battalion should be formed from the city's young men who were engaged in non-manual occupations. The scheme was backed by Birmingham's *Daily Post*, which invited youngsters to register their names at the newspaper's offices. The invitation was made on 28th August. By 1st September the *Daily Post* had more than 1,200 enthusiastic signatories. Within the week the register held 4,500 names. This upsurge in volunteers resulted in the deputy mayor reapplying to Lord Kitchener for permission to raise a second city battalion. When this was done, there remained on the register

enough names to form a third. The three Birmingham battalions –
known as the 1st, 2nd and 3rd City Battalions respectively – became
the 14th, 15th and 16th Royal Warwicks.

Walter Nash enlisted in the 14th Royal Warwicks, but not before
he looked at other Army units: 'I went to Worcester on 4th August to
join the cavalry, but they rejected me because of a rupture. I came
back and joined the 1st City Battalion.' Ernest Apps joined the 15th
Royal Warwicks: 'I was at a YMCA camp near Blackpool when war
was declared. We all rushed home to Birmingham to try to enlist. We
were afraid it would all be over before we could get into action.'

Harry Cohen had a different problem, magnified by a giant mock-
up of a barometer which stood on the City Hall steps, showing the
latest rise in Birmingham's recruitment drive. As a boy scout and
under age for enlistment, Harry Cohen's daily ritual was to push up
the barometer's red indicator to match the daily recruitment trend.
Desperately wanting to join up himself, he became increasingly
worried that the city battalions would be at full strength before he
could do anything about it. Decision time arrived one morning when
he was balancing on the top rung of a step ladder to raise the red
indicator. He thereupon walked to the special recruiting office for the
city battalions in Great Charles Street, but was stopped by a
recruiting sergeant in the doorway.

'He wanted to know my age and I replied that I was sixteen. He
then told me to go out again, walk round Birmingham and report
back when I was older. I left, waited round a corner and presented
myself again. Without batting an eyelid, the same recruiting
sergeant asked me my age. "Eighteen," I said. "That's better," he
replied. "Now follow me." I had arrived in the nick of time to be
accepted for the 3rd City Battalion.'

'Collectively the applicants form splendid material for fighting,'
noted the *Daily Post*. 'For the most part they are clean, well set-up
healthy-looking young men, well-educated and refined, intelligent
and vigorous.'

The 21st July found all three city battalions on the Somme: 14th
and 15th Royal Warwicks in 5th Division's 13th Brigade and the
16th with the 15th Brigade.

Men of the 15th Royal Warwicks were in reserve and had spent the
night in Caterpillar Valley, not far north of a cross-roads between
Montauban and Bazentin-le-Grand. Sleep had been nigh
impossible. Shelling was continuous and made worse by a nearby 60-
pounder battery firing directly over the battalion. Incoming shells

were plentiful, since the valley was overlooked by enemy positions to
the east at Ginchy. The rough shelters – no more than mere holes –
offered scanty protection against the 'Caterpillar Valley Barrage'
which periodically swept dispassionately over the ground. Even so,
Private Vincent Lissenden who was batman to the battalion's
medical officer, had tried to make himself comfortable with mixed
success:

> We were warned that the Germans were using a new type of gas
> shell, which could be identified by the fact that it exploded with a
> mild sort of 'plop'. On our first night in this sector, I found shelter
> in a shallow hole in Caterpillar Valley that was covered with one
> layer of sandbags and just deep enough to crawl into on my hands
> and knees. This hole was quite close to one of our artillery
> batteries, but I was able to identify the popping noise of the gas
> shells above the sound of this and many other batteries.
> Accordingly I donned my gas mask that consisted of a chemical-
> impregnated flannel bag with two eye pieces and a rubber
> mouthpiece for breathing purposes. Somehow I fell asleep
> wearing it.

Rawlinson slept soundly at Querrieu Château, but awoke to find out
that the previous evening's news of High Wood's capture was false.
His first action was to telegraph XV Corps which in turn contacted
its reserve division's commander, Major-General G.M. Harper,
warning him that his 51st (Highland) Division might have to relieve
33rd Division at short notice.

At 9.30 a.m., Rawlinson assembled his corps commanders to
discuss the scheme of attack for 23rd July. In view of the successes of
the 14th July style of assault, he opted for another night attack in the
early hours of 23rd July. It would be a general assault with III Corps
attacking the Switch Line in front of Martinpuich in conjunction
with an attack by Gough's Reserve Army against Pozières; XV
Corps to go for High Wood and the Switch Line on either side of it, as
well as securing the orchards at the northern end of Longueval,
leaving Congreve's XIII Corps to clear Delville Wood. Unless there
were any hostile counter-attacks before 23rd July, Rawlinson
expected the general assault to succeed. 'The Boches may make a
supreme effort, but I doubt it,' he wrote. 'All accounts say the Boches
are very tired.'

Congreve was not convinced. A day before his son was killed, he had observed that the 'enemy has undoubtedly got more guns and more men'.

Command of the German front was reorganised on the same day as Congreve made his observation. Enemy troops north of the River Somme became a new *First Army* under General von Below, and the two corps facing the British front were steadily reinforced with heavy artillery and howitzers. By the 22nd, these reinforcements would increase to 32 batteries. As for infantry divisions, since 1st July thirteen divisions had arrived to bolster the defences north of the Somme – and three more were about to enter the battle.

Lesser mortals at battalion level could reasonably have been forgiven if they thought the same thoughts as Lt-General Congreve. Among them on 21st July was the senior captain of the 15th Royal Warwicks, Captain C.A. Bill:

> In the morning we sat tight and watched the slaughter going on in Caterpillar Valley just below us. Guns, ammunition waggons, ration waggons, infantry marching up, wounded walking or being carried down – the road held a continual stream of traffic, with the German guns searching for it. At the crossroads a quarry was being used as a dressing station. I saw one large shell drop right into it and a dozen or so men came running out, but from the number of casualties continually being passed in and out that one shell must have done a lot of damage.[1]

Before its use as a RAMC advanced dressing station, this quarry was the headquarters of Kentish's 76th Brigade. The Germans had occupied it previous to 76th Brigade, but then the entrance faced away from the British lines. Detailed by the medical officer to work with the stretcher-bearers, Vincent Lissenden saw the devastation at first-hand:

> We passed another bearer party with a casualty on the way down. We picked up another casualty and, on our return, found the bodies of the party we had passed on our way up, together with the body of the man they were carrying. We had just left the quarry when a shell dropped in its yard, causing numerous casualties among men and also among the mules and horses harnessed to ambulances.

[1] Bill, C.A.: *The 15th Battalion Royal Warwickshire Regiment in the Great War* (Cornish Brothers Ltd, 1932).

It was but one example where the term 'in reserve' did not necessarily mean a rest. Private H.V. Drinkwater discovered this when he was detailed to help carry up the rations to the 1st Royal West Kents and 14th Royal Warwicks during the night:

> We kept on till 4 a.m., using the cover of old trenches wherever possible. The bags of rations kept swinging on the sides of the trenches, stopping our progress and adding to the delay. By this time we were getting close to our destination and on the fringe of a barrage. Shells were falling fast and to halt was impossible – it was either forward or backward. The leading man was dead in the trench with his head blown off, and the next man was raving mad on the trench bottom. The smell of everything was sickening.

In the daylight hours and after dark, patrols were sent by the 1st Royal West Kents and the 14th Royal Warwicks to ascertain, as far as possible, the exact location of the enemy. No one wanted to be caught napping when the order came to attack – as it surely would be given – but patrol work steadily added to the casualties; nor were the carrying parties immune. Lt-Colonel Dunlop, recognizing how dangerous was the rendezvous where rations and water were ordered to be brought, tried unsuccessfully to have the position changed. The refusal grieved him. His own battalion's casualties had risen to 90 officers and men, and they had yet to attack.

Company officers of the 15th Royal Warwicks, also of the battalion in close support – 2nd King's Own Scottish Borderers – crept forward to reconnoitre the front line. It was here that the cavalry charge had occurred and dead cavalry horses lay dotted about. The hot weather had blown them out and they stank to high heaven. Working parties, complete with gas masks, dug a pit alongside each dead animal after dark. The carcass was levered into the pit and covered with earth. The burials had to be done at night to avoid being sniped. Walter Nash nearly came to grief through one:

> An Indian lancer and his horse lay dead in the corner of these oats. I had no boot laces – only pieces of string. So I said to a mate that I was going to see what this Indian had got in his haversack in the way of spare laces. I stooped to get at his haversack when – bing! An oat stalk had toppled over no more than six inches from my head. Make no mistake; those Hun snipers were very patient and crafty.

Trying to obtain a fix on the German positions was no simple matter. The 1st Royal West Kents had a frontage of 400 yards from where their left touched High Wood. The 14th Royal Warwicks had a similar length of frontage next to them, but all that could be seen from the continuous trench, which was dug by their predecessors, was the cornfield. Admittedly the cornfield was cratered and tracts of it flattened from previous actions, but there was enough standing corn left to mask enemy snipers. To add to the frustration, it was impossible to observe the Switch Line without first breaching the German trench along Wood Lane. Unfortunately, even the lane was hidden from view, because the field sloped gently upwards for 350 yards to fall gently again for a further 50 to the lane itself.

Aerial photographs were the logical solution, but these were for staff use and rarely circulated at battalion level. Only trench maps were available, but recent aerial photographs of the sector had shown the Switch Line to be a well-dug, heavily-traversed trench protected by wire. It appeared that the Germans had not completed any deep dugouts, but the photographs did pin-point the shafts of several in the making. The biggest concern was that the photographs showed the Switch Line hardly affected by the constant artillery bombardments.

Another reconnaissance flight was made over High Wood in the morning of Friday, 21st July. At mid-day, Horne ordered Harper's 51st (Highland) Division to relieve Landon's broken 33rd Division that night, but Horne insisted that Landon should first make contact with III Corps' 19th Division on his left after dusk, thereby closing a 1,200 yard diagonal gap across the field from High Wood's southern corner to the right of the cross-roads, north-east of Bazentin-le-Petit. The field was in name only, cratered as it was beyond belief and literally spread with human flotsam that dated back to the 14th July engagements. It was, in essence, a vast graveyard with the majority of its occupants exposed to the elements.

Horne had demanded too much from a division whose casualties totalled 263 officers and 4,932 other ranks. In fact Landon was forced to inform Horne that his division was incapable of taking the line again for at least a fortnight, but Horne wanted 33rd Division up to strength and back by 30th July latest. He also wanted Landon's explanation as to why the wood was all but lost in its entirety after it had been virtually won.

The gap was left for 51st (Highland) Division to fill. Meanwhile its kilted 'Ladies from Hell' moved through the dust and stench of Flat Iron Valley to High Wood.

The division's 154th Brigade relieved the last of 33rd Division's troops at three in the morning of 22nd July. The change-over had not gone smoothly, because the trenches which the brigade had taken over were irregular, narrow and shallow, having evolved in a haphazard fashion during the past days. Came daylight and the Highlanders were even more disenchanted about their location:

To the left of the wood the trench lines, which were not continuously connected up, curved in a south-westerly direction towards Bazentin-le-Petit, leaving the wood as the apex of an acute salient. In this section of the front the trenches seemed to fulfil no tactical requirements. There was no depth to the defensive system; the trenches were little more than knee-deep, and were choked with dead.

The whole of this area had been the scene of repeated encounters, as the ground amply testified. In the undergrowth of the wood and in the standing corn, which covered the whole area, lay the dead of many different regiments. The result was that, owing to the scorching summer weather, the troops in the line lived in an atmosphere of pollution and in a positive torment of bluebottle flies. In one sap in particular, as one moved along it, the flies rose in such clouds that their buzzing sounded as the noise of a threshing-machine. In this sap, sentries could only tolerate the conditions by standing with their handkerchiefs tied over their mouths and nostrils.[2]

Brigadier-General C.E. Stewart's 154th Brigade had pulled the short straw to man the front at High Wood. The other two brigades of 51st (Highland) Division remained in support and in reserve; 153rd Brigade in Flat Iron Valley and 152nd Brigade further back between Fricourt Wood and Mametz Wood.

Stewart positioned the 4th Gordon Highlanders and the 9th Royal Scots in the front line, where it was found that in High Wood only 200 yards of it from the southern corner constituted British property. Not included was the all-important eastern corner. The Germans, fully appreciating its tactical value, had reclaimed it. More strongly fortified than before, they had garrisoned it again with machine-guns and surrounded the fortification with barbed-wire entanglements. The field of fire was superb. The Maxims could rake the cornfield to

[2] Bewsher F.W., Major: *The History of the 51st (Highland) Division 1914-18* (William Blackwood & Sons, 1921).

the east as well as sweeping the wood. In all respects the eastern corner posed a deadly threat to any attacking force.

Saturday, 22nd July, seemed full of unpleasant shocks. Aerial photographs taken the day before showed that a long trench had been dug to the north-west of High Wood. Aptly code-named 'Intermediate Trench', it lay halfway between the Switch Line and the forward positions of 19th Division's 57th Brigade. Connected to the Switch Line by a communication trench, it was observed to be full of Germans.

This new dimension threw the time-table for the general assault into some disarray. The trench was in III Corps sector, which meant that its 19th Division had to subdue it prior to attacking the section of the Switch Line in front of Martinpuich. After a hasty debate, III Corps headquarters made it known that Intermediate Trench would be 19th Division's first objective at zero hour instead of the Switch Line. The attack on the Switch Line would follow an hour later.

Zero hour for the infantry was originally set for 12.30 the next morning. Another hurried debate ensued. This time between the corps commanders. They concluded that to split the timing for the general assault could prove unwise, so it was agreed to delay the assault one hour which, hopefully, would give 19th Division enough time to secure Intermediate Trench beforehand. The artillery programme for the destruction of the Switch Line would merely be extended to 1.30 a.m. The compromise was put to Rawlinson.

The Fourth Army commander was already perturbed about the impending general assault. As well as wanting Congreve's XIII Corps to attack Delville Wood, he had arranged with the corps commander to assault Guillemont and Falfemont Farm. Since the farm was on the British right, an agreement was reached with the French for Balfourier's XX Corps to attack in conjunction with XIII Corps. However, Balfourier changed his mind at the last moment. Seething with indignation, Rawlinson cancelled the attack on Falfemont Farm. The Guillemont operation still stood, albeit an hour later if he sanctioned the change. He did agree after careful deliberation, but it was with much reluctance.

I do not like these changes of times, as it only means confusion in the units and doubts in their minds – especially in a night attack. However, I think that the Boche is tired and we may have an easier job than we expect.

Delaying zero hour to 1.30 a.m. was a step in the right direction for the infantry whose final objective was the Switch Line. Another hour's bombardment of it would also not go amiss – if the bombardment was accurate. The real worry was whether the assault on the Switch Line was too premature and too hastily organised to succeed? Everything pointed to the fact that this could be the case.

Major-General Harper at the 51st (Highland) Division's headquarters had his doubts about the forthcoming attack. With the relief of the 33rd Division only recently completed, he had received orders from Horne that very day to attack the enemy during the coming night. His division's objectives were High Wood's north-eastern and north-western edges, also the Switch Line through the wood and for 500 yards of it from High Wood's north-western edge. In concise terms, Horne expected Harper's division to capture the entire wood and 500 yards of the Switch Line too.

Harper detailed Stewart's 154th Brigade to carry out the attack. Stewart in turn detailed the 4th Gordon Highlanders and the 9th Royal Scots. Enemy activity restricted movement during the day and made patrol work impossible, but both battalions knew the enormity of their task. They gauged it by the number of dead strewn around their positions from previous engagements. Limitation of time denied the battalions the opportunity of studying the ground ahead or forming any specific plan of action, except to knock out the enemy redoubt in High Wood's eastern corner as their first priority.

Having learned of 7th Division's fate in the cornfield, Major-General Stephens of 5th Division was equally as anxious to see the redoubt neutralised. If it was not, there was little hope of securing Wood Lane, let alone the Switch Line behind it. Conversely, Harper knew from Stewart that the redoubt could hold up any advance through High Wood. The two divisional commanders eventually concurred on a special bombardment of the eastern corner and Wood Lane, followed by an infantry attack before zero hour on the redoubt and Wood Lane. Under the circumstances, it seemed the best possible course if both divisions were to reach the Switch Line. Zero hour was set for ten o'clock, and 19th Division no longer had a monopoly on preliminary attacks.

The bombardment started before dusk, assisted by spotter aircraft flying low over High Wood and the Switch Line. Until the light failed, their artillery direction was good and resulted in the enemy receiving some damaging blows. Yet several batteries were not notified of the attack until after dusk, when it was much too late for proper registration. Shrapnel was freely used, but in High Wood the decapitated trees acted as natural shields. Nevertheless the eastern corner had been marked out for special attention. There, Germans were badly hit although not mortally. It is sufficient to say that more machine-gunners survived than died.

Expecting the redoubt to be more or less destroyed in the barrage, a platoon of the 4th Gordon Highlanders was briefed to follow through and mop up. Ignorant of the fact that the wood was thick with enemy troops (in excess of two battalions), other Gordon Highlanders prepared themselves to inch forward in readiness to take the main objectives. The 1st Royal West Kents, being the nearest to the wood, detailed a platoon to move up the wood's south-eastern face and participate in finishing off the redoubt.

In the trench along the Martinpuich-Longueval road, officers and men of the 1st Royal West Kents and 14th Royal Warwicks checked their kit and fixed bayonets. Two companies from each battalion were to lead the 10 p.m. attack on Wood Lane in two waves, followed by a third company to construct support positions and communications. The fourth company from each battalion would then move up to the vacated trench along the Martinpuich-Longueval road, ready to carry wire and stores up to the new front line. In support and in reserve were the 2nd King's Own Scottish Borderers and the 15th Royal Warwicks. In command of the 15th Royal Warwicks' 'C' Company was Captain C.A. Bill:

> At 9.30 p.m., we moved up to another captured trench 600 or 700 yards behind the attacking line. This trench was already full of troops, and the congestion and confusion made it extremely difficult to keep in touch with one's men or to pass messages to one's officers. The night was pitch dark, save for the incessant flashes of guns and bursting shells and the glare from the star-shells in front; and the din of battle all round us was deafening.[3]

A moonless night; a barrage that was assumed to be doing an adequate job. What better combination than an infantry advance under cover of the darkness with small fear of retaliatory fire? The first to put it to the test were the specified companies of the 1st Royal West Kents and the 14th Royal Warwicks.

Leaving their trench system ten minutes before the barrage was

[3] Bill, C.A.: *op cit.*

due to lift off Wood Lane, they advanced 350 yards over the cornfield to the crest. For much of this distance they were protected by the lie of the land, but not when they breasted the crest as the guns stopped at 10 p.m. The moment the waves of infantrymen were seen in the light of the enemy's flares, concentrated machine-gun fire poured into them from High Wood's eastern corner.

Private Percy Hannibol of the 14th Royal Warwicks was waiting to leave his trench as part of the third wave when the hostile firing broke out:

> I can remember our soldiers going over the top to attack, two yards apart and wearing helmets. Obviously we had to be careful of our heads being seen over the top. After a short interval there was this terrific machine-gun fire and then silence. Eventually my platoon commander, 2nd Lt Turner, asked for a volunteer to go over and find out what had happened. Two of us volunteered and he chose my mate, Bob Farrell. Over he went, and that was the last we saw of him, a good friend and a brave soldier.

The story was no different inside High Wood. While their comrades tried to make ground through the wood, the platoon of 4th Gordon Highlanders attempted to take the redoubt. The strongly-wired fortification defeated them, besides which other machine-guns opened up with rifle support on the other Gordon Highlanders as they stumbled forward in the dark into unknown territory. The platoon of the 1st Royal West Kents, detailed to cover the battalion's left flank by helping to destroy the redoubt, met with the same fate as the platoon of the 4th Gordon Highlanders. The platoon was practically exterminated, with the platoon commander being the first to fall.

Troops of the 9th Royal Scots attacked up the south-western side of the wood, hoping to narrow the distance between them and the 500 yards of Switch Line allotted to them for the 1.30 a.m. assault. The ineffectual bombardment of the wood left too many Germans alive. In trenches well in front of the Switch Line in the wood, they traversed the open field with small-arms fire and down through the wood itself. To make it even more hellish for the luckless Royal Scots, a machine-gun began shooting at them from the eastern end of Intermediate Trench, which was not due to be attacked by 19th Division's troops until 12.30 a.m.

Soon after the ten o'clock attack was launched, orders were

received at the 15th Royal Warwicks' new position for Captain Bill's 'C' Company to move up to support it along with the battalion's 'D' Company, commanded by Captain Gough. Bill commenced extricating his men from the trench:

> Gough's company was lower down the trench, near where it was crossed by a track which led up to High Wood, and he took his men up along this track. To move my men down through the crowded trench to the same place I felt to be almost impossible, so I led them over the parapet from where we stood. We moved in single file and it was a slow and arduous business, for every man was carrying an extra bandolier of ammunition slung around him and a canvas bucket full of Mills bombs, in addition to his normal fighting kit. The Lewis gun teams carried, in addition to their guns and normal supply of ammunition, as many extra loaded drums as they could possibly manage.[4]

The 2nd King's Own Scottish Borderers, in close support to the 1st Royal West Kents, were called forward at 10.45 p.m. Their role should have been to develop a successful attack – to go through the Royal West Kents and on to the Switch Line at 1.30 a.m. Not any more. The Maxims had seen to that. Instead, their task was to support the initial attack on Wood Lane and chance their fate in the cross-fire; an act that could only lead to thickening a line already held up and which could only result in more slaughter.

A few Royal West Kents managed to fight their way into the lane and to its fiercely defended trench. It is even said that some Borderers joined them, but no one remained there unless they were dead. Not one of the Royal Warwicks could claim that small consolation, since most of them were strung out in still rows on ground made practically impassable by the volume of fire.

Private Hughes of the 14th Royal Warwicks was one of the luckier ones. He had gone through the stream of fire from High Wood's eastern corner when he became aware of a searing sensation in both his hands. He dropped his rifle before realising that his hands were useless, having been drilled through almost simultaneously by bullets. He looked around in the colourfully splashed light of soaring and falling star-shells to see that he was near the German wire and on his own. Incapable of further action, Hughes simply turned round

4 Bill, C.A.: *op cit.*

and walked dazedly through the cross-fire again to the battalion trench. Not another bullet hit him.

Walter Nash also found himself near to the wire:

I was a sharpshooter. They couldn't call me or any battalion sharpshooter a sniper, because we had not volunteered. On this occasion, however, I was on the left of the line with my bayonet fixed and four Mills bombs in my pockets. I got within 10 or 12 yards of the German trench when I fell into a shell hole. I was so near to them that I could hear them talking. I remember extracting the pins from two of my bombs and throwing both bombs into the trench. Then I was knocked senseless.

Bill had great trouble in leading his company to the front, until he tailed in behind a line of Highlanders of Stewart's 154th Brigade who were moving up to High Wood. He called a halt a short distance from the Martinpuich-Longueval road – their immediate objective – and then went forward with one man to the 14th Royal Warwicks' trench for information:

The trench from which the attack had been launched was very narrow and shallow and was obstructed by dead and wounded men. I could learn nothing here as to how the attack had gone, but further along towards High Wood I found a company of the 14th Royal Warwicks under Captain Bryson. Two of their companies had gone over and simply disappeared, apparently decimated, and they themselves made another effort to reach the enemy line while I was there, but were held up by heavy fire and forced to return. I told Bryson I would fetch my men up, though what to do with them when I got them there I didn't know. It was obvious from what had happened that the trench which had been attacked was untouched by our gun fire and to order the Company to attack would mean their utter decimation, as had happened to the 14th Warwicks and the West Kents. Yet we were sent up to support the attack![5]

He was pondering whether he should let his men merely occupy the 14th Royal Warwicks' trench and risk the wrath of higher command when his moral dilemma was solved for him. He was wounded by

[5] Bill, C.A.: *op cit.*

shell fire. Bill eventually found himself in hospital at Corbie prior to his evacuation to England. Three months would pass before he was fit again to rejoin his battalion.

Heroism flourished in the face of adversity that evening, also at 1.30 a.m. when the main assault was delivered – with the same tragic results. Officers and men performed feats of gallantry that certainly fulfilled the sanguine phrase: 'beyond the call of duty'. Corporal Hatch of the 1st Royal West Kents numbered among them.

Unable to use stretchers due to the traversing machine-gun fire, Hatch went out alone into the bullet-spattered cornfield and placed wounded men in the cover of shell holes in the expectation of bringing them in when the fire relaxed. It was a marvel that he did not become a casualty himself in the first five minutes, but fortune smiled on Hatch enough for him to continue his work for hours. Then his luck vanished when he received a wound which put to an end his diligence. He was later recommended for the VC which, in the opinion of all, he had repeatedly earned that night. To the great disappointment of every man in the battalion, it was not to be. Hatch was awarded the DCM and Médaille Militaire instead.

Captain Baines, medical officer to the 1st Royal West Kents, was another man whose work was classed as 'almost superhuman' by the battalion's commander, Lt-Colonel Dunlop. Baines attended to serious cases throughout the night and far into the day, his advanced dressing station being in the trench along the Martinpuich-Longueval road. Twice the trench fell in from shelling where he tended the wounded. On one of the two occasions his fingers were on a severed artery. Although he was partially buried, Baines maintained his grip and saved the patient's life.

No ground of any significance was gained in High Wood during the early morning attack, yet no blame could be attached to the 4th Gordon Highlanders for not trying. Shot at by unseen assailants, they scrambled forward amongst the fallen trees in their endeavour to get to grips with the enemy. In some instances there was bitter hand-to-hand fighting, but those who survived the bullets and bombs were defeated by the physical effort in negotiating dark shell holes, old trenches, thick undergrowth and patches of barbed wire. Yet they had made their presence felt for the enemy to reinforce the wood with infantry from the Switch Line.

Heavy shelling occurred to the left of the wood, just as the 9th Royal Scots advanced up its south-western edge to have another go at the Switch Line. Once more machine-gun fire was directed at them from Intermediate Trench where *3rd Battalion 93rd Regiment* was ensconced. The plan was for troops of the 19th Division to creep within 75 yards of the trench, but enemy forward machine-gun positions wrecked it. To compound the chaos, one of the battalions who should have taken part in the attack arrived too late. It became obvious by three o'clock that the attack was doomed and so a general withdrawal was put into motion under persistent shell fire.

The withdrawal of the 9th Royal Scots and the 4th Gordon Highlanders happened a little earlier. Both battalions were back at their old positions by 3 a.m., lighter by nearly 450 officers and men.

Far worse were the casualties suffered by the 1st Royal West Kents. The battalion lost 13 officers (including three company commanders) and 407 other ranks. Only some 250 survivors could be collected in the original front line trench after the action. The 2nd King's Own Scottish Borderers, who supported the battalion, lost 115 officers and men. As for the 14th Royal Warwicks, the night's work cost the battalion nine officers and 231 other ranks killed or missing presumed killed, plus seven officers and 238 men wounded – 485 casualties in all. One company of the 15th Royal Warwicks also suffered severely through machine-gun fire from High Wood.

A fraction of the troops were taken prisoner, which left the vast majority of those reported as 'missing' to have been either killed or mortally wounded. After the war, for example, Captain Bill heard that of the two companies who had 'simply disappeared', just three men returned from one and five from the other. One of the 'missing' was Lance-Corporal Vivian Hurley's eldest brother, Victor, serving with 'B' Company in the 14th Royal Warwicks. He survived the ten o'clock attack, but disappeared for all time in the 1.30 a.m. attack.

A Lewis gunner with the 16th Royal Warwicks in 5th Division's 15th Brigade, Vivian Hurley was in brigade reserve less than a mile away on the night his brother was killed:

> I saw my brother on the 19th July, as we were being marched up to take our positions. We shook hands and said 'God bless' to each other. Victor just disappeared in the attack, but I couldn't tell our mother that – knowing what 'reported missing' usually meant, like being blown to pieces by a shell. I couldn't tell her that, so I just said that Victor was killed in action.

At roll call for the 14th Royal Warwicks, Walter Nash was listed as missing presumed killed. Oblivious to the outcome of the 1.30 a.m. attack where he lay unconscious in the shell hole near Wood Lane, Nash came to in a groggy state, his face and tunic covered with blood from a fairly large wound near his left eye. As his vision cleared, he noticed that it was no longer night time. He also became aware of company:

There were two Germans in the shell hole, pointing their rifles at me. I picked up my rifle and they immediately gestured for me to drop it – I did! They escorted me through the wire, but I didn't go in their trench – just stood in the open at the back of it. As I stood there the two Germans relieved me of my cigarettes, but gave me some back. Then an officer spoke to me from the trench, in excellent English. 'Come down in here,' he said. 'You'll be killed up there by your own chaps with their artillery.'

His English was so impeccable that I really thought he was English! 'Never mind about that,' I replied, 'Just what the hell are you doing in that German uniform?' He looked at me and said: 'What do you mean? I'm a German officer!' 'Well,' I said, 'You speak better English than me.'

He then tells me that he spent 15 years in the north of England in the catering business. Since he liked it here, he intended coming back if he got out of the war still fit and well. After this chat, he tells me again to get down into the trench. Then I remembered that I had thrown two bombs at their trench, but still had two left with the pins straightened on my person. So I said to this officer, 'Look, I've got two Mills bombs in my pockets.' By this time there was a crowd of Germans by the officer and all were armed. He tells me to take the bombs out and drop them at my feet, but I was doubtful what his mates might do when they saw me with a bomb in each hand. So I told him what I thought. He turns to his mates and says something to them in German and then tells me to go ahead. I pull out the Mills bombs slowly from my pockets and drop them at my feet as he instructed, then I slid into their trench.

I found out that a German stick bomb was thrown at me in the shell hole, wounding me in the face and just missing my left eye. My helmet also had a large dent in it, so I must have been hit twice. The wound in my face was about half inch wide and one and half inches long, and whatever that was that hit me was still in there. Anyway, one of the Germans got hold of a pair of pliers and hooked it out. He showed it to me. Believe it or not, but the object was a compressed milk tin. I was bandaged up after that and escorted to the back area.

Walter Nash spent the rest of the war working in a Ruhr coal mine.

Sunday, 23rd July, was one colossal hangover for the Fourth Army, and certainly a day that Rawlinson would rather have forgotten. The attack on Guillemont had failed and every report Rawlinson read showed conclusively that the Bazentin Ridge was still the domain of the enemy. The only heartening news came from outside Fourth Army's left boundary, where the Australians had captured Pozières in Gough's sector. Significantly, Sunday was the day when Rawlinson ordered 2nd Indian Cavalry Division back to Querrieu, its chance of glory powdered in the chalky dust of the Somme.

In the XV Corps sector, Horne was very dismayed that the line his divisions held after the attack was exactly the same as before it. He issued an order to 51st and 5th Divisions to 'gain ground towards the enemy and establish a line from which the German Switch Line can be observed and captured. All work must be pushed on and patrolling must be very active in order to keep in touch with the movements of the enemy.'

The III Corps had loaned its 19th Division to Horne and, as a gap still existed between 19th and 51st Divisions, he ordered them to connect up to the former by digging a trench from Bazentin-le-Petit windmill while 51st Division dug westwards from its front line trench in High Wood. The 51st Division was also directed to complete the communication trench that the 18th Middlesex had started and which followed the line of the lane running from High Wood's southern corner to Crucifix Corner.

Harassed by artillery fire, infantrymen and pioneers worked at the trenches throughout the day and far into the night. It was dispiriting work, as the chalk below the soil was full of large flints. Virtually every spadeful had first to be loosened by a pick before it could be thrown out of the trench. What enthusiasm remained in the troops at daybreak was subsequently quashed when the enemy accurately bombarded the new Bazentin-le-Petit mill-High Wood trench. The communication trench escaped damage. By dawn, it was negotiable for human traffic to within 60 yards of the wood.

Opposite Wood Lane, 5th Division's 13th Brigade was relieved the same night as Stewart's 154th Brigade was ordered to extend 51st Division's frontage eastwards by taking over the 1st Royal West Kents' positions. The 154th Brigade now had a frontage of some 2,500 yards to hold, and Stewart's troops were growing weary by the hour. But there was more fighting to do. Horne had sent orders to divisional headquarters that he wanted the eastern and western corners of High Wood captured and secured at the earliest moment.

Division passed the orders on to 154th Brigade. Realising that his 9th Royal Scots and 4th Gordon Highlanders were all but crippled from the last attack, Stewart detailed the 4th Seaforth Highlanders. The battalion's first objective was the machine-gun redoubt in the eastern corner.

The 4th Seaforth Highlanders had the misfortune to have taken over the 1st Royal West Kents' frontage. They commenced their attack in the dark at 9 p.m., but were promptly enfiladed by such punishing machine-gun fire on leaving their trench that the attack had to be called off. Half the battalion had fallen victim, but the misery was not over. The Germans were roused and shelled the forward area throughout the night, mainly with gas.

Midst a bout of further gas shelling, Stewart's brigade was itself relieved by 51st Division's 153rd Brigade on 26th July. His war-torn battalions wended their way to bivouac in the reserve area, leaving High Wood to a triumphant if not equally weary enemy.

Having been in support, virtually every man from the battalions of 153rd Brigade knew the route to High Wood. They knew it, because they had made repeated journeys to the forward dumps at Crucifix Corner, where RAMC personnel waited with their wheeled stretchers to take the wounded to the advanced dressing station near Bazentin-le-Petit.

It always fell to the lot of the supporting brigade to furnish the men for the heavily laden hikes to the forward dumps in the face of artillery fire. Even water had to be carried forward in petrol tins, but there was no alternative under the circumstances. So the meandering human crocodile came and returned without respite. Always shelled on the journey, always shelled when in bivouac. Consequently the brigade in support lost much of its fighting edge before going into the line.

Nevertheless 153rd Brigade was now in the front line and had much to do. The first task was to cement a link with its front line counterpart in 19th Division so as to present an unbroken line of defence to the enemy. The 154th Brigade had left the task unfinished as indeed had the brigade which the 154th superseded. It was accomplished on the night of 27th/28th July when the brigade's 6th Black Watch joined up with 19th Division some 200 yards north-east of Bazentin-le-Petit windmill.

With hindsight this was the easiest task, because Rawlinson had delegated more difficult schemes against a broad landscape of imminent Fourth Army operations. Where 154th Brigade had failed so bravely, it became 153rd's turn to attempt the capture of the western and eastern corners of High Wood. When captured, both corners were to be connected by a trench. However, Brigadier-General D. Campbell who commanded 153rd Brigade was entrusted to do more by his divisional commander, Major-General Harper. He was expected to take half of Wood Lane. The remaining half, which led to Delville Wood above Longueval, was 5th Division's task. Next door in the XIII Corps sector, Major-General Walker's 2nd Division had meanwhile replaced Haldane's 3rd Division with orders to clear Delville Wood. All these operations were scheduled for 6.10 p.m. on Sunday, 30th July, after a preliminary bombardment timed to start at 4.45 p.m.

Allied aircraft were not slow in observing the enemy's build-up in Wood Lane. Semi-circular machine-gun positions positively dotted its length. The biggest obstacle was the infamous redoubt in High Wood's eastern corner. Seeming to bear a charmed life, would the planned artillery barrage destroy it along with the rest? It begged the question, as guns were wearing out from constant use. That and faulty ground observation made for erratic shooting – most undesirable where accuracy was essential for the good of the attackers.

The battalions of 153rd Brigade waiting to test the artillery's efficacy were the 5th Gordon Highlanders and the 6th Black Watch (Wood Lane) and the 7th Black Watch (High Wood). As 19th Division had been detailed to take Intermediate Trench at the same time, it was arranged for the big guns of III Corps to pound High Wood's western corner as well as Intermediate Trench. In 5th Division's sector, fate ordained that 13th Brigade would be in the line once more and supported by the division's 15th Brigade. The 2nd King's Own Scottish Borderers were to the right of 153rd Brigade with the 14th Royal Warwicks prolonging the line. In support were the 1st Royal West Kents (with a fighting strength of only 175 other ranks), leaving just the 15th Royal Warwicks in reserve.

The recently innovated creeping barrage was employed for the various attacks, so participating battalions left their trenches before 6.10 p.m. and pressed forward close upon the barrage before its first lift. In the case of 19th Division's troops, it worked well. The moment the barrage lifted from Intermediate Trench, they rushed the defenders and managed to capture the eastern half nearest to High Wood. The suddenness of their attack induced a captured German

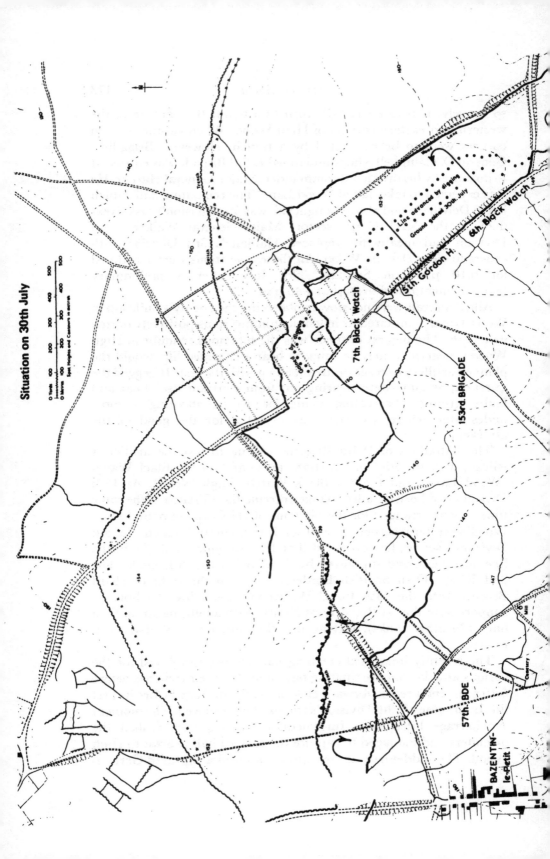

Situation on 30th July

0 Yards 100 200 300 400 500
0 Metres 100 200 300 400 500
Spot Heights and Contours in metres

7th. Black Watch

5th. Gordon H.

6th. Black Watch

Line advanced by digging
Ground gained 30th. July

153rd. BRIGADE

57th. BDE

BAZENTIN-
le-Petit

officer to remark that the British infantry came so quickly after the barrage lifted that his machine-gunners had no chance to fire. The machine-gunners in the other half of Intermediate Trench were luckier. They got their Maxims working in the nick of time, decimating the infantry in front of them. On the premise that half a loaf was better than nothing, those 19th Division troops who were victorious began consolidating their portion of Intermediate Trench.

A dominating factor in their success was the complete lack of enfilade machine-gun fire from High Wood's western corner. The III Corps heavy guns had pounded it to matchwood, but there was more: four mortar teams of the Special Brigade RE had fired nearly 80 smoke shells between the corner and Intermediate Trench, effectively screening the right of the advance.

High Wood, however, lived up to its reputation of being a natural fortress at the apex of a salient. Using mortars on the eastern corner redoubt without apparent effect, the 7th Black Watch tried their best to advance against severe machine-gun fire and remarkably accurate enemy shelling. Some gains were finally made, but were so infinitesimal that the troops withdrew to their original positions.

To the right of High Wood the 5th Gordon Highlanders and the 6th Black Watch advanced up the mangled cornfield to the low crest which hid them from Wood Lane. Ahead of them the barrage danced and spurted in the lane's vicinity. It looked impressive, even when it started creeping back to the Switch Line from the lane. They topped the crest in wave formation where the awful truth thudded home in a bank of bullets – enough defenders had lived through it.

The attacking force's predicament considerably worsened when the left flank received the attention of the machine-gunners in High Wood's eastern corner. Wiped out on the left, isolated groups of survivors went to ground in the centre and right of the attack, digging in about 200 yards in front of their starting line.

It was later learnt that the assault was expected and preparations made to defeat it; small recompense for the diminished battalions of 153rd Brigade, or for the attacking battalions of 13th Brigade to their right, whose advance was watched by Private Drinkwater and his pals in the 15th Royal Warwicks:

We understood that the Jocks [2nd KOSB] and the 14th Royal Warwicks were going over the top, with the West Kents in support and we in reserve. From our position we could see our front line trenches on the slope of ground from where the attack was to commence. Half way back were the support lines where we knew the West Kents to be.

Our big guns started bombarding the German positions over the ridge. We heard the shells go over and there was a line of smoke where they dropped. We saw the West Kents move out of their trenches to get closer to the front. The skyline by this time was one mass of smoke. Promptly to the minute, we saw the Jocks and 14th Royal Warwicks leave their trenches to slowly double over the crest of the hill and into the smoke, where they were lost from view, their places being taken by the West Kents who followed on behind.

A thrilling sight to see lines of men rise from the ground and go forward to what after all is the apex of war, then to be lost in the smoke of battle as they're followed by another line and yet another. In these instances one can think of the glories of war; and there was some glory, for the men went steadily. The staging was also appropriate – a landscape of undulating ground.

The horrors of war I saw next day. Those lines of men whom I saw go so steadily were nearly all dead, and scattered over the ground.

The 14th Royal Warwicks had received the same treatment from the enemy in Wood Lane as the unfortunate battalions of the 154th Brigade to their left. Heavy rifle and machine-gun fire checked their whole line on the reverse side of the crest, no more than 50 yards from the lane. They too went to ground in whatever cover there was available. The 2nd King's Own Scottish Borderers managed to push past Longueval, but were badly shelled on the north-western edge of Delville Wood. The 1st Royal West Kents, in support of the Borderers, shared the incoming bombardment.

Reports were received at XV Corps headquarters of the failed assault in High Wood and on Wood Lane. Horne wanted to mount a fresh attack in High Wood the same evening at 9.45 p.m., but his orders did not reach 51st Division's headquarters in sufficient time for them to be relayed to the front line. The divisional commander, Harper, felt that High Wood could only be taken after a special bombardment of heavy artillery, and suggested this measure in his report of the action. His suggestion passed without comment at XV Corps headquarters.

That Sunday evening, Private Drinkwater's eyes took in the battlefield as darkness fell:

High Wood on the left of our position was on fire, the Germans still holding one corner. On the right, Longueval village had been set on fire by German artillery, and the ground between the two extreme points was lit up by the explosion of shells and German Very lights. In the dusk of the evening it all looked very weird.

Under the mantle of night the remnants of the 14th Royal Warwicks drifted back to their starting point. It was later logged that of the 14 officers and 454 other ranks who had earlier gone over the trench parapet, just eight officers and 289 men returned. A message arrived at the 15th Royal Warwicks' position to relieve their hard-hit sister battalion. Drinkwater buckled on his kit:

We moved off, our pockets bulging with bombs; down the slope, across the valley and up the other side. Shrapnel was falling everywhere. At 4 a.m. we were in the front line trench and relieved what remained of the 14th Battalion. It was rather a pathetic sight, a few straggling men black with grime and hardly able to drag their feet along. As a battalion, they practically ceased to exist.

On arrival we set about strengthening our position; reopening the trench and making shelter from observation. At such times many incidents of a diverse nature take place, from the stretcher bearer who crawls out on all fours into No Man's Land, binding up the wounded and, pulling and tugging, brings them in, to those who volunteer to carry messages or fetch rations. In the case of the latter, rations had to be fetched up from the rear – some three miles away and the journey lay through a storm-swept area of falling shells.

Imagine for a moment yourself set on the breast of a hill, the ground stretching away from you for some three-parts of a mile, a gradual slope downwards to culminate into a narrow neck of land through which runs a road. Your eyes are focussed on this road and, presently, those whom you have been looking for, emerge. The ration party, now heavily laden.

The ground they have to travel over before they reach you is hard searched by shells. Enemy artillery are probably firing at random, knowing that this area of ground is seething with activity because of its close proximity to a road. So shells are, almost in the literal sense of the word, poured over. Shells of every calibre.

Now it was through this that our men had to walk. They did not get far when over came the shells. For a moment they were obliterated by the dirt thrown up by the shells exploding. They could, if they had wished to do so, have dumped the rations and made off somewhere for cover, but they continued to come on. We could see the bags of rations swinging from their shoulders, their hands holding petrol cans of water. The journey was uphill and with their luggage the pace was slow. Twenty minutes is a long time to face such an ordeal of one's own free will. It was cold courage and well done.

Gradually they got nearer and nearer, and then had passed through the shell zone. We gave them a cheer and then got at the food and water.

Monday, 31st July, being the day on which Private Drinkwater witnessed this episode, was remarkable for a violent bombardment of the country that was practically continuous throughout the day. The Germans were angry. Longueval was completely in British hands and nearly all of Delville Wood.

High Wood, however, was impenetrable as ever.

CHAPTER EIGHT

Enter the Tanks

As July bowed out in bloody fashion, thoughts turned to alternative methods than local attacks to oust the High Wood defenders. The change in attitude was influenced by Haig's decision to step up the pressure on Guillemont. Rawlinson favoured going for High Wood and the Switch Line again, but Haig won the day and the Fourth Army commander transferred his priorities to Guillemont.

More than two weeks of bitter fighting had left High Wood a complete shambles. The few trees still standing were mostly shorn of branches and looked distinctly skeletal. Here and there were forlorn clumps of discoloured undergrowth among the mass of large, small and over-lapping craters. Uplifted tree roots protruded from the smashed· and blackened timber that once was a leafy haven midst cultivated fields. Suspended everywhere was the cloying smell of death from whole and dismembered bodies. The ghastly aroma afflicted the nostrils of the Highlanders from 51st Division's 152nd Brigade when relieving the 153rd on Tuesday night, 1st August.

The 152nd Brigade commander, Brigadier-General Pelham Burn, knew what was required of his men. They were to gain as much ground as possible in High Wood and opposite Wood Lane through minor operations, but mainly by sapping forward in advance of the existing front line. With less cover to be had in front of Wood Lane, Burn was advised to dig posts in No Man's Land at night and then link them up to form one continuous trench line.

He was thankful that his divisional commander, Harper, had been given orders not to deliver any set piece attack involving a large number of troops. Harper was glad too, because there was no reason to suppose that 152nd Brigade would meet with any more success with that tactic than its predecessors. Both officers' opinions were shared by Major-General Haldane, who heard about the latest failure at High Wood when his division was on route for rest and replenishment:

Attack on High Wood failed, that on Guillemont will be difficult. It is a great pity that piece-meal attacks are being made. They are quite unsound and very costly. The Germans can concentrate much artillery on them and shell us out of captured trenches, but the high authorities never seem to learn lessons which are obvious to those who have to carry out their plans, even if they had not learned the folly of such tactics in the infancy of their military careers.

Haldane's scathing remarks were not aimed at his corps commander, Congreve, whom he considered to be 'a gentleman and a true soldier', but stemmed in part from his time under General Allenby and part from 3rd Division's sacrifices on the Somme. His division's casualties for the period 11th-27th July were 248 officers and 5,854 other ranks.

High Wood and the attacks on Wood Lane had taken their toll too. A fortnight in the line had cost Stephens's 5th Division about 220 officers and 5,400 other ranks. On his reporting that his brigades were exhausted, the XV Corps brought up 17th Division as a replacement. Due to XIII Corps' continuing operations against Guillemont, Rawlinson ordered Pulteney to extend III Corps' right boundary to the western edge of High Wood, while Horne's XV Corps' boundary shifted again to the right to accommodate Delville Wood.

Having extended his sector to the western edge of High Wood, Pulteney arranged for Nicholson's 34th Division to relieve 19th Division. The changeover was desperately needed, since 19th Division's casualties for July ran to 337 officers and 6,260 other ranks. The outcome of this movement left Harper's 51st Division with High Wood and the greater portion of Wood Lane.

The enemy's defence of High Wood and the ground in its vicinity had not come cheaply. July's casualty figures for six of the German regiments employed in its defence amounted to 1,860 killed, 6,679 wounded and 964 missing.[1] The suffering on both sides illuminated High Wood as a classical case of an irresistible force meeting with an immovable object. No matter. Brigadier-General Pelham Burn had his orders to lay the foundations for its eventual capture.

[1]
26th Regiment:	200	killed,	1,241	wounded,	446	missing.	
27th Regiment:	302	" ,	1,182	" ,	158	"	.
165th Regiment:	495	" ,	1,310	" ,	104	"	.
72nd Regiment:	256	" ,	1,122	" ,	125	"	.
93rd Regiment:	219	" ,	921	" ,	49	"	.
153rd Regiment:	388	" ,	903	" ,	82	"	.

Sapping forward in High Wood was slow and arduous in the extreme, not so much from enemy activity (very little attention was paid to the working parties), but from the maze of tree roots beneath the surface. In many instances the roots proved too stout to be severed by a spade and so axes and bill-hooks had to be employed, as well as picks and shovels. The diggers also had to contend with the heat and the swarms of buzzing bluebottles during the day – a greater nuisance value it seemed at the time than the periodic burst of machine-gun fire which kept the diggers on their mettle.

Burn, an innovative commander, believed in turning a difficult problem upside down and studying it from all angles. Recognising that the ever-present machine-gun redoubt in the wood's eastern corner was a most formidable stumbling block to any advance, he suggested that a shaft should be sunk without delay and a shallow gallery driven towards it with the object of placing a mine under it. His suggestion was adopted at once by divisional headquarters. In less than three hours, Royal Engineer tunnelling officers were at his brigade headquarters where it was agreed that mining operations would begin the next day.

The first week of August was full of innovations, some of which meant the use of weapons never seen before at High Wood. Among them was an apparatus known as the Barratt Hydraulic Forcing Jack – promptly called the 'pipe-pusher' – which was designed to drive iron pipes loaded with tin canisters of ammonal (2 lbs of ammonal per foot run) through the ground at a depth of four to five feet. When a sufficient length of pipe had been driven through the ground in the required direction, the charge was exploded. It was hoped that the five feet deep fissure created by the explosion would provide an instant semi-covered way for troops to move along.

Nine pipe-pushers were to be employed: eight inside High Wood and one just outside its south-eastern edge towards Wood Lane. The not so good news was that the heavy equipment had to be carried to the wood and large emplacements made to accommodate them. It was also planned to employ two flame-throwers for the next big attack against the defenders of High Wood. Unlike the German *Flammenwerfer*, an infantryman's weapon, these each weighed two tons. The parts had to be brought up in 50-lb loads and assembled on the spot – an unappealing prospect for the ranker.

The 152nd Brigade commander had an alternative scheme to the mooted plan of sapping towards Wood Lane, digging 'T' heads at the ends of the saps for the posts before connecting the 'T' heads together so as to form a continuous fire trench. He gave instructions for a large working party to 'jump' a trench some 250 yards in front of the existing front line during the night. If the enemy could do it with Intermediate Trench, so could he.

Working as quietly as they possibly could to a backdrop of artillery fire, hundreds of troops of the 152nd Brigade beavered away at the trench. No more than 50 yards ahead of the line of diggers was the crest which hid them and their work from the enemy in Wood Lane. Even the men in the machine-gun redoubt were unaware of their activity. The trench was garrisoned by dawn and a communication trench dug back to the previous front line, which now became the support trench. Come morning and the Germans awoke to find that the whole of the 51st Division's front, exclusive of High Wood, had advanced towards them.

Landon's 33rd Division had marched up to relieve 51st Division on 7th August, and Baird's 100th Brigade took over the line that day from the 152nd Brigade. The division's losses sustained in the two fruitless attempts on High Wood were approximately 120 officers and 2,000 other ranks, but during its time at the front its troops had closed the dangerous gap between Bazentin-le-Petit windmill and the wood. What is more, Burn had at last done something positive in advancing the front as well as sowing the seeds of destruction with respect to the German strongpoint in the wood's eastern corner.

Baird and Burn made the changeover in broad daylight for the first time ever. It was a deliberate move due to the enemy's nightly barrages on Flat Iron Valley, which was still the route to and from High Wood. There was some apprehension caused by three German aircraft flying low over the lines during the movement, but nothing happened and the experiment proved very successful. The 152nd Brigade did not lose a single man.

Stormonth-Darling's Glasgow Highlanders were the first of 100th Brigade's battalions to take up position in High Wood. They arrived there via High Alley; the communication trench shallowly dug by the 18th Middlesex and deepened by 51st Division's 8th Royal Scots. Trenches had appeared by accident or by design, criss-crossing the landscape. A far cry from three weeks before, when the Glasgow Highlanders first set eyes on the wood.

They were a changed battalion too. From the fresh drafts which arrived during 33rd Division's spell in corps reserve, Stormonth-Darling's battalion had soaked up 421 of the reinforcements. Not all the battalion's intake were Glasgow Highlanders; many came from other Scottish regiments. It was unnecessary, but the War Office ordained it in expectation of fostering an 'Army spirit' at the expense of the regimental *esprit de corps*. The policy was a recent one and every regiment shared a common dislike for it. The time out of the line was too short for a thorough 'shake-down', but Stormonth-Darling had done his best. Now his battalion was back at High Wood.

The wood's appearance had changed out of all proportion. 'Just a hedge,' was one pithy comment, but the British line in its southern half was roughly the same as when 33rd Division had left it. The troops noted the saps hard dug by Burn's 152nd Brigade, and soon the Glasgow Highlanders were actively trenching the ends of the saps together. Keeping them company were the Royal Engineers, busily tunnelling towards the German redoubt. Artillery fire was heavy from both sides, and British shells were falling short. The battalion was relieved by the 1st Queen's on 9th August, by which time the Glasgow Highlanders had lost three officers and 45 men from British and German guns.

King George V visited the Somme front the next day, where he was met by Rawlinson:

I took him up to the Bois Française craters and showed him the Boche front line and some of the German dugouts into which he descended. He was very cheery, looked well and was certainly in good form. He told me many things, the chief one being that there was a cabal at home led by Lord French, Winston and F.E. Smith decrying D.H. and saying that the present offensive was a waste of life and energy. It is disgraceful that people should be able to do such unpatriotic deeds, and all through jealousy.

Congreve was a prominent member of the Royal entourage during the morning, but he was far from enjoying the experience. He felt wretched and, unknown to the King, had slipped away three times to be violently sick. The XIII Corps commander was back at his headquarters by noon where his condition rapidly worsened. He took to his bed, racked with cramp and in a feverish state of mind. The medical officer's diagnosis was acute gastro-enteritis, and Congreve was wrapped up in hot blankets and injected intravenously with liberal doses of salt and water.

Rawlinson called in at XIII Corps' headquarters after the King had left his sector and was alarmed at finding Congreve so dangerously ill. He telephoned Haig's chief of staff at once, requesting a replacement and suggesting Lt-General the Earl of Cavan who commanded XIV Corps. The matter was referred to Haig. He agreed to the appointment and Cavan was summoned to Querrieu where Rawlinson explained the situation. Cavan promised to take over Congreve's command in the morning and was allowed to bring his XIV Corps staff with him.

That evening Congreve was evacuated to No 5 Casualty Clearing Station at Corbie, not to figure actively again in the Somme offensive. His departure coincided with Joffre about to pen a letter to Haig that piecemeal attacks were a waste of time. He wanted to revert to large scale combined operations with a view to capturing the line Thiepval – High Wood – Ginchy – Combles, after which to assault Grandcourt – Courcelette – Martinpuich – Flers – Morval – Rancourt – Bouchavesnes around 1st September.

Haig responded by proposing that the first step should be a combined attack from High Wood down to the Somme on 18th August, but made it conditional on the French attacking simultaneously all along their front north of the Somme.

There was one weapon which he dearly would like to have for the operations: tanks. He and his staff had been pressing for them, even a few, to be sent out to France. Their very presence would give the infantry a terrific fillip and arguably tip the balance in the Allies' favour.

Haig's eagerness for tanks was only matched by his impatience. At home the people involved in the development and production of the 'landships' were more reticent. Their invention was an infant and suffered from growing pains. They wanted to see it mature into something better before its Western Front debut. Another worrying factor was that every completed tank was being extensively used for trials and practice – all would need an overhaul by September. Besides, tank commanders and crews could not be trained overnight. Yes, 150 tanks might be ready for September, but come the New Year and 350 could reap a surprise on the enemy if used in mass. The French were not enamoured with the thought of British tanks being used prematurely. They too were working on a tank design which would not be in production until spring 1917.

An early advocate of the tank, Albert Stern, who rejoiced in the title of Director of the Tank Supply Department, aired his colleagues' doubts to Robertson and to the Secretary of State for War, Lloyd George. On 3rd August, Stern pursued the subject in a letter to the Rt Hon E.S. Montagu, Minister of Munitions:

I believe it is intended to send small numbers of these machines out at the earliest possible date, and I beg to inform you that the machines cannot be equipped to my satisfaction before the 1st September. I have therefore made arrangements that 100 machines shall be completed in every detail, together with the necessary spares, by the 1st of September. This is from the designer's and manufacturer's point of view, which I represent.

I may add that in my opinion the sending out of partially equipped machines, as now suggested, is courting disaster.

Stern's September date was reflected in a message to Haig on 11th August, which stated that 'accessories for tanks' would not be delivered until 1st September. It met with his disapproval: 'This is disappointing as I have been looking forward to obtaining decisive results from these "Tanks" at an early date.'

So August was out with regard to tank involvement, but he could see no reason why tanks should not be deployed in a large-scale attack that he and his staff were secretly planning for mid-September.

Rawlinson would hear of his commander-in-chief's intentions within the week, whereby Haig proposed to exploit the surprise effect of the tanks in 'securing the enemy's last line of prepared defences, between Morval and Le Sars with a view to opening the way for cavalry.' This ambitious scheme pivoted on one grey point, namely that he wished to see this assault launched from a line that included Bazentin Ridge and High Wood.

The heat wave was about to break, but activity at High Wood was steaming ahead with the tunnelling to the German machine-gun redoubt. The troops employed on the pipe-pushers were not having too much luck due to the numerous tree roots which handicapped their efforts. However, more communication trenches had been dug and it was now possible to go from Crucifix Corner to High Wood without stepping into the open. Large carrying parties used them to move up supplies from the forward dumps. Relief battalions hacked their way through them, as the enemy smothered the whole area in shrapnel, high explosive and gas shells. In the course of relieving Baird's 100th Brigade, Arthur Russell, machine-gunner with the 98th Brigade Machine-Gun Company, made the journey late on 12th August:

It was night-time when we took our Vickers machine-guns into the line, but thanks to the labour of dismounted cavalrymen and men of the pioneer battalions a well-dug communication trench gave us a reasonably easy passage up the gentle slope beyond Bazentin-le-Grand and so to the front line trenches in that awesome wood.

My team mates and I had our gun mounted in a shell hole-like position some 20 yards behind our advanced infantry outposts and about 60 yards from the German trenches. When daylight came we saw that we were isolated from all other troops, and to get into our close support trench 40 yards behind us there was only a ditch about three feet deep, which meant that we could not leave the position in daytime, except by crawling on our hands and knees – otherwise it was a bullet in the head from the ever alert Boche snipers. In the event of an enemy attack our job was to give covering fire to our infantrymen, but should a British withdrawal take place we stood an even chance of being over-run and taken prisoner, or worse. Soon after dark on the first day, however, we received the most welcome order to dismount our gun and move back and take up a position in the close support trench.

We had just carried our gun, tripod and boxes of belted ammunition to the site of our new position when there was a sudden flurry of action on our front. An exchange of rifle fire and the throwing of hand grenades out in No Man's Land, where apparently one of our infantry patrols had run into a German one, soon set off a steady ripple of rifle fire from both British and German front line trenches. There had been little shell fire coming over from the German batteries until this incident, but very soon a regular barrage of enemy shells was falling on our trenches, and shells from our own batteries away down in Mametz Valley were screaming over our heads to crash down on the German front line and supports. The noise from exploding shells, grenades, trench mortars and the rattle of musketry was now terrific. As we struggled to mount our machine-gun on an improvised platform on top of the parapet the question came to my mind: was Jerry about to launch a night attack?

At the height of this excitement and without warning, I was blinded by a vivid flash. A blast of air sent me reeling on my back and earth came tumbling down, half burying me. . . Looking around at one another in the bright glare of numerous German parachute type of Very lights, we saw that there were only four of us. One man was missing, Humphreys, a new-comer just out from the Grantham Training Camp. We soon spotted an arm sticking out of the piled up earth in the trench. With our hands and the careful use of an entrenching tool, we revealed the much torn and mutilated dead body of our comrade. He had received the full force of the explosion and most of the steel shell fragments had smashed into his head and back. At the time of the explosion we were all quite close together and it was a miracle that the rest of us should have escaped at least some extensive shells wounds, or even death.[2]

Private Frank Richards of the 2nd Royal Welch Fusiliers, who relayed messages from the windmill during the 20th July attack, later found himself in the wood with his battalion:

Our trench ran from just inside the wood to the centre of it and we dumped our telephone on the fire-step in a bay by ourselves. Anyone leaving the centre of the wood would have to pass us to make their way to the communication trenches. Some parts of the parapet had been built up with dead men and, here and there, arms and legs were protruding. In one bay only the heads of two men could be seen; their teeth were showing so that they seemed to be grinning horribly down on us. Some of our chaps that had survived the attack on the 20th July told me that when they were digging themselves in, the ground being hardened by the sun and difficult to dig away quickly, if a man was killed near them he was used as head cover and earth was thrown over him. No doubt in many cases this saved the lives of the men that were digging themselves in. The troops who relieved them would immediately begin to deepen the trench and since that time the rain and shells had exposed the bodies in their different ways.[3]

High Wood was heavily shelled while Richards was there. Trench walls collapsed and shallow dugouts were hit with devastating results. The bombardment was so bad that his company alone had close to 60 casualties in under two hours. As the bombardment tailed off, Richards joined in removing the Royal Welch bodies from the blocked trenches. 'We were throwing our dead on the back of the parapet, from where in some cases they were blown up again and

---

[2] Russell, Arthur: *Machine Gunner* (The Roundwood Press (Publishers) Ltd, 1977).
[3] Richards, Frank: *op cit.*

thrown further afield.' The ghastliness was not remedied in the slightest when the troops heard that the ration party coming up to their position, and bringing mail too, had been shelled into oblivion.

Not all was doom and gloom on neighbouring fronts. In III Corps sector some gains were made, although at some expense. A further 300 yards of Intermediate Trench had been wrested from a recalcitrant enemy by daybreak on 11th August, followed on 17th August with the capture of the greater portion of a new German trench that ran westward for about 600 yards across the Bazentin-le-Petit road from High Wood. A German counter-attack early next morning managed to retrieve about 90 yards of it. The counter-attack came from the direction of High Wood.

On the left of III Corps, Australians of Gough's Reserve Army had even bitten into the Switch Line and, inside the III Corps sector, three battalions won another 400 yards of it and made touch with the Australian forces to their left. After a good deal of see-sawing, a 46th Brigade battalion of III Corps' 15th Division assaulted a forward bulge in the Switch Line (known as 'The Elbow') just east of the Contalmaison-Martinpuich road. The troops cleared it at bayonet point after the artillery had all but flattened the position and prevented supplies reaching the defenders. Indeed the defenders were in such a parlous state, they resorted to drinking the water from their machine-gun jackets.

All were positive gains, but the length of the Switch Line that bisected the road from Bazentin-le-Petit to Martinpuich and which swung up and into High Wood's north-western edge stayed secure in the enemy's possession.

At Querrieu, Rawlinson was busily making final preparations for the 18th August Anglo-French assault. Except for XIII Corps signals company, he had sent Congreve's headquarters staff away to rest, replacing them with Cavan's XIV Corps staff. He was beginning to regret his decision, as Cavan had also fallen ill – 'a great nuisance' – and was forced to bring in Lt-General Morland to understudy Cavan until he was fit again. The Fourth Army commander hoped that XIV Corps would accomplish Guillemont's capture on the day despite its commander being indisposed. Of the three Fourth Army corps, the new XIV Corps worried him the most.

The guns were already drumming out their deadly messages, but there was not to be a crescendo to place the enemy on his guard for the infantry attack – just a methodical bombardment for 36 hours until zero hour at 2.45 p.m. At that time the field artillery would lay down a curtain of fire 100 yards in front of the infantry. One minute later, having estimated that the infantry would be 50 yards from it, the barrage would lift forward at the rate of 50 yards a minute with the infantry advancing close behind. Such a plan called for good gunnery at the best of times, but artillery pieces had become worn from use. Worse, the enemy's constant barrages on the static gun emplacements in Flat Iron Valley and Caterpillar Valley had taken an above average toll of artillerymen. It was not for nothing that one artillery officer had turned to an infantry officer earlier in the month to make the telling remark: 'If we fire over you, God help you – we've only one trained gunner per gun left.' Prophetic words for the 2nd Argyll & Sutherland Highlanders who were to advance through High Wood.

Battalions of Heriot-Maitland's 98th Brigade were to attack the German positions in the wood and along the main portion of Wood Lane. The 2nd A&SH went into High Wood's front line trenches on the 17th. By midnight they had lost three officers wounded, four men killed and 46 wounded with two missing presumed killed – all from enemy shell fire. Three companies were to attack at zero hour with one company in support. They were told to expect some assistance from the gigantic flame-throwers, also from the pipe-pushers that were due to explode under the German trenches and create instant communication trenches back to their front line positions. To round off the 'Heath Robinson' devices, flaming oily rags were to be shot forward on the mortar principle. Agog with curiosity, more than a few Jocks awaited zero hour with bated breath.

Troops of the 4th King's Liverpool Regiment were detailed with two companies of the 4th Suffolks to storm Wood Lane. They went into the front line trench at 7.30 a.m. Heavy calibre shells rocketed overhead to explode on the other side of the crest, but some fell short to spew earth on to the British positions. A decision was taken to evacuate the front line trench until zero hour came a little nearer, and so the troops crowded back into the close support trench some 50 yards behind.

Arthur Russell belonged to 'A' Section of the brigade's machine-gunners, which comprised 23 men and an officer with four Vickers machine-guns. Their orders were to move into the saps that had been dug out 30 yards into No Man's Land from the front line position. Once there, to mount their guns and cover the 4th King's advance.

Minutes before the appointed time, everyone started squeezing their way down the narrow support trench and into the front line

position via a short communication trench. Russell's machine-gun
team had the ill fortune to finish up in the rear. Subsequently they
were on the point of entering the front line trench when the whistles
blew for the attack. The infantry scrambled over the parapet as 'A'
Section frantically searched and found the saps into No Man's Land.
Their discovery coincided with the thunderous noise of German
artillery opening up in concert with trench mortars, rifle and
machine-gun fire together with showers of stick bombs from the
enemy front line. Midst the sounds of battle, Russell and his mates
started making for the 'T' head of their sap:

> My gun team of six men, five gunners and one ammunition carrier
> had barely moved 10 yards when a terrific explosion blew me off
> my feet; earth and sand bags cascaded down, and the sides of the
> trench caved in on me. Stunned and dazed, I dragged myself out
> of the tumbled debris and retrieved the Vickers gun which had
> fallen off my shoulders. Two yards in front of me the gunner who
> had been carrying the tripod lay face down in the bottom of the
> trench, a large gory gash across the small of his back where a large
> piece of shell had ploughed its way through. He was groaning and
> just conscious.
>
> Turning round I saw another gunner on his knees, a great
> wound at the back of his neck from which blood was spurting
> freely. His head had gone forward and his steel helmet, held
> suspended by its strap, was hanging down below his face. It was
> full of blood and overflowing – he was dead. Then I saw the
> attached infantryman extricate himself from the tumbled heap of
> earth and sand bags, apparently unhurt. There were still two of
> the team to be accounted for. Pulling at the sand bags and earth
> piled in the trench soon revealed their limp and lifeless bodies.
>
> Most of the infantry were now 'over the top', but quite a
> number had been killed or wounded, as had my mates. Only a few
> yards from the spot where my gun team had been decimated was
> the shattered and bleeding body of a sergeant of the King's
> Liverpools, who barely half an hour ago had told the men of his
> platoon and myself that he was 'for it' this trip.[4]

None of the 4th King's reached Wood Lane. Whole platoons were
blasted apart by the retaliatory barrage, while individuals who

[4] Russell, Arthur: *op cit.*

managed to get close up to the enemy's line perished on the barbed wire. To continue was futile. Survivors dodged from shell hole to shell hole, gradually making their way back to the starting line. Others stayed put in No Man's Land, using the shell holes for cover and preferring to wait for darkness before scrambling back. The 4th Suffolks, between High Wood and the 4th King's, did a little better when a group of them actually penetrated Wood Lane's defences. For all their effort and pain, they were quickly bombed from both flanks and raked with machine-gun fire from the wood's feared eastern corner.

Those survivors of the attacking force would have found it incredible if someone had told them that, in mid-July, No Man's Land was a golden carpet of corn, colourfully splashed with scarlet poppies, yellow mustard and the blue of the occasional cornflower. To them it was an unmitigated disaster area of chalky earth, broken bodies and discarded equipment.

The 2nd Argyll & Sutherland Highlanders in the wood were beaten even before the onset. British artillery fire had 'walked' through their positions, destroying men and burying the bulky flame-throwers which carrying parties had sweated to bring up the line. The so-called 'oil firers', 30 in all, looked impressive in action and yet gave the defenders nothing more than a passing fright. As for the much vaunted pipe-pushers designed to create instant trench cover, just one exploded at zero hour. To the Jocks' horror, it blew a crater in their own line, which attracted German snipers like bees to the proverbial honey pot.

With superhuman will, three ragged companies advanced at the given hour to be greeted with machine-gun fire and bombing parties. They tried their damndest to get forward through the wood, but made no headway on the centre and right. The Maxims in the redoubt, in lethal harmony with other machine-gun positions in the path of the advance, had made any movement virtually suicidal. Attacking up the extreme left of the wood, some troops of 'B' Company actually attained the capture of a small advance German trench as the attack in the centre and on the right was being repulsed. Their victory was brief. Cross-fire swept their position, causing them to withdraw just as a storming party rushed them, hurling stick bombs. 'B' Company's tiny contingent fired into the oncoming figures. Lance-Corporal William Preston worked the bolt of his Short Lee Enfield, in a kill or be killed mood: 'We got most of them,' he recalled. 'It was the first time we saw the Germans with steel

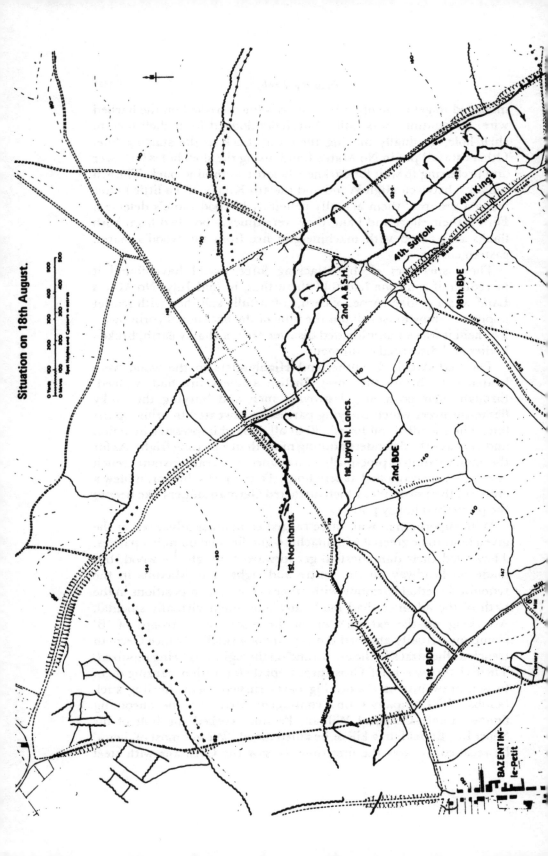

Situation on 18th August.

helmets.' Their antagonists were infantrymen of the *1st Battalion, 134th Regiment* who later reoccupied the trench after 'B' Company's withdrawal.

Too powerful a resistance, they were too few in number – that was the stark reality. The Scottish troops were forced back to their own front line to seek cover in tumbled-in trenchworks. Trembling fingers groped in tunic pockets for a calming cigarette. They were scared, they were angry and they had much to say about the parentage of generals who ordered the attack. All companies were badly hit, but fate had decreed that one 'B' Company subaltern should miss the gory show. He was Lieutenant Gordon MacMillan of MacMillan, who later became a general in World War II:

Fortunately for myself, I was attending a Lewis gun course at Le Toucquet on 18th August. I say 'fortunately', because all the officers in my company were killed in action in High Wood at that time. I think that only 37 men out of the 100/120 [in 'B' Company] were not casualties of some sort. It was not much fun to return to the battalion after a cushy time at Le Toucquet and to find out the sad news of the loss of all my friends in 'B' Company.

In the 4th King's jumping-off trench, hard by the entrance to the collapsed sap that jutted into No Man's Land, Russell and the other survivor of his machine-gun team were pondering on their next move. Their section officer decided for them after he had approached them on all fours, crawling his way down the trench. He gave orders for the evacuation of the Vickers to a support position some 50 yards back. The short communication trench that led to the support line had partly fallen in from shell fire, but by crawling down it and half carrying and half dragging the Vickers and tripod – the former weighing 38 lbs and the latter 40 lbs – they eventually reached their destination. Their next step was to make a return journey and salvage what they could in the way of ammunition. This they did with bullets snapping the air inches above them. The two men managed to retrieve four belts of ammunition; also a sandbag containing tins of bully beef, a large hunk of cheese and a number of hard army biscuits, all of which constituted the team's rations for 48 hours. The team's petrol tin of water was empty, punctured by shrapnel. To make good the loss, they salvaged bottles of water from the equipment of two dead men. Russell noticed that the gunner with the huge gash in his back was still alive. He made the man as comfortable as possible and tried to cover the wound with a field-dressing to keep out dirt. The man was moaning quietly to himself as they left. Russell doubted that he would last the day.

Back in the support trench, Russell mounted the Vickers on the parapet and weighed down the legs of the tripod with sandbags. He set and sighted the machine-gun to fire in an arc right and left to cover the enemy front line and supports. German machine-gun and rifle fire was an intense as ever, but their artillery barrage had lifted from the immediate area to plaster the rear supports and reserve lines. Walking wounded filed past his position, but he and the attached infantryman, who was Russell's team's ammunition carrier, failed to spot any stretcher cases. Evidently a lot of stretcher-bearers had also been hit in the course of the attack.

On the left of High Wood, where 1st Division had attacked at zero hour, ground had been gained. Two companies of the 1st Loyal Lancs went forward at zero hour to seize the trench on the wood's north-western edge. The troops of the right hand company were felled almost to a man by the British bombardment, but the company on the left entered an extension of Intermediate Trench without much opposition. With assistance from the 1st Northamptons, they bombed eastwards along the trench towards High Wood. They were 100 yards short of the western corner when progress ground to a halt through 33rd Division's failure to take the wood.

Any optimism lingering at 33rd Division's headquarters was entirely dissipated by the evening. No staff officer worth his salt could ignore the shambolic mess at High Wood and in front of Wood Lane, and 98th Brigade's repeated calls for reinforcements only served to strengthen the feeling of defeat. After much thought, Major-General Landon prudently opted for Mayne's 19th Brigade to relieve the whole of 98th Brigade's line. Mayne then ordered up the 1st Cameronians to relieve the 4th Suffolks and 4th King's opposite Wood Lane, and the 2nd RWF to replace the 2nd Argyll & Sutherland Highlanders at High Wood.

For six days the 2nd RWF had supplied large working parties for trench digging in addition to finding men for carrying parties. Weary from their labours, they trudged forward under the darkening sky to the Contalmaison-Longueval road that crossed the top of Flat Iron Valley. They stayed there without food or sleep before moving up to High Wood at first light via the communication trench near Crucifix Corner. Bleary-eyed the men took over the line from the Scottish battalion whose total casualties were 187 dead, wounded and missing – approximately half its pre-battle strength. When the 2nd RWF's companies were in position, its medical officer, Captain Dunn, fetched out a note book and scribbled down his initial impressions of the morning:

'B', 'C' and 'D' Companies hold a trench about 100 yards from the Germans, 'A' is again in support. In the autumn heat the air is fouled with the smell of the innumerable dead so lightly covered that in unsuspected, though extensive places, one's tread disturbing the surface uncovers them, or swarms of maggots show what one is seated near.

While awaiting orders to dismount his machine-gun and proceed out of the line, Russell had the opportunity to visit the scene of yesterday's tragedy:

The gunner with the gash across his back was dead. Several infantrymen were working in the trench at this point; they had already moved the other three dead machine-gunners into shell holes at the back of the trench, and they now proceeded to do the same with the man who had just died of his wounds.

The 98th Brigade's headquarters was in an old German deep dugout in Bazentin-le-Grand. It was here that the CO of the 2nd Argyll & Sutherland Highlanders spoke to a staff officer compiling intelligence on the abortive attack. The information tendered induced the staff officer to write:

The battalion in High Wood report that the men holding the line opposite were dressed in new uniforms and were well grown, healthy looking specimens of humanity. They wore shrapnel helmets of a shape similar to a fireman's.

To everyone, except the enemy, it was a dispiriting observation.

Recovering in a London hospital from wounds received near Bazentin-le-Petit cemetery before the 2nd RWF entered High Wood on 20th July, Captain Robert Graves had also spoken to a staff officer on his evacuation to Heilly. The staff officer – a 'brigade-major' – was wounded in the leg and Graves found himself next to him. The staff officer related to Graves his personal impressions of the 20th

July battle, and how the troops of the 2nd RWF had conducted themselves with such panache. This chance meeting was to plague Graves for years after the war.

On route from Heilly to London, after his talk with the staff officer, Graves was shuttled into a military hospital at Rouen. There he met a wounded colleague with less dramatic consequences in later life, although his personal account of that day's action was no less engrossing:

> Next to me lay a Royal Welch second-lieutenant named O.M. Roberts, who had joined the battalion only a few days before the show. He told me about High Wood; he had reached the fringe when he got wounded in the groin and fell into a shell hole. Some time during the afternoon he recovered consciousness and saw a German staff officer working round the edge of the wood, killing off the wounded with an automatic pistol. Some of the Royal Welch were, apparently, not lying as still as wounded men should, but sniping. They owed the enemy a grudge: a section of Germans had pretended to surrender but, when within range, started throwing stick-bombs. The officer worked nearer. He saw Roberts move, came towards him, fired, and hit him in the arm. Roberts, very weak, tugged at his Webley. He had great difficulty in getting it out of the holster. The German fired again and missed. Roberts rested the Webley against the lip of the shell hole and tried to pull the trigger, but lacked the strength. The German had come quite close now, to make certain of him. Roberts just managed to pull the trigger with the fingers of both hands when the German was only five paces off. The shot took the top of his head off. Roberts fainted.[5]

Four weeks had passed since that day when the 2nd RWF's momentum had all but carried the wood into British possession. New troops had joined, many of whom had never participated in an attack. Physically and mentally the battalion had undergone a change that affected regimental morale. No better example of this change occurred on the night of 19th/20th August, when a 'stunt' was arranged by brigade headquarters for the 2nd RWF to clear the trench on the south-western edge. Dunn and the battalion CO, Crawshay, thought the scheme senseless and were not at all

[5] Graves, Robert: *op cit.*

impressed with the artillery back-up. 'D' Company was detailed for what could only be a suicide mission, but the new soldiers lacked the necessary motivation. The night attack, as Dunn observed, 'was a washout from the start; the men didn't follow their officers out of the trench'. The Official History was kinder, calling it 'an abortive attempt'. The same night, but with more chance of success, men of the Glasgow Highlanders moved up on to the extreme right of Wood Lane and captured a partially completed trench without loss.

In the morning, Rawlinson conferred with his corps commanders at Horne's headquarters. Fully briefed on Haig's intentions to take the last German line of prepared defences between Morval and Le Sars, he explained to them that just three weeks remained to reach the high ground from where he would launch the assault. Relentless pressure must be maintained along the whole of the Fourth Army front, including surprise night attacks. Anything, in fact, that would push the front forward.

On 21st August the 100th Brigade, prolonging the 19th Brigade's right, attacked a German trench that went eastwards from Wood Lane to the Flers road. Strongpoints in Delville Wood were also attacked while, in XIV Corps sector, Guillemont was assaulted again. All failed.

The 2nd RWF were relieved early on the 22nd, and went into support at Crucifix Corner. The battalion's departure coincided with preparations for another attempt by 100th Brigade to take the trench between Wood Lane and the Flers road. This time the brigade would employ three attacking battalions: 1st Queen's, 16th King's Royal Rifle Corps and the 2nd Worcesters with the Glasgow Highlanders in support. For the new assault the brigade commander was determined that nothing should be lacking in effective covering fire. In addition to an artillery barrage, he intended to make history with the 100th Machine Gun Company under the command of Captain G.S. Hutchison.

Ten Vickers machine-guns were to be grouped in a trench that gave a panoramic view of the enemy line at a range of 2,000 yards. From this vantage point, Hutchison was instructed to maintain rapid fire continuously for twelve hours to cover the attack and consolidation. The attack was due to start at 6.45 p.m. on 24th August. Appreciating the Herculean effort required to carry out the order, Hutchison promised a prize of five francs to each of the members of the gun team firing the greatest number of rounds.

On the dot the infantry went over, protected from the ever-alert

German machine-gunners in High Wood's eastern corner, half a mile away, by a billowing smoke-screen. Strictly observing regulations on barrel-changing, Hutchison's ten gun teams collectively fired 250 rounds short of a million. Four two-gallon petrol tins of water, the company's water bottles and all the urine tins from the neighbourhood were emptied into the gun jackets to keep them cool. The company artificer, assisted by a private, maintained a belt-filling machine in action without cessation for the whole of the period. At the end of the twelve hours, the winning team had fired more than 120,000 rounds.

It was a prodigious feat that reaped rewards. The objective was taken and a number of Germans captured. The prisoners told their captives that the effect of the machine-gun barrage was annihilating. Troops trying to concentrate east of High Wood for the purposes of counter-attacking were met with a rain of death.

Soldiers of the 2nd RWF wended their way back to High Wood on 26th August, but their stay was to be brief. In the words of their unofficial diarist, Captain Dunn: 'High Wood is to give lustre to another.'

He was right. Every battalion in the division's three brigades was tired. With casualties nearing the 4,000 mark for the month of August, Landon's 33rd Division was due for a rest. Influenced by Haig, Rawlinson decided to shift the corps' boundaries eastward again so that XV Corps became responsible for Ginchy's capture and not Cavan's XIV Corps. Delville Wood remained a thorny problem for XV Corps, but the task of capturing High Wood and Wood Lane was given to Pulteney's III Corps. Pulteney in turn detailed his 1st Division for the job, under its commander Major-General E.P. Strickland. 'Flame projectors and other gadgets are on the ground to ensure a spectacular capture of the Wood by the 1st Division,' noted Dunn with the aside: 'A current view among those who knew the GOC 1st Division as Brigadier in the 33rd is that if hot air be the further means to success, he has a never-ending supply in himself.'

To Haig's joy, tanks were arriving in France and being transported to an improvised training centre at Yvrench, near Abbeville. The innovator of the tank concept, Lt-Colonel E.D. Swinton, originally had in mind three battalions of tanks to be used on the battlefield in mass formation. GHQ quashed his proposal in favour of tactical units, namely six companies of 25 tanks each in four sections of six with one tank in reserve. Three of the tanks in each section were armed with two 6-pounder guns ('male' tanks), while the other three ('female') carried four Vickers machine-guns capable of firing 1,200 rounds a minute from each side. The 'male' tanks were the 'destroyers', whereas the 'female' versions were the 'man-killers'. All six companies were prefixed with a letter ('A' to 'F') for identification, and the tanks in each company numbered 1 to 25 with the relevant prefix.

The tanks of 'C' Company were the first to reach Yvrench, where their crews hoped to get them mechanically fit for battle. Instead the officers and men of the newly designated Heavy Section, Machine-Gun Corps found themselves in a circus-like atmosphere as star performers. On 26th August, they 'performed' in front of Haig and Rawlinson. Both were favourably impressed, but Haig more so:

> A Battn of infantry and five tanks operated together. The Tanks crossed ditches and parapets representing the several lines of a defensive position with the greatest ease, and one entered a wood, which was made to represent a 'strong point' and easily 'walked over' fair-sized trees of six inches diameter! Altogether, the demonstration was quite encouraging. . .

Knowing intimately the limitations of the tanks' capabilities, Swinton was appalled by the frequent demonstrations:

> Some of the machines were asked to force their way through a wood and knock down trees – tricks which they had not been designed to play and which were likely to damage them seriously. I protested against these 'stunts' and the frequent exhibitions, which were wearing out both machines and personnel. In addition to the almost continuous work of repairing, cleaning and tuning their Tanks, the men barely had time to eat, sleep, and tend themselves. I speculated as to how many machines would be one hundred per cent fit to go into action when their day arrived; and wondered how the Royal Flying Corps would have fared if it had made its début during the War with fifty aeroplanes of the first type produced, and had had to submit to similar preliminaries before it went into action. As had been the case in England, it seemed impossible to establish a realization of the fact that the New Arm was a mass of complicated, and in some ways delicate, machinery in an embryonic shape, and not the fool-proof product of long trial and experience.

Besides the effect of wearing out valuable tanks and crews, a world of difference lay between a young wood untouched by war and a more mature one savaged by it. Even so, two tanks broke down in the 26th August demonstration and one driver had fainted. With the break-through assault firmly fixed for 15th September, with winter on the door-step, Haig hoped that the tanks – any tanks – would give him the edge. He expressed these thoughts in a letter to Robertson: 'Even if I do not get so many as I hope, I shall use what I have got, as I cannot wait any longer for them, and it would be folly not to use any means at my disposal in what is likely to be our crowning effort for this year.'

Accepting Swinton's justifiable protestations, but mindful that the Somme campaign was one of attrition, it is difficult not to feel a degree of sympathy with Haig's reasoning. Swinton was one of the few men of the time to understand the future role of tanks, but the numbers were not there in late August, nor would they be for 15th September to implement the role. And his Commander-in-Chief was fully prepared to make do with what tanks he could get, but not in the way that Rawlinson initially proposed.

Haig's idea was for Gough's Reserve Army to push the enemy off the northern end of the plateau, clear of Pozières and Thiepval, while Rawlinson breached the third and last main line of defence with the aid of tanks. On establishing a defensive flank facing eastwards from Morval to Bapaume, Haig intended for Rawlinson to send five cavalry divisions northwards through the gap created by the tanks and infantry. The bone of contention was that Rawlinson wanted to use the tanks cautiously and achieve the break-through in three stages on successive nights, 'Attempting too much, we run the risk of doing nothing,' whereas Haig took the opposite view: 'I think we should make our attack as strong and as violent as possible, and plan to go as far as possible.'

The Fourth Army commander suspected that Haig would not like his plan and was not in the least surprised when Haig rejected it. On losing the argument, he recorded:

The Chief is anxious to have a gamble with all available troops with the object of breaking down German resistance and getting through to Bapaume. . . We shall have no reserves in hand, but tired troops. If we succeed, it may bring the Boche to terms; if we fail we have all the winter to recuperate. . .

First, however, there was to be an 'offensive before the offensive' on Sunday, 3rd September, so that British and French armies could secure advantageous positions beforehand. Meanwhile, small but useful gains were being made on the Fourth Army front. Delville Wood was captured on 27th August and the occupants of the remaining enemy-held section of Intermediate Trench surrendered to troops of 15th Division, after 1st Division had taken over at High Wood and along the front facing the greater part of Wood Lane.

There had been a good deal of wet weather of late, but the last day of August was sunny and bright. The Germans chose it to lash the front and back areas from High Wood to south-east of Delville Wood with shells of all calibre. The bombardment continued all morning until 1 p.m., when they mounted a vigorous attack on a 3,000 yard front. The assault – the severest yet made by the enemy on the Fourth Army – was repulsed, but the Wood Lane junction north-west of Delville Wood was lost. The Germans also managed to regain a foot-hold in Delville Wood's south-eastern corner, but only after attacking three times. Met everywhere by rifle fire, massed machine-gun and concentrated trench mortar fire, not to mention artillery fire, the attacks ceased by late evening with heavy losses to the enemy. The retaliation proved such a shock to the system that, in a letter home, one soldier of the *17th Bavarian Infantry Regiment* wrote:

We are actually fighting on the Somme against the English. You can no longer call it war, it is mere murder. We are at the hottest place of the present battle, in Foureaux Wood [*sic*]. All my previous experiences in this war, the slaughter at Ypres and the battle in the gravel pit at Hulluch, are the purest child's play compared with this massacre, and that is much too mild a description. I hardly think they will bring us into the fight again now, for we are in a very bad way.

Accompanied by Lord Derby, Haig attended the Church of Scotland morning service at Valvion on Sunday, 3rd September. Politician and soldier listened intently to the preacher, Mr Duncan, expanding on his text: 'Thy will be done on Earth as it is in Heaven.' Miles away at High Wood an RE officer detonated the mine beneath the German redoubt in its eastern corner, blowing the machine-gunners into oblivion.

The 'offensive before the offensive' was under way.

CHAPTER NINE

A Fearful Victory

Working against the clock, sappers of the 178th Tunnelling Company RE had dug down 25 feet to burrow out a gallery 310 feet in length which brought them under the German redoubt. They had laboured in hazardous conditions and all material was brought over the devastated battlefield. Their work culminated in the placing of 3,000 lbs of ammonal at the end of the gallery, and the mine was exploded 30 seconds before zero hour.

Before the last smoking clod of earth had hit the ground, hard-bitten Regular troops of the 1st Black Watch had rushed the lip of the vast crater. They started consolidating the position as other troops bombed westwards along a German front-line trench that once had fed into the strongpoint. Thanks to the efforts of the tunnellers, theirs was an easy operation compared with the remaining companies of the Black Watch, who were poised to sweep through the wood with the help of blazing oil drums, pipe-pushers and gigantic flame-throwers. As luck would have it a Stokes mortar, firing short, prematurely ignited the oil drums. To compound the misfortune, none of the pipe-pushers worked in the way that they should have done. Instead of creating instant rough and ready trenches to the enemy front inside the wood, all blew back with tragic consequences. The sum result was complete confusion which retarded the moment of advance. On moving forward, they were met with machine-gun and rifle fire. The delay, brief as it was, had given the Germans time in which to recover their wits.

High Wood was not bombarded prior to zero hour, because of the close proximity of the British front line to that of the enemy's. There was more tolerance between the Wood Lane defences and the opposing British positions. Aided by an unusually accurate creeping barrage, four companies of the 1st Camerons with an 8th Berkshire detachment on their right, arrived in the Wood Lane trenches close behind the barrage. With no vicious machine-guns from the eastern corner to stop them, they clashed with the defenders in hand-to-hand combat and ousted the Germans from a 200-yard section nearest to High Wood.

The barrage had knocked in parts of the trench, but the Camerons expected a carrying party to appear at any moment with tools and material for them to consolidate the section they had won. Consolidation was a priority, because everyone knew the enemy would counter-attack. To the Camerons' chagrin, no carrying party appeared. The men comprising it had gone off course. When the inevitable counter-attack came, it was launched from the Switch Line north-east of High Wood, but not directly at the Camerons. The Germans knew that the Camerons' Achilles heel was the wood's eastern corner and, like a deadly game of chess, they pressed through the wood towards the crater.

Their losses were frightful, but they kept advancing until they had bombed the Black Watch from the crater. A machine-gun was quickly set up and a stream of fire was brought to bear in enfilade on the Camerons in the Wood Lane trench. To stay was to die. Those Scotsmen still alive scrambled out to avoid the sward of bullets tearing at the damaged trench. The only gain of the day was a clutch of Bavarian prisoners who were captured in the first rush. Otherwise, all that could be said was that 1st Division had that day tasted the same experience of previous divisions sent in to subdue the wood.

The furthest end of Wood Lane was the boundary line between the fronts of III Corps and XV Corps. During the night, two battalions of the 165th Brigade of Major-General H.S. Jeudwine's 55th Division moved in next to III Corps (and 1st Division's) boundary. They were the 1/6th and 1/7th King's Liverpool Regiment.

Sunday, 3rd September, was notable for one important gain – that of Guillemont. It had been a bitter fight and the surface of the razed village was thick with enemy dead. It was the first real success for Cavan's XIV Corps and Rawlinson was pleased. The French successes bolstered his confidence and he was in an optimistic mood when he conferred with his corps commanders at Querrieu on 5th September. The Fourth Army was not quite on the desired jumping-off line for the larger operation on 15th September, and Rawlinson had called the meeting to discuss how it could be done. After informing his corps commanders that he had arranged with the French for another combined push on 8th September, he turned to Pulteney whom he knew was proposing to attack High Wood again on that day.

The III Corps commander was asked whether he could carry out the task allotted to him on 15th September, if his attack on High

Wood was a success. Pulteney, who intended using Strickland's 1st Division to secure the western half of the wood in conjunction with a 15th Division brigade, answered in the affirmative, adding that 1st Division would go for Wood Lane on the 9th.

Rawlinson wanted Horne's XV Corps to capture Ginchy before 15th September. Horne reckoned that he could do it and, on being asked if he had considered the question of moving his artillery forward in readiness for the 15th, Horne replied that High Wood and Wood Lane prevented any immediate move. Rawlinson suggested that he should do it after 8th September. Morland, who was standing in for Cavan, told the Fourth Army commander that XIV Corps guns were moving forward in a few hours time, not having the same problem as Horne. A discussion on the state of the roads to the front followed before Rawlinson broached the subject on how tanks were to be employed on 15th September.

'An experiment with tanks was carried out this morning,' he said. 'I understand from Colonel Elles that it was fairly satisfactory.'

Lt-Colonel Hugh Elles, present in the room as the representative of GHQ on tanks, assured the corps commanders that a tank travelled at the rate of 100 yards in five minutes without a check.

'The difficulty,' continued Rawlinson, 'is to get them to go fast enough in front of your infantry. If the infantry overtake them, they will not be of much use. If you have got 300 yards to go from your trench to the enemy's trench, they will take a quarter of an hour to reach it. Therefore you will have to start them off at least ten minutes before time, if they are to have a reasonable chance of getting to their objectives before the infantry arrive. This means you will have to get the tanks up during the night or late in the evening before.'

'Won't they draw the enemy's barrage?' interjected Morland.

'Yes, but I am not at all sure that a barrage on a front of 9,000 yards will be a very serious obstacle. What we hope to do is to start them at such an hour in the morning that they will not be visible at any great distance. I think you should have a hiding-place for them about 200 yards behind the starting-off point.'

'They will not be visible at all in the early dawn,' said Elles in support of Rawlinson's idea, knowing that the tanks were specifically painted for camouflage purposes.

The method of employing the tanks on the day took much consideration. There was no experience on which to call; no benchmark whatsoever save for the field trials and what could be gauged from the frequent demonstrations. With Swinton's scheme invalidated by GHQ and by the small number available, it was left to Rawlinson to step gingerly into the unknown: 'I want to get them working in fours, so that you will only have one commander to deal with, who can have a watch to start them at the right moment. If they succeed in starting from their 'stables' half an hour before zero – making zero at early dawn – they will go on to their first objective: the strongpoints in the intermediate line. The moment the infantry have captured this by assault, the tanks ought to proceed to the next objective in similar formation. The artillery will have to study this, and arrange to leave an opening in the barrage for the tanks to go through.'

His corps commanders noted his recommendations, particularly about leaving 'lanes' in the artillery barrage for the tanks.

The troops ordered to secure the western half of High Wood on 8th September were the 1st Gloucesters and the 2nd Welsh of 1st Division's 3rd Brigade. Two companies of the 2nd Welsh advanced up its left hand side at 6 p.m. while, further to the left, the 1st Gloucesters attacked the wood's south-western face. Helping both battalions were two companies of the 9th Black Watch from 15th Division who assaulted a trench that ran from the western corner.

After a short fight the 2nd Welsh company nearest to the centre of the wood gained its objective, but the other company was checked by fire. As for the 1st Gloucesters, it was a disaster. Weak in numbers even before the attack, they had to winkle the enemy from wired shell holes at bayonet point. Isolated with no chance of being reinforced and reduced to three officers and 96 men, they withdrew to their original line after dark. The two companies of the 9th Black Watch were successful in their endeavours. They occupied the trench at the western corner and captured 30 infantrymen of the *18th Bavarian Regiment* and one machine-gunner. After beating off a counter-attack, they were also forced to retire due to 1st Division not being able to maintain its gains in the wood. Both company commanders were wounded and an officer reported missing. Among the men, 24 were killed, 14 were reported missing presumed killed and 59 were wounded. A watery dawn showed the slaughter in gruesome light and gave a fair indication of how the Germans had suffered too.

A 19-year-old corporal by the name of H.F. Hooton heard of the abortive attack and knew that his battalion was destined for High Wood. He was in 'D' Company of the 1st Northamptons, currently in the reserve trenches near Mametz Wood. Included in a draft of 30 men, Corporal Hooton had come to the Somme to join the battalion on 31st August. He had no need to ask any veterans what High Wood was like, because he had tasted its horror when the 1st Northamptons entered the trenches there the next day. His most indelible memory of his first spell at High Wood was rounding a bend in the trench and passing a dead soldier who stood embedded in the side of the trench. Most of his body was exposed and Hooton recognised him as someone he had known in England. The macabre experience visibly shook him.

Hoping forlornly – as it transpired – that the wood's western side would be free of the enemy in readiness for the 9th September attack, Major-General Strickland intended clearing the whole of High Wood during the attack on Wood Lane. Plans were hurriedly changed on learning that the enemy still controlled the western side. Strickland ordered up the 10th Gloucesters of 1st Brigade to attack the western corner when the 2nd Royal Munster Fusiliers of 3rd Brigade advanced up the left hand side with the 1st Northamptons of 2nd Brigade to their right. The Germans were still garrisoning the lip of the crater in the eastern corner. To help the Northamptons retake that area, Royal Engineer tunnellers had cleared the old gallery of debris and had placed another charge of explosives beneath the crater's near side edge. The charge, a further 3,000 lbs of ammonal, was timed to be touched off 30 seconds before zero hour.

Hooton and his comrades had breakfast at midnight in the expectation of parading at 2 a.m. for the trek to High Wood. They cut off chunks of meat with jack-knives from a huge joint and did their own cooking over concealed fires. The midnight feast was washed down with tea with scant regard that they were using up the whole of their tea ration. When 2 a.m. arrived, however, no order came for them to parade. It was the first sign that something was not what it should be, and everyone's imagination started working overtime. After a long period of uncertainty, they eventually paraded at 11 a.m., when greatcoats and water-proof sheets were handed in. Then, dressed in battle order and with a longing for the tea which they had quaffed at midnight, Hooton's company marched off with the rest of the battalion:

On the way through the communication trenches, we had one sorry mishap. Having at one stop drawn our twelve Mills bombs for each man; these being packed in wooden boxes, the drill was to take these out carefully, one by one and turn back the split pins to prevent them slipping out. All twelve would then be put into a sack provided and, with six bombs each side, the sack would be tied up at the centre and at both ends. The sack was thus slung over the shoulder with the weight evenly distributed. The trenches were full of muddy water, up to and over the knee in some places. There was cable wire underneath and overhead. Frequently a warning was passed along the single file of men: 'Wire under' or 'Wire over'. Many men tripped in spite of this warning and one man's bombs exploded about twelve men ahead of me. Several were killed.

'D' Company reached a point just left of its previous position in High Wood at 3 p.m. It was here that Corporal Hooton exchanged verbal promises with a good friend, Harry Woodhams, about conveying news home should only one of them survive. They could scarcely hear each other for the noise of the bombardment that was designed to wreck the German positions. The plan of attack was brutally and optimistically straightforward, commencing with the first wave going over the top at 4.45 p.m. Participating in the first wave would be the Northamptons' 'B' Company and Hooton's one. If all went well, they were to reverse the fire step in the captured enemy trench and start strengthening the new position as the following wave (troops of 'C' Company) passed them, leaving 'A' Company in reserve and to dig communication trenches up to the new front. Meantime, those left alive had three days' supply of iron rations – hard biscuits and water – for sustenance until the completion of the action.

To everyone's consternation, many of the shells intended for the enemy's trenches were dropping short to smother the Northamptons' and Munster positions. Soldiers scurried along the trenches in an attempt to find shelter whilst officers busied themselves on field telephones, entreating the gunners to lift their fire. When the crisis had passed, Hooton was put in charge of a listening post which was at the end of a trench that jutted out towards the German lines and which carried two pipes to fuel a flame-thrower. A periscope was positioned at the end of the trench for observation.

The distance from our front trench to the German line was the closest of all along the front, being a matter of 40 yards. A disturbance would have brought quick results and disaster. I had six men and was told to post two at a time at the periscope and to

Situation: 3rd — 9th September

change men at 15 minute intervals. A nerve-racking job, but the noise of hob-nailed boots treading backwards and forwards on the iron pipes made it more hazardous. The firing of a trench mortar was to signal zero hour, but I was to withdraw the men 15 minutes before and return them to their attack positions. All very orderly if it worked. I thought of other Saturday afternoons, playing cricket.

A few minutes before I called off the watch, a lad came to me and said he was only 16. I could only say, 'What a time to tell me that!' Then I sent him back to find a sergeant. What happened to him I never knew. At 4.45 the Stokes mortar boomed.

On scrambling over we were met with concentrated machine-gun and rifle fire from the German trenches, covering every inch of the attack and the German barbed wire was intact! Most of our men rolled back into the trench and Harry Woodhams and I got into a shell hole, bullets pinging fast over our heads. We carefully peeped out and saw soldiers lying all around. Terrific machine-gun firing continued. Looking out again, we realised that every man around us was dead – there was no movement whatsoever.

We somehow got back. It seemed that there was no one but dead and dying in the front line trench, so we decided to go forward again. As we tried to find a break in the barbed wire, my foot caught in wire beneath and sprawled me on to the entanglement. My companion unhooked my clothing and, free again, we moved along when an explosive bullet shattered my left elbow. I dropped my rifle to clutch my broken arm, staggered back across No Man's Land to fall headlong into our front line trench. Harry followed me back. He ripped open my tunic with his jack-knife to get at the stitched-in bottle of iodine and then poured the lot into my wound. He then went over again.

The bones above and below the elbow were badly broken, but holding the left arm with my right I negotiated the trench as best I could and found a stretcher-bearer who supported my arm with the tape of a puttee. He gave me a sip of water from his carrier and, thus refreshed, I joined many other wounded soldiers on the long trek down the communication trenches. This had all happened so quickly that I found myself passing what I took to be the men of the second wave waiting to go over. One man, whom I recognised as Ben Griggs from Wollaston, asked me: 'What's it like over there?'

'Like Hell!' I said. I understand that he was killed some minutes afterwards.

In the turmoil of battle, Corporal Hooton had missed the blowing of the second mine adjacent to the crater in the eastern corner. It did a most thorough job, but the men reaching the new lip were so few in number that the area was again lost when the enemy counter-attacked 90 minutes later. The previous crater was large, but the combined craters measured 135 ft x 85 ft x 35 ft deep.

A battalion each of the *4th* and *5th Bavarian Regiments* were defending High Wood that day, and defended it well although at 'the loss of many, good, irreplaceable men'. Their defence was so spirited that neither the 1st Northamptons nor the 2nd Royal Munster Fusiliers could make any headway, nor could the 10th Gloucesters who attacked the wood's western corner. They managed to enter the wood, but were thrown back by bombing attacks and by the cross-fire of machine-guns.

Wood Lane had a different ending, but the attack which resulted in its capture was no less bloody. Infantrymen of the 2nd Royal Sussex advanced past High Wood's eastern corner to capture their section of Wood Lane, but finally had to dig a defensive flank to link up with the British line inside the wood. Private Walter Grover, who had joined the Royal East Kent Mounted Rifles for 1/2d a day before volunteering for France with the 2nd Royal Sussex at 1/- a day, was in the attack:

> We could see High Wood on our left, all battered and shell-torn, and the barrage from our own artillery and that of the Germans on that afternoon was indescribable. The ground over which we attacked was swept by machine-gun and field gun fire – whizzbangs – with 5.9s for good measure. I did not know at the time what they were, having only been in France since the 8th August, but I soon learned. Seeing my friends shot down on each side of me gave me a feeling of dread. I wondered when it was going to be my turn.

Walter Grover was lucky. He survived the attack unscathed and soldiered on to win the MM in April of 1918.

Advancing towards Wood Lane on the right of the 2nd Royal Sussex were the Regulars of the 2nd King's Royal Rifle Corps. They captured their objective in breathtaking style, although absorbing considerable punishment from the defenders before doing it. Watching the nightmarish spectacle was a sniping and intelligence officer, 2nd Lieutenant Victor Russell, who was at the time attached for rations to 'B' Company, 1/6th King's Liverpools:

We had just returned to the line and had taken over a stretch of the front below the ridge upon which High Wood stood, and to the left of a sunken road running up the hill, across which the Germans had built a strongpoint or roadblock. It was surrounded by barbed wire with a couple of machine-guns mounted there. Some 150-200 yards to its rear and covering it, lay a switch trench[1] that was heavily manned and containing more machine-guns.

Our side kept up a continuous, heavy artillery barrage on the German positions all along the ridge. In return, they plastered us with counter-fire, which was not quite so heavy as ours, but bad enough. The noise was simply horrendous and stunning, and its effects shattering. In a queer sort of way, we got used to it. On Saturday, after a series of small, local skirmishes, 'A' Company and a company from our 1/5th Battalion to the right of the sunken road advanced on each side. Both companies attacked under a Stokes mortar barrage while a bombing party worked up the road itself. My snipers were out on each side trying for targets of opportunity.

The Stokes barrage stopped abruptly and without warning – they had run out of ammunition. The first attack failed with heavy losses, as the bombers on the road came up against uncut wire. Dead and wounded lay out in the open and, as the wounded were being attended by three or four chaps who hadn't been badly hit, machine-guns from the switch trench suddenly opened up on them. The machine-gunners traversed backwards and forwards until all movement ceased.

I went up the road to see what was happening and got stuck in a shell hole. A little later the Stokes mortars received a fresh supply of ammunition and the strongpoint was taken. A short time afterwards, a mine was blown in High Wood. Huge clouds of debris shot into the sky as the artillery barrage rose to a shrieking crescendo.

Suddenly it stopped and, though the ground still trembled, an eerie silence fell – broken by a skylark high above us, singing its heart out! We all looked up in wonder, but before we had time to take the little miracle in, a barrage from massed machine-guns began along the small ridge behind us. Under this cover the

---

[1] Wood Lane trench, not the Switch Line which lay behind it.

KRRC on our left, with the Guards Brigade on our right, rose and started up the hill in three waves, their bayoneted rifles held at the high port and the sun flashing on their blades. Each wave dressed by the right as though on parade, and they moved forward and upwards in perfect order.

At first, there was no response whatsoever from the stunned Germans. Then their machine-guns started to chatter; one after another the men began to fall. I remember seeing the Guards' sergeants checking the dressing and filling the gaps as more and more fell. Then they were all at the top of the ridge and all the bayonets flashed down, as though at a word of command, before they disappeared into the pall of dust and smoke which crowned the ridge.

In this attack the Guards by-passed the roadblock and veered in behind the German positions. As they did so, about 150 Germans clambered out of their trench, threw their rifles away and came downhill towards us with hands up. A machine-gun officer pushed me to one side, plonked himself down behind a Vickers and growled, 'By God – no you don't.' Before we could stop him, he had pressed his thumbs down on the firing studs and was traversing left and right along their line.

You see, he had witnessed the massacre of our wounded earlier in the afternoon.

The 9th September operations rolled Ginchy into the British net and made the Germans relinquish their toe-hold on Delville Wood's eastern point, but they kept a grip on some nearby trenches that made a nasty re-entrance into the British front. Wood Lane was finally neutralised, but the British line through High Wood remained as before. High Wood – as an observer aptly described – was like a tightly fitting cork in a bottle. It could neither be drawn out nor pushed in. Piece by piece it had to be crumbled away. The capture of Wood Lane had assisted the process.

Rawlinson touched on the subject at a meeting of his corps commanders the next morning. On the whole he was satisfied, because Fourth Army had improved its position sufficiently enough for him to view optimistically the outcome of the 15th September offensive. He had laid down four lines of objectives, labelling them the Green, Brown, Blue and Red Line. Depending on launch locations along his front, it would mean an advance of something in the order of two to three miles if the Red Line was reached, plus a

gaping hole in the enemy's defences of nearly three and a half miles
wide through which the cavalry would ride. Inclusive of Gough's
Reserve Army divisions, but discounting the five cavalry divisions, it
was expected that ten British divisions would confront five German
ones in the initial attack. With the help of the artillery (double the
density attained on 1st July), Rawlinson expected to have his troops
on the Red Line by noon in readiness for the cavalry to advance.
Then, of course, there was the secret weapon to ensure a decisive
success – tanks.

He was given to understand by GHQ that 42 tanks were being
allotted to the Fourth Army, of which he intended giving Horne's
XV Corps the majority. He informed Pulteney at the meeting that he
was allotting fewer tanks to III Corps, since its objectives were not so
distant. With that, he asked Pulteney how III Corps planned to use
its tanks. The III Corps commander replied that he proposed using
six against the southern end of Martinpuich, possibly sending one
tank up the Martinpuich road to deal with a likely barricade.

'Can you tell from photographs whether the road is negotiable?'
asked Rawlinson. Pulteney admitted that he could not tell. Pressing
on, Rawlinson said: 'You will have to put the tanks right into the
village in front of your infantry. You will have to start them very
early, because the infantry will move faster than them. Now what
about the barrage?'

Rawlinson had ordered a three day 'softening up' bombardment
to precede the infantry assault at 6.20 a.m. on 15th September, after
which to employ a creeping barrage. He was in two minds whether
'lanes' should be left in the barrage for tanks to go through, or
whether it was best for the tanks to advance irrespective of the
creeping barrage and go to their objectives whilst the barrage was
behind. Pulteney favoured the former, but to Rawlinson's question
he did confess that owing to the slowness of the tanks, it would be a
difficult matter to implement it. He then made the startling remark
that the tanks would go quickly through High Wood, because they
would have cover all the way.

What compelled him to say such a thing is hard to imagine, unless
he was drawing on the demonstration attended by Rawlinson and
Haig where tanks forced their way through a wood to the detriment
of two of the tanks. By 10th September, High Wood was a lethal
tank-trap. Liberally studded with deep-rooted tree stumps, it was
full of shell holes of varying depths and diameters and also interlaced
with trenches.

Elles, who was again present, swiftly saw the danger and spoke up. 'I took a tank out for an experiment. It went 15 yards a minute over badly crumped ground. I do not think tanks would be able to get through a place like Trônes Wood,' he added, citing a comparison.

The Fourth Army commander looked hard at Pulteney.

'This is a matter for consideration. You had better settle whether it is worth going through the wood, or whether it is better to ignore it and go round it.'

But Pulteney had already made up his mind. He intended leaving High Wood as a vast 'lane' for the passage of four precious tanks and without a hint of a barrage.

Another tank company had arrived in France – 'D' Company under the command of Major Summers – and it followed the tracks of 'C' Company to Yvrench. 'C' Company in the meantime had departed to a rail centre called the Loop near Bray-sur-Somme. Summers was ordered to take his tanks there too. The move began on the 7th and was not completed until 13th September. With the offensive so close, tank crews really did think that the move to the Loop would spell the end of their circus routines. They could not have been more wrong. A tank commander bitterly wrote:

> When we got there we found that the Infantry Brigade had been notified that the Tanks were to perform daily from 9.0 to 10.0 and from 2.0 to 3.0, and every officer within a large radius and an enormous number of the staff came to inspect us. We were an object of interest to everyone. This did not help one's work.

He spoke with sincerity. Only half a company could squeeze in a meagre day's firing practice. The time snatched between the performances in which to service the 30-ton monsters was equally as limited.

Yet no one could blame Haig in not giving Rawlinson his wholehearted backing. He sent the Fourth Army commander every man and gun that could possibly be spared from the other British fronts. Fresh infantry divisions marched south to the Somme during the late summer. Among their number was 47th (London) Division to join III Corps. A Territorial division, its three infantry brigades comprised battalions of the London Regiment, whose titles echoed many of London's districts and institutions from where their ranks were largely recruited.

There were the lads of the 6th and 7th Londons, colloquially called the Cast-Iron Sixth and the Shiny Seventh respectively. In the same brigade (140th) were the Post Office Rifles (8th Londons) and the Prince of Wales' Own Civil Service Rifles (15th Londons). In the 141st Brigade were the Poplar and Stepney Rifles (17th Londons), London Irish (18th Londons), 19th Londons from St Pancras, and the 20th Londons from Blackheath and Woolwich. The division's third brigade (142nd) embraced the 1st Surrey Rifles (21st Londons), also the 23rd Londons from Clapham and the 24th Londons (The Queen's).

The battlefields of Festubert, Givinchy, Loos and Vimy Ridge had marked the battalions, but enough Territorials remained for the absorption of new drafts without losing the London character and spirit. Commanded by Major-General Charles Barter, all battalions were up to strength as the division arrived to relieve 1st Division at High Wood on 10th September:

> We walked into a new world of war. We passed through Albert for the first time, under the Virgin, holding out her Child, not to heaven but to the endless procession below. Fricourt, where the line had stood for so long, was now out of range of any but long-range guns, and we could see the freshly devastated country without being in the battle. All round the slopes were covered with transport of all kinds, and whole divisions of cavalry waiting for their opportunity. Further forward in Caterpillar Valley heavy howitzers stood in the open, lobbing their shells over at a target miles away. Up near the line by Flat Iron Copse and the Bazentins the ground was alive with field-guns, many of them hidden by the roadside and startling the unwary. All these things, later the commonplace of a successful 'push' were new. But we never saw anything quite like High Wood.

With the British front-line position running through its southern half to fall away by the huge crater, it was – as an officer observed at the time – 'a wood only in name – ragged stumps sticking out of churned-up earth, poisoned with fumes of high explosives, the whole a mass of corruption'. The country outside the wood was a featureless wilderness:

> Imagine Hampstead Heath made of cocoa-powder, and the natural surface folds further complicated by countless shell holes, each deep enough to hold a man, and everywhere meandering

crevices where men live below the surface of the ground, and you will get some idea of the terrain of the attack.

Thus ran a contemporary description and one with which carried the unanimous agreement of every infantryman under Barter's command. There was nothing to commend the perverted landscape, nothing at all. And they were going to attack over it.

The truculent Switch Line and the defences linking it with Martinpuich featured in the Fourth Army's first objective, while its second objective included a vital part of the enemy's third main defence line that lay in front of Flers, as well as a series of subsidiary defences between Flers and Martinpuich. As Pulteney's III Corps bordered the Fourth Army's left flank, its three infantry divisions were detailed to sweep on to the ridge where High Wood and Martinpuich stood, and cover the advance northwards of Horne's XV and Cavan's XIV Corps on the right. To expedite the advance, Haig belatedly instructed the Canadian Corps of Gough's Reserve Army to capture Courcelette the moment that Martinpuich fell.

Barter's 47th Division was on the right of III Corps and next to the New Zealand Division, which had moved into the Wood Lane positions secured by 55th Division. In command of 47th Division since September 1914, Barter was told to make a line clear of High Wood and then to attack the Starfish Line, about 500 yards north of the wood and the Switch Line. After capturing the Starfish Line, his troops were to join up with the New Zealanders and continue through the remaining German positions between Martinpuich and Flers. The 50th Division, on Barter's left, had orders to break through a section of the Switch Line called Hook Trench and help 15th Division take Martinpuich.

Eight tanks were allotted to III Corps, four of which were given to 47th Division to assist the clearing of High Wood, and two apiece to 50th and 15th Divisions for the assault on Martinpuich. Rawlinson had advised his corps commanders to regard the tanks as infantry 'accessories'. Because of their limited speed and because they were to be used in 'penny packets', he judged that the tanks' surprise value would be at the greatest when capturing the first line of objectives. All tank commanders and crews were inexperienced in battle, and Rawlinson also advised his corps commanders that tank representatives should be given a chance to reconnoitre the front.

Since the opposing lines in High Wood were too close to allow for an artillery bombardment on the wood, Pulteney hoped that the tanks would prove their worth there. On seeing the condition of the wood, however, tank officers formed the opinion that the jagged tree-stumps made it nigh impassable. Their doubts were expressed to Barter, who paid a personal visit to the High Wood front with the 141st Brigade commander, Brigadier-General R. McDouall. Faced by the wood all along his front, McDouall fully concurred with the tank officers' feelings.

Two of the division's three infantry brigades were to attack at zero hour on 15th September, but the other assaulting brigade, 140th under Brigadier-General Hampden, would only be sending two companies of the Civil Service Rifles up the east side of High Wood. His other battalion for the initial attack, 7th Battalion, was clear of it and would be attacking the Switch Line next to the New Zealanders.

Barter was not happy with Pulteney's plan of attack from the beginning, since he preferred to withdraw his front temporarily to give the artillery a free hand with the wood. Then, just prior to zero hour, he could send his quota of tanks up the sides of High Wood and pinch it out. He had made his views known, but the staff of III Corps were disinclined to change anything. This time he made his representation with more vigour, believing that his recommendations could aid the complicated and difficult operation that his division was required to do; complicated because the route of the advance lay in a north-easterly direction and yet involved a final twist due north; difficult because the operation's success depended on McDouall's 141st Brigade first taking High Wood. Should McDouall fail, Hampden's 140th Brigade, advancing on the right, would be exposed to flanking machine-gun fire from the wood's eastern edge.

Unfortunately for Barter, his immediate superiors again refused to listen. He had orders to put his tanks through High Wood, and through the wood they were to go.

No one could accuse the division's battalions of not being well-rehearsed for the coming battle. Before arriving at the front, they had practised daily over a taped course at a training ground near Franvillers. The training had been strenuous and the attack was practised with zero at every possible hour of the day and night. Trench mortar teams participated and so did the contact aircraft attached to the division. Only the tanks were missing, because their shrouded forms were still being transported to the Somme. On the whole, it was the widespread impression that the division had never been better prepared for battle.

Suitably attired for the morrow, battalions of the 141st and 140th Brigades moved into the assembly and front line trenches at High Wood and to the east of it, relieving 142nd Brigade as they did so. The relieved battalion withdrew to the support and reserve trenches to await the call should it come. Meanwhile, tanks trundled at snail-like pace to the front as dusk fell, their numbers steadily reducing through mechanical trouble or when a forgotten dugout caved in under their weight. Dawn would see 36 tanks on their markers for the whole of the Fourth Army front, but further mechanical trouble was ready to reduce this number to around 30 for the actual advance.

There was no darkness on the skyline. The exploding shells of the British barrage ensured it. High Wood was an oasis in a maelstrom for its defenders, and the troops of the London battalions in its proximity experienced a weird silence as they sat packed in the trenches. High Wood's reputation was universal along the Somme front, and the thought of attacking it in a few hours was enough to keep a man quietly awake. In a peculiar way, the arrival of dawn was welcomed. So too was the issue of rum that came with it.

The battalions detailed to advance through the wood were, from left to right, the London Irish, Poplar and Stepney Rifles and two companies of the Civil Service Rifles. Scheduled to attack the Switch Line in four waves on High Wood's eastern side were the Civil Service Rifles' other two companies, also the 7th Londons who extended the attacking front to the nearest New Zealand battalion on their right. On capturing the wood and their allotted section of the Switch Line, troops of the 19th and 20th Londons and the Post Office Rifles were to go straight through to the next objective (Starfish Line), followed by the 6th Londons to capture the final objective.

In preparation for the 19th and 20th Londons to take over their front line positions, officers and men of the London Irish and the Poplar and Stepney Rifles attempted to lie forward of the trenches. Morale was good and those of the London Irish were proud of their nationality, at least by adoption. It was said that McDouall had once asked the CO, Lt-Colonel Concanon, if it was true that most of the men in his battalion were Irish. 'Certainly, sir,' he replied, turning to his orderly room sergeant. 'Sergeant Levy, bring the roll.' Hurt by the brigadier-general's mirth, Concanon ruled that, in future, the NCO in question should be known as Sergeant Leary.

The anecdote was far from their minds as they waited in No Man's Land with the Poplar and Stepney Rifles. As for their CO, he had set up his HQ in the same nearby support trench as the officer commanding the Poplar and Stepney Rifles. Due to the crookedness of the assembly trenches, troops of the Civil Service Rifles' 'B', 'C' and 'D' Companies crept into No Man's Land to make a straight line with 'A' Company on the extreme right when the attack started. There was less than an hour to go to zero, but where were the tanks?

Briefed to leave their starting points along its south-western edge at staggered time intervals before zero, the tank commanders for the High Wood operation had three routes mapped out for them. Taking these routes through the wood – coded A, D and E – they were to arrive on the German front line trenches at one minute before zero. Three minutes was the waiting peiod in which to create havoc on this line, by which time the infantry should be with them. Afterwards they were to proceed up to the Switch Line in the northern part of the wood, reaching it at zero plus 32 minutes: 6.52 a.m. Pausing there for one minute, they were to drive from the wood via its north-eastern edge and assist the infantry in capturing the remaining defences, including the strongly-manned Flers Line that went between Eaucourt Abbey and Flers itself.

One 'male' and one 'female' tank from 'D' Company, under the commands of Lieutenants Robinson and Sharpe, were to take Route A, which began at High Wood's southern angle and ran up the inside of the south-eastern edge to brush the huge mine crater on its right. Another 'D' Company tank, 'female' and commanded by 2nd Lieutenant Sampson, who had christened his lozenge-shaped monster with the name of Delilah[2], was ordered to go through the wood just right of centre. This route (D) merged with Route E on leaving the north-eastern edge. Route E took a parallel course with the north-western side and was scheduled for a 'C' Company tank, commanded by 2nd Lieutenant Strother. His was the only 'C' Company tank with either III or XV Corps.

With strictly limited vision and deafened by the loudness of the centrally-mounted 105 horse-power petrol engine, the heat and fumes of which all but stifled the eight-man crew, each tank was extremely uncomfortable and most awkward to drive at the best of times. Attempting to navigate it over a barren landscape pitted with shell holes and riven with trenches was a feat of endurance. The upshot was that all four tanks temporarily lost their way and were

[2] All 'D' Company's tanks had nick-names beginning with the letter 'D'. They also had individual company numbers. Robinson's and Sharpe's tanks were D22 and D21, Sampson's was D13 and Strother's, being a 'C' Company tank, was C13 and had the name of Clan Ruthven.

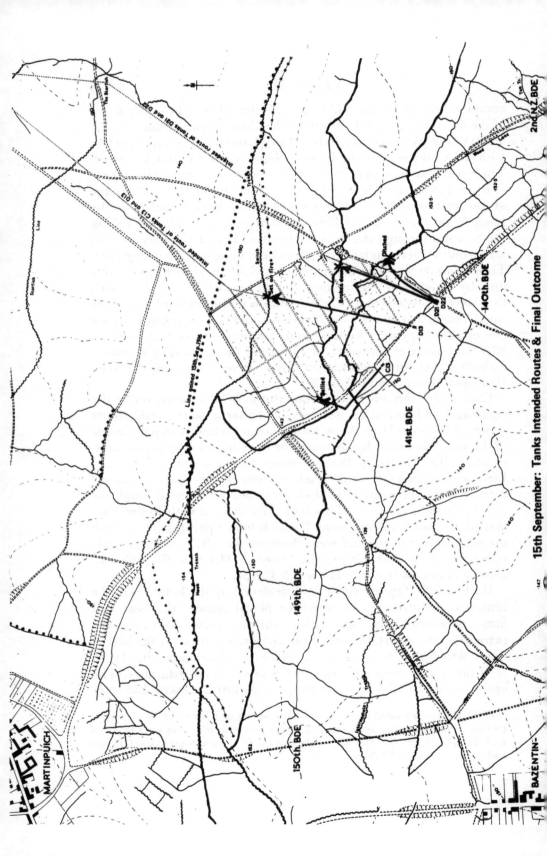

15th September: Tanks Intended Routes & Final Outcome

still disorientated when crawling through the British support lines literally minutes before zero hour. One tank – Robinson's – actually fired several shots from its 6-pdr guns before halting close to the Post Office Rifles' battalion headquarters. Thereupon, Robinson alighted to ask the way to the crater. On being told, he climbed back into his tank and drove off. Another tank, according to the Civil Service Rifles, nearly smashed up their headquarters. The tank stopped and its commander, going into the battalion headquarters, asked the CO, Lt-Colonel H.V. Warrender, where High Wood was. It could have been the same incident, but viewed from a different angle. Whatever it was, Warrender's exasperated reply went unrecorded.

He had good reason to be angry, because three of his companies in the growing light, together with the Poplar and Stepney Rifles and the London Irish, were being swept by machine-gun and rifle fire where they lay outside the trenches – and zero hour had yet to come. To compound everybody's plight, German artillery opened up on the assembly trenches. The tanks lumbered up to their starting positions virtually on the stroke of 6.20 a.m., and were promptly left behind as the first wave of infantry tried to advance.

They walked straight into the murderous fire from the untouched German front line trenches. In platoon formation, wave after wave of Londoners tried desperately to bridge the narrow strip of earth between them and the enemy in High Wood. The attack was soon held up and, although 'A' Company made some headway on the extreme right, the other three companies of the Civil Service Rifles lost four-fifths of their number and all three company commanders became casualties before everyone went to ground. Captain Leslie Davies of 'B' Company was killed within seconds of the assault taking place; Captain Arthur Roberts of 'D' Company lived long enough to crawl with some of his men to within 20 yards of the enemy. He rose up to give the charge and was instantly shot dead. The officer leading 'C' Company, Captain Geoffrey Gaze, was wounded and yet refused to throw in the towel. Gaze, in fact, was the only officer in these three companies to remain at duty.

Most of the NCO's were hit, including Corporal M.J. Guiton in Gaze's 'C' Company who lost a leg. The incidents and sights at High Wood were still with him two years after the Armistice, when he wrote:

That day I saw sights which were passing strange to a man of peace. I saw men in their madness bayonet each other without mercy, without thought. . . I saw men torn to fragments by the near explosion of bombs, and – worse than any sight – I heard the agonised cries and shrieks of men in mortal pain who were giving up their souls to their Maker.

The mental picture painted through the medium of the eye may fade, but the cries of those poor, tortured and torn men I can never forget. They are with me always.

All the survivors of the battalions attacking High Wood could do was to scramble back into their trenches and reform for another effort. The 19th and 20th Londoners had previously moved up, expecting to find the assembly trenches vacated for them. They were obliged to shift into the support line that was already crowded with HQ staff of their sister battalions.

To the east of High Wood, having attacked in four waves at zero hour over a 400 yard front, troops of the 7th Londons topped the ridge and took the Switch Line. Admittedly they experienced machine-gun fire from the wood, but they had been covered by a terrific artillery barrage which crashed down on the German positions ahead of them. The barrage moved on at 50 yards a minute during their advance, and the vast majority of the 7th Londons' casualties occurred in the two companies nearest to the wood. Lance-Corporal W. Robertson was advancing in that area as a member of a bombing party:

My position with the bombers was on the left of the battalion. We went over in the second wave and skirted the edge of High Wood. Lt R.E. Taylor MC was in charge of the first wave and he, together with Sgt G. Steele DCM, went after an enemy machine-gun post which they silenced, but were both wounded in the effort.

The ground we attacked over was just fine powder; shells did not so much as make shell holes but merely moved them. Of the German trenches, there was no trace.

By this time the four tanks had long since gone forward into High Wood and, as Barter and McDouall had feared, had come to grief.

Robinson's tank started out on the right course, but the tree stumps proved too much for it. The tank careered off-course, turned due east and came out of the south-eastern side to ditch in a British front-line trench, known as Worcester Trench, after firing on some unfortunate Londoners who happened to be near it. A heated altercation between an infuriated company commander and Robinson immediately broke out. For Robinson, it was truly an ignominious ending; he and his crew stayed with the tank for 14 hours – digging it out under shell fire, during which time one of his crew was wounded.

Sharpe's tank went forward, but broke the axle of its two-wheel steering 'tail' when trying to manoeuvre through the mass of shell holes and tree stumps. Just ten minutes in action, it finished about 50 yards west of the crater. Repeatedly shelled but not hit, Sharpe and his crew used the stationary tank's guns to good effect. Sampson in his Delilah and following Route D, actually crossed the enemy's front and was enfilading the support trench in the middle of the wood when a shell struck the tank, setting it on fire. The crew, three of them wounded, bailed out into the hostile trench and captured some fifteen Germans.[3] It was later reported that one of Sampson's wounded crewmen was shot in the leg before the tank was shelled. Apparently a German infantryman had crept up to the tank as it was moving, opened a loop hole and fired into the vehicle.

The fourth tank, Strother's, entered High Wood along Route E where it met with a stubborn tree stump which pressed up its belly. The tank was ditched about 50 yards inside the south-western face, a shell destroying it around mid-day on 21st September.

To the left of High Wood, along 50th Division's front, infantrymen entered Hook Trench – their first objective – at 7 a.m. Try as they might, the next wave could not get to the next objective in the Starfish Line on account of hostile machine-gun fire from the wood's north-western edge. At one stage, groups of Germans started counter-attacking from the wood. Confusion broke out as 50th Division troops found themselves threatened on their right flank. Attempting to neutralise the threat, a battalion of the Northumberland Fusiliers sent bombing parties to its north-western edge. They contained the threat as other Northumberland Fusiliers set about providing a defensive flank, such was the potency of High Wood – a fact not lost on the 19th and 20th Londoners, and the Post Office Rifles, when they were thrown into the mêlée.

Pulteney anticipated the clearance of High Wood by 7 a.m. If it had happened, then these battalions were scheduled to swan through the wood and east of it and take their objective in the

[3] PRO: W095/674

Starfish Line, being a trench called Flag Lane. The ineffectual tank advance in place of a barrage, not least the defenders' courage, had pulped the time-table beyond recognition. Assembly trenches on the High Wood front were so congested with the dead, wounded and unwounded soldiers of the first abortive attack, that the press of men for the second attack made them almost untenable.

Lt-Colonel Hamilton of the 19th Londons, worried about his battalion not being in position in time for their assault, clambered from a back trench and called to the men nearest to him to follow him. All who did, including Hamilton, were cut down within seconds of being exposed to machine-gun fire.

The attacking path of the Post Office Rifles lay half in and half out of the wood, more or less in the footsteps of the hapless Civil Service Rifles. Battalion officers were in broad agreement that, at no time in the war, had their men been better trained or more closely knit by mutual trust or understanding than those waiting to go over the top on Friday, 15th September. Their CO, Major W.J. Whitehead, had personally devoted numerous hours in cutting and pasting a cardboard relief of the site of their proposed attack. He had a deep pride and confidence in his battalion and wanted the attack to go right. His second-in-command, Major W.B. Vince, echoed his feelings. Vince's allotted place for this attack was as a reserve officer in the transport lines, but he had come up on his own accord to see how well the battalion would do.

Both officers had picked up scanty and conflicting accounts on how the Civil Service Rifles had fared, one of which informed them that they had reached the Switch Line. The right-hand company of the Civil Service Rifles had indeed arrived there in reduced condition, but the remnants of the other three companies were either back in the trenches or pinned down in No Man's Land. On that note the Post Office Rifles' personnel, who were about to attack, made last-minute adjustments to their equipment. Placed in charge of a section of rifle bombers, Lance-Corporal James McIntyre animatedly discussed with a colleague whether it would be good policy to wear their entrenching tools at the front as a protection against wounds. Finally, being fatalists, they decided to leave them on their backs. Further along the trench to the right, Rifleman Don Cree of 'C' Company had earlier seen the tanks sluggishly coming up, but knew nothing of how they were faring. Yet the very thought of what they might do to the enemy had boosted his morale, as he and his mates waited for the 'off'. Suddenly the whistles blew and Cree's crowd went over the top with yells of bravado:

> The yells were soon death-screams, as man after man went down before that awful machine-gun fire of the enemy. Within 50 yards of the trench we left, there was but a bare handful left of half a company. I looked behind, to see the second half of the company come on, led by the company officer, who I remember as he neared us shouted, 'Get on damn you!' Just then he fell dead.
>
> Our platoon officer led us on. He had a walking stick in one hand, a revolver in the other, and his face fixed in a set smile. A big fine-looking man he was. Men were falling on all sides, some in death agony and, between the groans and cries of men and the eternal awful fumes of cordite, that hundred yards to Fritz's lines is the most fearful memory of France I have.
>
> In the group near at hand, I recollect the officer's runner stop with a terrible scream. He crumpled and fell behind a tree stump. The platoon sergeant next collapsed and began crawling back to our lines. A lance-corporal who, as we reached the trench, laughed and coldly walked away with blood spurting from his trouser leg.
>
> Germans were lying all over and at the back of the trench. A group of six or seven had been hit together by a shell. They were the bloodiest and most battered human beings I had until then seen. Some of the less severely wounded put up their hands, while their comrades in the trenches behind kept up machine-gun and rifle fire amongst friend and foe alike.
>
> When I got clear of the trench I could only see the officer with about half-a-dozen men. He waved me over, but a shell landed beside him before I could move and practically smothered him with earth. All I could see was his helmet, which had been covered with a piece of sacking to stop it glinting in the sunlight. But there was damned little sunlight that morning at that time.

McIntyre had a slightly easier passage at first:

> We came across many of our own wounded, but were under orders not to stop for anyone. There were many unburied dead too, and I noticed that some of the corpses had 'turned' black. So far, my section was still intact.
>
> On we pushed and suddenly we saw a near-straight trench full of men from another battalion, and a machine-gun blazing down

it. Their officer was by the trench, exhorting his men to climb out. I dropped on one knee and fired my rifle grenade at the machine-gun. My aim proved good. The grenade burst at the point from where the machine-gun was spluttering. The firing ceased, but I fired another grenade for good measure.

The officer took my name. I did not recognise him, but from his black buttons I judged him to be from another rifle regiment. Either he or I was off-course. I never heard any more of the incident.

Completely unaware, McIntyre's section had caught up with an isolated party of the Civil Service Rifles and was on-course.

Rifleman 'Porkie' Knight was with the Post Office Rifles' 'A' Company, which had been badly hit by heavy machine-gun fire on leaving the British front line positions. He saw his company commander and two lieutenants go down, as well as two of the company's sergeants. As the survivors scattered, Knight ran towards some smashed trees and took cover. The machine-gun fire never slackened and, after what seemed ages to him, he glanced over his shoulder and noticed an officer approaching him whom he recognised as Captain Webb from a different company:

Captain Webb appeared alone with a revolver in his hand. This was about 9 o'clock. He said, 'Up Knight and at them.' We rushed the machine-gun post. He was killed and I was slightly wounded in my right thigh. A small lull followed and I saw Rfn G.P. Merlin and CSM Carty crawling away, both wounded. I proceeded at the high point and came across a dead German by his machine-gun.

Webb's death took the toll of company commanders killed in the Post Office Rifles' attacking force to three – all excellent officers whose talented leadership was more than ever needed at that moment.

The 6th Londons were due to attack on a 500 yard frontage in four waves at 8.20 a.m. Platoon commanders were to accompany the first, second and fourth waves, and company commanders with company sergeant-majors would go with the third. Advancing on High Wood's right, they were expected to pass through the Switch and Starfish Lines and take a Flers Line trench, north-east of a knot of trenches named the Cough Drop. Unless the reserves were called forward, because of the emergency, their battalion would be the last

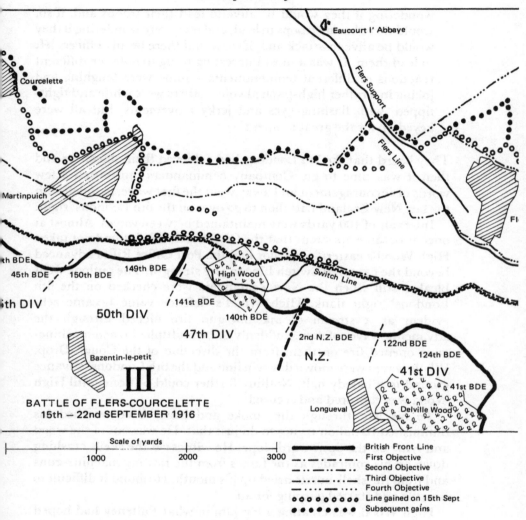

Courcelette

Eaucourt l' Abbaye

Flers Support

Flers Line

Martinpuich

45th BDE   150th BDE   149th BDE

High Wood

Switch Line

th DIV

th BDE

5th DIV   **50th DIV**   141st BDE

140th BDE

47th DIV

2nd N.Z. BDE

122nd BDE

124th BDE

Bazentin-le-petit

N.Z.

41st DIV

41st BDE

III

Longueval

Delville Wood

BATTLE OF FLERS-COURCELETTE
15th — 22nd SEPTEMBER 1916

Scale of yards

1000   2000   3000

British Front Line
First Objective
Second Objective
Third Objective
Fourth Objective
Line gained on 15th Sept
Subsequent gains

to attack in 47th Division. They had seen the other battalions
advance, and they had watched the walking wounded drift back,
mingling with dazed and frightened prisoners. A 6th Londons'
officer in the assembly trenches expressed everyone's feelings:

> We had to wait an hour before 'going over', and the enemy's
> retaliatory barrage was hitting the trenches with unpleasant
> frequency. It was a most unnerving experience; officers were

wondering if they would be alive to lead their troops and, if so, would there be any troops to lead, and men were wondering if they would be alive to attack and, if so, would there be any officers left to lead them. It was a most interesting thing to note the different reactions of different temperaments – some were laughing and joking in a rather high-pitched voice, others were white and tight-lipped, with flashing eyes and jerky movements, but all were keyed up for the great moment.

They heard that the 7th Londons had achieved their objectives and then it was time to go. Company commanders murmured a few words of encouragement and away went the first wave, in touch with the last New Zealand battalion to go over on the 6th Londons' right.

Intervals of 100 yards were maintained between waves. Almost at once it became apparent that the Civil Service Rifles had not taken High Wood's eastern edge, nor had the Post Office Rifles advanced beyond the captured Switch Line in any strength. The outlook went bleaker still when the New Zealanders were checked on the 6th Londons' right flank. High Wood's defence value became self-evident as a stream of machine-gun fire flicked through the advancing waves of men, suddenly to be multiplied when machine-guns opened fire on them from the direction of the Cough Drop. Whole waves were mown down in line and the 6th Londons' advance ground to a bloody halt. Nothing further could be done until High Wood was captured and secured.

To his left, through the smoke and haze, Cree watched his diminished battalion trying to do just that. He was out of the wood and lying on the downward slope. He witnessed the shells crashing down on his comrades as the fumes from the rattling machine-guns and from the shell-bursts dried up his mouth. He found it difficult to breathe and started gasping for air.

High Wood was creating a log-jam in what Pulteney had hoped would be a smooth-running operation for his corps. He had, after all, heard that tanks had assisted greatly in entering Martinpuich that very morning, and one of the four tanks had broken down before the attack. Due to 47th Division's failure to clear High Wood on schedule with four tanks, 50th Division's right flank was getting hung-up and not achieving its objectives to the operational time-table. Similar difficulties were being encountered by the New Zealanders on 47th Division's right. Pulteney was determined that someone's head should fall for the foul-up, but in the meantime he had no choice but to seek Fourth Army's approval to make the Starfish Line as the main position for consolidation. Fourth Army gave its approval and III Corps headquarters issued the message at 10.30 a.m.

To a neutral observer, there was no question that Barter's division was not doing its utmost to capture the wood. Mid-morning found no less than five battalions simultaneously engaged in trying to take it, but the defenders met them with bombs and rifle fire from their trenches, while machine-guns – some ensconced in undamaged concrete emplacements – scythed the attackers down in volume. With the tanks out of action, McDouall let it be known at divisional headquarters that the wood's western and north-western areas should be subjected to an artillery bombardment. Barter complied with the 141st Brigade commander's wishes.

About the same time, in order to quell resistance in the eastern part of the wood, Hampden's 140th Brigade headquarters gave the word for its trench mortar battery to come into play. The battery, commanded by Captain G.L. Goodes, had eight 3-inch Stokes mortars situated close to the front line. His men had previously stock-piled 125 rounds next to each mortar during the night, as well as bedding the mortars in. Goodes was anxious to give the attacking infantry some support at zero hour, but surprising the enemy with the tanks was the keynote and, like the artillery, he was told to keep his mortars silent. When his men finished their work at two in the morning, he sent them to rest and to shelter in nearby dugouts. One TMB member, Jack Richbell, was not over-impressed: 'Ours had been hit and knocked in by a shell, and was only held up in places by very thick tree trunks about three feet from the ground. The Germans were shelling us pretty heavily.'

Out of the blue, Goodes ordered them to man the mortars and bombard the eastern part of the wood. They responded magnificently, firing more than 750 rounds in 15 minutes – a feat afterwards described as the most brilliant piece of work in the history of trench mortars. A Post Office Rifleman, as interested in the outcome as any Civil Service Rifleman, later commented that he observed eight or ten of the cylinder-shaped shells going through the air like a row of single sausages. The remnants of two Civil Service Rifles' companies re-attacked, one of which was led by the already wounded Captain Gaze. Soon afterwards, Germans started coming into the British lines with their hands above their heads. Gaze was not to see the outcome. He was killed before his troops reached their objective.

The shelling of the opposite side of the wood showed its result when bombing parties worked around the enemy's flanks on completion of the bombardment. Tired prisoners, mostly from the *23rd Bavarian Regiment*, staggered in with and without escorts. After two months and one day of bitter fighting, enemy resistance at High Wood was at last collapsing. By 1 p.m., its collapse was complete, but the residual effect of the wood's belated capture continued to be felt for the rest of the day.

Out there, some 700 yards beyond High Wood, was the Starfish Line. A few groups from once-proud battalions had reached it over to the right and, indeed, had broken through it. A small detachment of the 6th Londons, for instance, heroically broke through it as High Wood was captured and managed to take the Cough Drop. Of the small band who assaulted the strongpoint, an even smaller band pushed on to the Flers Line where it suffered 100% casualties. The 6th Londons' whole complement at the Cough Drop numbered just two officers and 38 other ranks – all that was left alive and unwounded of the battalion's original attacking force.

Cree nearly reached the Starfish Line after watching Goodes' mortar battery's performance from outside the wood's north-eastern edge. Thinking that there was no one alive around him, he spied a group of khaki-clad figures through the smoke and heat-haze on his right. He doubled across to join them. The group consisted of an officer, a sergeant and about a dozen men. Cree went forward with them to the Starfish Line, but they came under fire before they had gone 60 yards. The officer ordered them to retire 50 yards back and to dig in.

We started to run the gauntlet two at a time. The officer and myself were last. Just as we made our dash, one of the two in front was hit and dropped. We got to him and pulled him into a shell hole. He was hit through the shoulder and was moaning. 'Don't leave me,' he pleaded.

That officer was a brick. He got hold of the chap and ran with him to where the others were digging in. I was left with two rifles to make the last dash. I got there, but it was awful expecting to get one in the back all the time. As I dropped beside the others, I remember thinking that I was lucky not to be killed with my back to the enemy. That seems weird when I think of it now, because it would have made little difference how I was facing if I had been killed.

German artillery batteries were hard at work, shelling the captured ground and placing barrages on all approaches to the new forward positions, but the attack was going ahead on both sides of 47th Division's flanks. The enemy, however, still held a long section of the Starfish Line opposite High Wood and which endangered the progress of the 50th and the New Zealanders. The 47th Division had to take it, but the two brigades in the front line were in no fit state to do it. McDouall's 141st Brigade was a case in point. The Poplar and Stepney Rifles had lost 332 killed, wounded and missing; the London Irish casualties were 223, and the 19th and 20th Londons had lost 361 and 263 all ranks respectively. Because of these casualties, there was such disorganisation that a composite battalion was temporarily formed under the command of the Poplar and Stepney Rifles' CO, Lt-Colonel Norman.

As the capture of the Starfish Line was considered essential, two battalions belonging to Brigadier-General F.G. Lewis's 142nd Brigade, in reserve, received orders at 3.30 p.m. to carry out the attack. The battalions, 1st Surrey Rifles and the 24th Londons, went forward an hour later to High Wood from their reserve positions near Bazentin-le-Petit mill. The 1st Surrey Rifles and one company of the 24th Londons had orders to make their attack on the east side of the wood, leaving the remaining 24th Londons' companies to attack from High Wood's north-western face. There was no opportunity for any reconnaissance work, nor could they expect any meaningful artillery cover. The time factor also eliminated any chance of a simultaneous assault, since the 24th Londons had to negotiate the wood before attacking. The final coffin nail was the weather. The heat-haze had dissipated during the afternoon and the autumn sun showed everything with clarity.

As the 24th Londons trekked through the human detritus in the wood, so the 1st Surrey Rifles and the attached company of the 24th Londons rapidly shook out in platoon formation. The movement took place on the shallow incline just below the crest made infamous from earlier days, except this time the objective did not lie a short distance from its top, but way ahead and without the element of surprise.

A total of 569 officers and men of the 1st Surrey Rifles were present for the attack that afternoon, the 19-year-old Lance-Corporal Harold Silvester was one of them. A veteran of Vimy Ridge, he had taken the precaution of attaching wire cutters to his rifle barrel. Like the majority of the men, he had positioned his trenching spade with the blade upwards between his pack and his shoulder blades. The lack of artillery support made him feel uneasy and, if given a choice, he would have opted for an attack at dusk – not in brilliant sunshine.

They advanced at about 5.30 p.m. On topping the crest, they came into full view of the enemy and seconds later were on the receiving end of a veritable tornado of shells. Their immaculate dressing was seen by Major Lord Gorell of the 19th London Battery, who was in a forward observation post. As the first salvo of shells landed, he telephoned back the message: 'The 1st Surreys have gone over just if they were on parade.'

There were other eyewitnesses to the battalion's splendid resolution – Cree and his tiny party in No Man's Land. They were beginning to feel somewhat lost as they could find no one to link up with.

All of a sudden the German batteries opened up, and all the ground on the slope we were on was churned up with hissing metal. We were amazed to see coming over the ridge a battalion in platoon formation. As they neared us, they extended first into little bunches of sections and then into something like lines. They nearly all had their rifles slung over their right shoulders. Shells dropped among them and they must have lost hundreds by the time they reached our position. As they passed, one said: 'Cheer up, boys, we'll see you right.' Another beside him had a pipe in his mouth and a bag of bombs or rations on his back. Mostly the faces were set and white, but not a falter as they went to the hell in front.

German machine-guns fuelled the carnage. One bullet struck Silvester low in the leg. He toppled into a shell hole already crammed close to capacity with wounded men. Silvester pressed his face to the earth near the rim of the crater, as bullets screamed off the blade of his spade.

Statistically, it should not have been possible, but a few of the 1st Surreys actually succeeded in entering the Starfish Line to capture a strongpoint. That in itself was a remarkable achievement, because of the hideous losses suffered in the advance. Two officers and 60 other ranks remained unwounded from the 17 officers and 550 men who attacked. The number of killed and missing went well into treble figures. The 24th Londons, attacking from High Wood, met with similar opposition and were forced to dig in 200 yards from the captured Switch Line. The afternoon's operation had, in all respects, proved to be an ill-fated and costly venture.

Cree, who had watched the 1st Surreys' advance with unbounded admiration and incomprehension, saw the aftermath from his position in No Man's Land:

> Some returned late that night, and went right back as our officer would not take responsibility for them – a mere handful, a few whimpering, a few crying like babies. Poor devils, they had it rough.
>
> Our officer decided that we must find our own battalion. We set out with only a very faint idea of where their objective was. We scrambled over trenches and shell holes, dead and wounded, barbed wire and dugouts. After carefully watching for hidden posts, we found a strongpoint with a number of trenches around it. There we found the remains of the battalion. I remember seeing our CSM who I had not seen since leaving our own trenches. He was dead and lying behind the trench that we were in. A fatherly man who was respected by all ranks.

The 47th Division was relieved by Strickland's 1st Division on Tuesday, 19th September. Its battalions, previously fit and strong and full of confidence, came out exhausted and desolated. Divisional losses exceeded 4,500 officers and men. For Pulteney, it was the last straw. Someone must be answerable. Protesting his innocence, Major-General Barter was dismissed for 'wanton waste of men'. He returned to England under a cloud, determined to vindicate himself.

The roll calls when the battalions came out of the line were heart-rending to say the least. Rifleman Cree, having noted the wastage of his battalion, summed up the whole nightmare:

> We were a pitiful sight when we got back to safety and marshalled together. Our company was about two dozen strong, had no officers and only one sergeant.
>
> I will never forget High Wood.

His sentiments were shared by all who had endured its horrors and emerged alive.

CHAPTER TEN

The Twilight Years

In his dispatch from the field of Waterloo, Wellington wrote: 'Nothing except a battle lost can be half so melancholy as a battle won.' High Wood was a stark example, because the price paid in human misery for its capture was terrible. Corpses lay everywhere, especially by the hotly contested mine crater where the Civil Service Rifles experienced their heaviest losses. The burial of the dead began after dark on the 15th, but the bodies gathered in that night were generally of soldiers within convenient reach. Priority, after all, had to be given to the wounded who were scattered in the wood, on either side of it and beyond to the Starfish Line itself. The limited gains had to be consolidated too, in readiness for counter-attacks. Yet special parties were detailed for the sombre work and graves were dug in High Wood. The dead company commanders of the Civil Service Rifles, Captains Gaze, Davies and Roberts, were buried together. The CO, Lt-Colonel Warrender, in a letter of sympathy, informed Roberts' father that 'the grave has been properly marked and the position notified to the Graves Registration Committee.' Sadly, over two years of war lay ahead and the ground had not seen the last of battle, nor had it that night, as an officer, who was there, graphically described in later years:

The night of the 15th September presented a very striking contrast to the previous night, when peace and quiet had reigned in High Wood. The heavy artillery, with which the enemy was so well supplied, pounded away continually at the new trenches and at the supporting field gun batteries on the edge of the wood. Amid the noise of the shells could often be heard the groans of the wounded who had not yet been brought in, the shouts of the search party of stretcher-bearers, and the curses of a ration or carrying party who had got lost. But above all was the ceaseless wail of the field guns, echoing over the wilderness. Listening to them on that night one could almost imagine that they too, were mourning for the gallant fellows who had lost their lives that day, and who were now being laid to rest. To many who were there the peculiar echo of the field gun ever afterwards brought back vivid memories of those terrible nights in High Wood.

More bodies were buried on 18th and 21st September. On one of these dates 47 officers and men from the various London battalions found a final resting place in a large shell hole, roughly opposite the midway point of the wood's south-western face and a few feet on the other side of the Martinpuich-Longueval road. Other graves were added later. A padre who officiated at some of these burials was the Rev David Railton, chaplain attached to 141st Brigade. The Union Jack which he used at the funerals of many men of 47th Division in the field was also used on Armistice Day, 1920, at the funeral of the Unknown Warrior. The very same flag was solemnly dedicated the following year and placed above the grave of the Unknown Warrior in Westminster Abbey.

Representatives of 47th Division were chosen to place it in position at the dedication ceremony; a great honour, but how many of them were aware that the division's brave performance at High Wood, which culminated in its capture, was looked upon with jaundiced eyes by higher authority? 'Lack of push' was the description and even Haig believed it. On 2nd October 1916 he commented in writing:

The 47th Divn failed at High Wood on 15th September and the GOC was sent home! Barter by name. Now Gorriage [*sic*] has taken over Command. He arrived on Sunday, so has not had time to make his personality felt. I told him to teach the Divn 'Discipline and Digging'.

Pulteney had done his job well, but Barter had no intention of letting the matter rest. Refused an official investigation, an unofficial inquiry subsequently revealed the true facts, entirely exonerating him from responsibility for the division's huge casualty rate at High Wood. On being cleared, he was knighted by King George V and sent on an important military mission to Petrograd. The nature of his dismissal still rankled with him, even in his retirement after the war. Speaking at a dinner in honour of the 47th Division in 1919, he had this to say about the affair:

I was charged with wanton waste of the men entrusted to my command at the battle of the Somme. I repudiate that charge with indignation. The measures taken which led to this loss were either in opposition to my representations, or I was not responsible for them.

I was dismissed at an hour's notice with disgrace from my division. I was dismissed at an hour of the most brilliant achievement of the division – the capture of High Wood, which several other divisions had made futile attempts to take.

I think it is unexampled in military history that a military commander should be disgraced in the hour of the success of the troops under his command without any attempt at investigation. . .

His quest for an official inquiry, whereby the facts of the matter could be made public, eluded him all his life. A bachelor, he died in Madrid on 22nd March 1931.

Fortunately for the troops' morale at the time of his dismissal, only the new divisional commander, his closest colleagues, and those above him knew of the slur on the division's reputation. Rifleman Bill Harfleet of the Post Office Rifles certainly did not:

Pride, discipline and some sort of faith and 'stick it out' feeling kept me going. Certainly not the almost daily recital in battalion orders during our march to the Somme battles, solemnly read out and searing my memory with disgust: 'At a Field General Court Marshal on the blank of July, Private Blank of the Blank Regiment was found guilty of (desertion or cowardice) in the face of the enemy and sentenced to be shot at dawn. The sentence was duly carried out.'

I knew of only one deserter, poor lad, after High Wood. He kept moaning 'All mothers' sons' before he disappeared for three or four days. He was back with us just before the Le Sars battle and under arrest, but went into action and was badly wounded. I forget his name and always hope that his 'crime' was not recorded.

Bodies were still exposed to the elements on 47th Division's return to the front in September 1916. A London Irish officer, Captain R.G. Appleby, went to rejoin his unit after a brief spell in hospital. He travelled to the front line via High Wood, where he noticed some canvas screens erected not far from the road. 'We – the infantry – were told that the screens hid tanks. Water-filled shell holes, many containing dead bodies, were to be seen all over the area.'

The Somme campaign continued for another two months, during which time the ridge between High Wood and Delville Wood became packed with artillery batteries. From High Wood itself, two German 10.5-cm field howitzers, captured on 15th September, were removed in October. The tanks were recovered, but the broken hulk of Strother's tank, Clan Ruthven, continued to rust 50 yards inside the wood's south-western edge. German shells still pitched into the wood and one of their aircraft, on 20th October, was shot out of the sky to crash into it. During this period, artillery officers observed from the wood, signal wires were draped across and a bogie track was laid past it.

As the fighting died down on the Somme, so the task of clearing its battlefields commenced. Both British and German arms and equipment were salvaged wherever possible and, whenever possible, burial parties consigned the dead to graves. Yet as late as June 1917 soldiers returning to England wounded or on leave were complaining bitterly about the number of bodies left unburied on the Somme.

In memory to those who fell at High Wood, a number of wooden crosses were erected there. The 47th Division put up one in December of 1916. Then came the turn of the 33rd Division when its battalions were in the area in January 1917. The 20th Royal Fusiliers found themselves located near the wood. It was considered a favourable opportunity to erect some form of memorial to those members of the battalion who were killed there. Suitable materials were scarce, but timber was obtained from some sympathetic Royal Engineers and a rough cross was made. Six men from the battalion erected it among the shell holes and shattered tree stumps. Similar wooden memorials were erected about that time by four other battalions and by the 1st and 51st Divisions.

When the Germans withdrew to the Hindenburg Line in early 1917, High Wood and other centres of conflict rediscovered the meaning of tranquillity – a tranquillity shattered by the German March offensive of 1918. Again the wood was fought over and, again, battalions of 47th Division eerily found themselves amongst its brambled waste of decaying trenchworks, rusty wire entanglements, tree stumps and weed-infested shell holes – 'An ironic joke of Fate, surely, to send us back through High Wood.' The troops did not tarry long, as the division was in very real danger of being outflanked. As they retired, they passed by the division's memorial cross of 1916.

Fate once more played a cynical hand when the tide of battle flowed back, but this time it was the turn of 33rd Division. The date was late August and pressure on the flanks forced the enemy to abandon his line in front of the division. Its infantry immediately advanced and took up a line from north-east of High Wood to Longueval. On 28th August, curiosity compelled two 2nd RWF subalterns from 19th Brigade to visit the wood:

> We found the graves of several men of ours who had fallen there in 1916, and recalled the tales we had heard from survivors of that sanguinary period. We met the Brigadier who had gone there with the same object as we, for he had fought over it in those days.

Soldier poet Philip Johnstone also visited the wood, but earlier in the year and before the German offensive. The sights he saw motivated him to write a satirical poem called 'High Wood'; satirical, because he had a vision of tourists flocking to the battlefields after the war. His poem, first published on 16th February 1918 in *The Nation*, was a portentous protest against any attendant commercialism.

The memorial crosses at High Wood were largely untouched by the 1918 fighting, but the changing seasons did their best to camouflage the marked graves. More often than not, nature succeeded in doing it. An American relation of Captain Roberts was serving with the US Army in Paris after the Armistice. He travelled to High Wood in the summer of 1919, but was unable to locate Roberts' grave.

High Wood was never cleared when the Somme battlefields were methodically combed by military exhumation parties after the Armistice. The thickness of its young and thrusting undergrowth, coupled with the large quantities of live ammunition within its perimeters, made the wood too impenetrable for anything beyond a cursory search. It is said that the wood is the final resting place of over 8,000 British and German dead. The only dispute about this figure is that it is possibly on the conservative side.

With High Wood reluctantly left as a grim relic, the clearing of the surrounding countryside continued unabated. The Imperial War Graves Commission had expected to complete the exhumations by March 1920, but the work went on until November 1921, by which date some areas had been searched up to twenty times. Smaller battlefield cemeteries were also exhumed so that their dead could be brought together in officially designated cemeteries. The tiny battlefield cemetery at High Wood, which encompasses the 47 officers and men buried in the large shell hole, was preserved and called the London Cemetery. This cemetery holds 101 bodies, mostly from the 15th September attack and not all with headstones. A larger cemetery – London Cemetery Extension – backs up to it.

London Cemetery Extension gradually became filled with the dead until its burials numbered 1,606. The bodies of Captains Gaze and Davies, but not of Arthur Roberts, were eventually found to the west of High Wood in 1920. London Cemetery Extension was full and the two officers were reinterred in Caterpillar Valley Cemetery. Containing 5,511 graves, two-thirds of them unnamed, this cemetery is positioned on a ridge from which High Wood is clearly visible.

The land in 1920 was useless for agriculture, but the returning population persevered. One man who returned was a French war hero, Gaston Mathon, whose land included High Wood. The sight which greeted him was disheartening to say the least, but he and his wife set to work with a will. As he tilled the field to the west of the wood in 1925, where Gaze and Davies were found five years before, he came across the remains of five soldiers. They were subsequently identified as belonging to the Civil Service Rifles and one was Captain Arthur Roberts. All five were reburied at Cerisy-Gailly French National Cemetery as Caterpillar Valley had also been closed to further burials.

In the 1920's thought was seriously given to replacing the wooden crosses at High Wood with memorials of a more permanent nature. The wood itself was threatening to obscure the crosses with its annual growth, and there were no sources of income with which to pay for their upkeep. There was a flurry of fund-raising activities in Great Britain and the first of the permanent memorials was unveiled at High Wood on Sunday, 13th July 1924. The memorial, a granite slab that commemorated the attacks of the Cameron Highlanders and the Black Watch on 3rd September 1916, replaced two crosses which were erected in December of that year. The ceremony was performed by Lt-General Strickland, who commanded the 1st Division at the time of the battle. The 51st Division's wooden cross was transferred to the preserved battlefield at Beaumont Hamel, which the division took in splendid style during November 1916. The cross was positioned in front of the division's Highland Memorial which looks across to the village of Beaumont Hamel.

Having decided to bring home 47th Division's wooden cross at High Wood, also another cross from Eaucourt l'Abbaye, and set them up at the Duke of York's Chelsea barracks, committee members of 47th Division commissioned the building of a monument that would show against the very long line of woodland on High Wood's south-western side. The memorial was the centre of dedication on 13th September 1925. In bright sunshine, representatives and colour parties of units which served with the division during the war were in attendance. Present also was the division's DAA and QMG, Major C.R. Congreve, whose cousin, Billy Congreve VC DSO MC, was shot and killed a few hundred yards from where the dedication ceremony took place. At the ceremony, buglers of the 1st Surrey Rifles were chosen to sound the 'Last Post' and 'Reveille', a minute of silence being observed between the two calls. The day ended with the unveiling of a school playground at Martinpuich, which the division had built for the village.

The 20th Royal Fusiliers' cross also found a home in England. It was taken to Hounslow Barracks after its arrival in 1926, where it finally succumbed to woodworm and was destroyed in 1955 with much sadness. The cross held a special meaning for the few veterans left who fought at High Wood, because the cross had become more than a memorial. It was a symbol of their pride and of the battalion's reputation. A reputation that was nearly shattered in 1929. In the autumn of that year a war book burst on the literary scene and immediately became a runaway best-seller. The book was *Goodbye to All That* and its author was Robert Graves.

Its sensational revelations upset his family, his old school (Charterhouse), counties, regions, continents (Australia), but most of all the 1st Cameronians and ex-members of the disbanded 5/6th Scottish Rifles and the 20th Royal Fusiliers. The controversial passage that angered them was the one where Graves met a wounded staff officer in hospital, who described the 2nd RWF's 20th July attack on High Wood to him. When Graves asked whether the 2nd RWF held the wood, the staff officer replied:

They hung on to near the end. I believe what happened was that the Public Schools Battalion 20th RF came away at dark; and so did most of the Scotsmen. Your chaps were left there more or less alone for some time. They steadied themselves by singing. Afterwards the chaplain – R.C. of course – Father McCabe, brought the Scotsmen back. Being Glasgow Catholics, they would follow a priest where they wouldn't follow an officer. The centre of the wood was impossible for either the Germans or your fellows to hold – a terrific concentration of artillery on it. Late that night a brigade of the Seventh Division relieved the survivors; it included your First Battalion.

Generally sniped at throughout the book, the passage was the last straw. It infuriated them and lifted *Goodbye to All That* from the literary pages of the press to send it skidding across the editorial columns. Readers wrote in and their letters – for and against – were printed to fuel the furore. It transpired that the two Scottish battalions, far from being 'Glasgow Catholics', were virtually all Protestants. Moreover the Roman Catholic chaplain was Father McShane – not McCabe. McShane, no longer an army chaplain but a parish priest, denied that the two Scottish battalions had 'legged it' *en masse* from the wood. Graves, meanwhile, was under attack from a Protestant journal which accused him of a bias towards Catholicism, while simultaneously being accused by a Catholic journal of nourishing a virulent animosity against Catholicism. His old battalion's medical officer, who had taken up general practice, wrote to him directly to inform him that the two Scottish battalions stood fast at High Wood, although the 'Public Schools Battalion of the Royal Fusiliers disappeared.'

The *Daily Mail* gave Graves the opportunity to reply to his critics and, in its edition of 17th December 1929, Graves repeated the main points of the good doctor's letter. The article was read by a 20th Royal Fusiliers' veteran of High Wood, Harold Tyson. He promptly wrote to Graves in defence of his battalion, whose casualties at High Wood were 22 officers and 375 men. The controversial passage was not deleted from future editions of *Goodbye to All That*, but Tyson's detailed account induced Graves to insert the following text immediately after it:

This was not altogether accurate. I know now that some men of the Public Schools Battalion, without officers or NCOs, maintained their positions in the left centre of the wood, where they stayed until relieved by a brigade of the Seventh Division twenty-two hours later.

In fairness to Robert Graves, his book with all its inaccuracies in the first impression was nearer to the naked truth of front line warfare than the overall newspaper reportage of 1914-18. With few exceptions, newspapers gave the distorted and jaunty view that 'a

battle was just a rough jovial picnic'.[1] Even a respected journalist as
Philip Gibbs (later knighted for his craft) embellished his dispatches
to the point of ridicule for the sake of home consumption, none more
so than his description of the tanks at High Wood:

> . . . then to their great joy saw the Tanks advancing through High
> Wood and on each side of it.
> 'It was like a fairy tale!' said a Cockney boy. 'I can't help
> laughing every time I think of it.'
> He laughed then, though he had a broken arm and was covered
> in blood.
> 'They broke down trees as if they were match-sticks, and went
> over barricades like elephants. The Boches were thoroughly
> scared. They came running out of shell holes and trenches,
> shouting like mad things.
> 'Some of them attacked the Tanks and tried to bomb them, but
> it wasn't a bit good. O Crikey, it was a rare treat to see! The
> biggest joke that ever was! They just stamped down the German
> dug-out as one might a whops' nest.'

Such journalism might deceive readers at home, but not the troops at
the front. They knew better, and because they knew better, how
could they believe in what they read in newspapers again? For the
masses, it was the start of a credibility gap between them and Fleet
Street. Besides, there was Strother's tank stuck in the wood as
evidence. A rust-eaten wreck, half-submerged in the earth and
covered in brambles, Strother's tank was still there when Europe
entered the next Great War.

German panzers snarled cross the old front lines of a previous
generation, passed the neatly laid-out military cemeteries to occupy
Albert and other Somme centres. It was May 1940, and their
advance over the battlefield sites had taken a day. During the period
of German occupation, several decoy aircraft were built and
positioned on the Longueval side of High Wood; except for this
negative intrusion, High Wood stayed aloof from the occupation.
The war made it impossible for British pilgrims to visit the continent,
but nothing could stop the old comrades of the 1st Surrey Rifles from
honouring their High Wood dead at home. They paraded as usual
every year on the Sunday nearest to 15th September, as they had

---

[1] Montague, C.E.: *Disenchantment* (Chatto and Windus, 1922).

done since 1920, to march to St Giles Church in Camberwell. After the service they would reverently lay a wreath at the battalion's war memorial. The ranks are thinned out, but the homage continues today.

World War II once more evaded High Wood when British divisions pursued the enemy across the Somme countryside in September 1944. London Cemetery Extension, however, was temporarily reopened for the reburial of 165 1939-45 casualties in 1946. Mainly of 51st Division from June 1940, they had been recovered from various burial grounds where permanent maintenance was not possible. A generation later another memorial was erected at High Wood. Rather late for World War II, one would assume – and it would be a correct assumption, because this memorial hallows the Glasgow Highlanders who fell there in July 1916.

Legend has it that when a Scottish clan assembled for battle, each man brought his weapons and a stone. The stones were piled and, after the battle, each survivor removed one stone from the pile. The remainder were built into a cairn. Since there was no memorial to the Glasgow Highlanders' epic action, save for the collective names on the Thiepval Memorial to the 'Missing of the Somme', a Glaswegian military historian, Alex Aiken, felt that the omission should be put right. By coincidence, there is a High Wood about two miles east of the Culloden battlefield. After a good deal of careful planning, he and his wife transported enough stones from High Wood, Scotland, to High Wood on the Somme and, there, constructed a cairn on an already prepared slate-covered concrete foundation – courtesy of the Mathon family. The ceremony was conducted in pouring rain on Tuesday, 21st November 1972, when Mme Mathon unveiled the memorial's Gaelic inscription, which in English reads: *Just here, Children of the Gael went down shoulder to shoulder on 15th July, 1916.*

The cairn's facia contains 192 stones in honour of the 192 Glasgow Highlanders killed that day. Its height is 5 feet 7 inches, being the minimum height for enlistment in the Glasgow Highlanders. On 14th July each year, the French tricoleur and the St Andrew's Cross are flown to commemorate the day the Bastille was stormed and the night when High Wood was approached by the Highland battalion.

High Wood today is not unlike the wood first seen in the distance by the troops of Shea's 30th Division on 1st July. It is at its former height, has the same perimeter and would certainly be recognisable to the troops of 7th Division who entered it a fortnight later. The one major change, but tastefully built, is the Mathon family's farmhouse in its southern angle. The double-mine crater is now a deep pond and, near it in 1970, a trench was uncovered which yielded up a fully charged Colt revolver and the remains of twelve rifles with bayonets attached. A serious effort was made to clear the wood of its war *matériel* in the 1960's, during which time the remains of Strother's tank, Clan Ruthven, were cut up for scrap metal. It was impossible to entirely clear the wood and no one would countenance lighting a fire. Admittedly High Wood is private property, but its nameless and numerous dead lie at peace beneath its undulating surface, respected by the local population and vigilantly protected by the wood's owners – souvenir hunters enter it at their peril. Philip Johnstone would have been pleased.

The surrounding land is intensively farmed and mementos of that war, including unexploded shells and mortal remains, are annually uncovered during the ploughing season. Flat Iron Valley, alias Happy Valley alias Death Valley, where the vast majority of the soldiers waited to move up to High Wood, contains its share of grass-covered shell holes and trenches. Much to the author's amazement the original crucifix is still in position at Crucifix Corner. Ripped by shell fire, pierced by bullets, it stands on the bank in a clump of trees. When seen in the summer of 1983, an unexploded 18-pound shell lay at its base.

In spite of the area's violent past, there is an atmosphere of dignity and compassion. To experience it, simply walk through the gate of the tiny London Cemetery at High Wood. The first white headstone to the left is that of 9194 Private J.R. Luker of the 19th Battalion, London Regiment. The only son of Mr and Mrs James Luker, he was 21 when he was killed on 15th September 1916. If the visit is in mid-summer, glance down at the base of his headstone and admire the delicate blooms of the flowers growing there. The flowers are London Pride. Whoever chose them had chosen well.

Bibliography

Military Operations France & Belgium, 1916, Vol 1: Brigadier-General Sir J.E. Edmonds (Macmillan, 1932).

Military Operations France & Belgium, 1916, Vol 2: Captain Wilfred Miles (Macmillan, 1938).

Military Operations France & Belgium, 1918, Vol 1: Brigadier-General Sir J.E. Edmonds (Macmillan, 1935).

My War Memories 1914-18: General Ludendorff (Hutchinson).

Schlacten des Weltkrieges, Somme-Nord II: Reichsarchiv. (Stalling, Oldenburg, 1927).

The Somme: A.H.Farrar-Hockley (Batsford, 1964).

The First Day on the Somme: Martin Middlebrook (Allen Lane, 1971).

Courage Past: Alex Aiken (privately published, 1971).

Birmingham City Battalions Book of Honour: Sir W.H.Bowater (Sherratt & Hughes, 1919).

Battles of the Somme: Philip Gibbs (Heinemann, 1917).

The 7th Division: C.T.Atkinson (Cassell, 1927).

The 15th Royal Warwickshire Regiment in the Great War: Major C.A.Bill (Cornish Bros, 1932).

The 15th (Scottish) Division 1914-18: Lt-Colonel J.Stewart & John Buchan (Wm Blackwood, 1926).

5th Battalion Reminiscences: CSM P.Docherty (Covenanter, Vol XV, 3).

The 47th Division: Ed. Alan H.Maude (Amalgamated Press, 1922).

Pilgrimage: Lt-Colonel G.S.Hutchison (Rich & Cowan, 1935).

Machine Guns: Lt-Colonel G.S.Hutchison (Macmillan, 1938).

The War the Infantry Knew: Anon (P.S.King & Son Ltd, 1938).

Terriers in the Trenches: Charles Messenger (Picton Publishing, 1982).

The Tanks, Vol 1: Captain B.H.Liddell Hart (Cassell, 1959).

The Private Papers of Douglas Haig: Ed. Robert Blake (Eyre & Spottiswoode, 1952).

Invicta: Major C.V.Molony (Nisbet & Co Ltd).

Goodbye to All That: Robert Graves (Jonathan Cape, 1929).

But It Still Goes On: Robert Graves (Jonathan Cape, 1931).

Machine Gunner: Arthur Russell (Roundwood Press, 1977).

The World Crisis by Winston S Churchill – A Criticism: Colonel The Lord Sydenham of Combe *et al* (Hutchinson).

Old Soldiers Never Die: Frank Richards (Faber & Faber, 1933).

Field Marshal Sir Henry Wilson, Vol 1: Major-General Sir C.E.Callwell (Cassell, 1929).

Up the Line to Death – The War Poets 1914-18: Compiled by Brian Gardner (Macmillan, 1964).

The Unending Vigil: Philip Longworth (Constable, 1967).

Armageddon Road – A VC's Diary 1914-16: Ed. Terry Norman (William Kimber, 1982).

Disenchantment: C.E.Montague (Chatto and Windus, 1922).

The Drinkwater Diary (unpublished).

INDEX